BOLLINGEN SERIES LXXXV

Selected Works of Miguel de Unamuno

Volume 7

Selected Works of Miguel de Unamuno

Edited and Annotated by

Anthony Kerrigan and Martin Nozick

1. *Peace in War*
2. *The Private World*
3. *Our Lord Don Quixote*
4. *The Tragic Sense of Life*
5. *The Agony of Christianity*
6. *Novela/Nivola*
7. *Ficciones: Four Stories and a Play*

Miguel de Unamuno

Ficciones
Four Stories and a Play

Translated by Anthony Kerrigan

With an Introduction and Notes
by Martin Nozick

Bollingen Series LXXXV · 7
Princeton University Press

THIS IS VOLUME SEVEN OF THE
SELECTED WORKS OF MIGUEL DE UNAMUNO
CONSTITUTING NUMBER LXXXV IN BOLLINGEN SERIES
SPONSORED BY BOLLINGEN FOUNDATION.
IT IS THE FIFTH VOLUME OF THE
SELECTED WORKS TO APPEAR

Printed in the United States of America by
Princeton University Press
Princeton, N. J.

Table of Contents

Translator's Foreword

AGONY, SPIRITUAL STRUGGLE, is present in all of Unamuno: in this volume we have it in "fictional" form in, among other works, the drama of an unbelieving priest, an ancient theme in Christian literature (even painted by Raphael in *The Mass of Bolsena* at the Vatican). The living martyrdom of Saint Manuel Bueno is none other than the Tragic Sense of Life and the Agony of Christianity, the best known titles of Unamuno's work, given embodiment here in the person of a priest.

All his life, Unamuno played a role exactly opposite to that of Dr. Guillotin, who strove to cut death, the death-throes, short. Unamuno drew it out as a lifelong agonic struggle and proposed it as a constant in every thinking man's life.

Josef Ignace Guillotin had merely made adjustments in the interests of speed in the diabolic machine already invented by others and he strove to have it used on aristocrats only, on those who were eligible to engage in a duel. The French doctor spent his life in protesting the misnomer, the misuse of his name as eponym. In truth, he was lucky enough in those Red days not to be guillotined on his guillotine. For his part Unamuno strove to force all men to ponder the fact that we are all under sentence, condemned to death in advance and that we all inhabit a Death-Row, the entire world one vast Death-Row, and in his polemic, in his tortuous reasoning—which was his agonic device, his equivalent to a spiritual guillotine—

he flung his admonitions to the wind in every genre: drama, "fiction," and essay, and in verse, lyrical *memento mori*. His work is farthest possible from a well-constructed guillotine, from a "humane" one. He agonized (in the Greek sense of struggle) all his life against death, for he believed that Agony and the Tragic Sense were concomitant with the course and length of one's entire life. He cries out and agitates against death, protests Death, knowing all the while that his head—and that of all his listeners and readers —is already lying on the block, with no way out, UNLESS . . .

Unless there is an eternity, which implies a necessary Godhead, Agony is nothing but agony, nothing but senseless struggle in a permanent death-throes; *unless*, instead of absurdity, there is some logic of a higher kind, the other logic, the logic of the head, of this world, of all modern, up-to-date philosophies and of Science shows us that there is no ulterior sense at all, no prescient *human* sense in our lives, in the life of each and every one of us.

And so for him, a Pascal and his holy water— even a Saint Theresa and her mystical ecstacies— were more important for Spain than a Descartes and his inflexible guillotine-logic could ever be. Even an Ave Maria is more important than a scientific formula for our spirit in the middle of the night of our dreams, or in our intimate revery amid the shadows in the shade of our phantom life. Sacred mystery itself is more important than inventing a better light bulb to shine into and show up the dark corners.

"Let the others invent!" he cried, the other Western nations (though nowadays even tribal Africans—let alone Iberians—are sent to Paris or Kansas City to master "Science").

The Agonies here assembled in the form of "fiction" and a play have the following bibliographical history:

La tía Tula (in *OC²*, IX, 521-634), was first published by Renacimiento, Madrid, in 1921, though its first draft in manuscript dates from 1902. By 1928, it had been translated into German, Dutch, and Swedish.

Saint Manuel Bueno, Martyr: San Manuel Bueno, mártir (in *OC²*, XVI, 561-628), dated Salamanca, November 1930, was first published in the literary weekly *La Novela de Hoy* (No. 461), March 13, 1931; later it was published by Espasa-Calpe, Madrid, in 1933, as the first of four narratives: *San Manuel Bueno, mártir, y tres historias más*. The other three tales are *La novela de Don Sandalio, jugador de ajedrez* (*The Novel of Don Sandalio, Chessplayer*, included in this volume), *Un pobre hombre rico o El sentimiento cómico de la vida* (*A Poor Rich Man or The Comic Sense of Life*), and *Una historia de amor* (*A Love Story*). *San Manuel Bueno* was translated into French in 1934, and again in 1936; into Dutch in 1935; into English, by the present translator, in 1956 (Chicago)—revised in this edition—and by other translators in 1957 (London); the first of these translations into English was first anthologized in the book *The Existential Imagination* (Greenwich, Conn., in 1963) and appeared in later anthologies. It was also translated into Italian in 1955 and into German in 1961.

The Novel of Don Sandalio, Chessplayer: La novela de Don Sandalio, jugador de ajedrez (in *OC²*, XVI, 629-70), is dated Salamanca, December 1930, and is one of the stories included in *San Manuel Bueno, mártir, y tres historias más* (1933). The story of a vacuity, to paraphrase Julián Marías in his book on Unamuno, of a character who exists only insofar as he is a chessplayer, evolved from an essay on chess by Unamuno published in Buenos Aires in 1910 ("Sobre el ajedrez," *Contra esto y aquello, OC²*, IV, 900-10), according to the author himself, who points out that twenty years passed until its fruition as a "fiction." The story is Giacometti-like in that two human beings confront each other only in their existential roles as players, confront each other in daily life devoid of any notion of each other except as players around a board, just as Giacometti's attentuated sculptured figures are bent on passing each other in life as fellow pedestrians—and nothing more. The critic Ricardo Gullón holds that the two chessplayers are each The Other One, the Other to each other. Perhaps Don Sandalio is only a figment of the Other's imagination, Gullón writes (in "Don Sandalio o el juego de los espejos," in *Autobiografías de Unamuno*, Madrid, 1964). A French version was made in MS in 1936, but there is no record of its publication. An Italian translation was published in 1955, and a Dutch version in 1959.

The Madness of Doctor Montarco: "La locura del doctor Montarco" (in *OC²*, III, 685-700), dated February, 1904, was first published in *La España Moderna* (año XVI, no. 182, Madrid, February 1904). The first translation into English, by the present translator, appeared in magazine form (in *The New Mexico Quarterly Review*, Summer-Autumn 1955, Vol. 25, nos. 2, 3, pp. 145-60), and in book form (in *Abel Sánchez and Other Stories*, Chicago, 1956). No other translations of this story into any other language are known to the present editors. The translation in this edition is a revision of the earlier translation.

The Other: the play *El otro* (in *OC²*, XII, 800-63) was originally composed in Hendaye, in 1926, during Unamuno's exile, and received its première in Madrid on December 14, 1932, the year of its first publication in book form in Spain. It was issued in Argentina in 1946. Numerous Spanish editions followed. There have been translations—most of them unavailable for examination, even in the Unamuno Library in Salamanca—into German, into English (and even news of a production in the English language in Dublin: but no version in English has been uncovered by the present editors), into Italian (Rome, 1955), and into modern Greek. The play is produced from time to time in Spain, and there has been a good film of the drama produced for RTE (*Radio Televisión Española*).

ANTHONY KERRIGAN

New York City
1975

Introduction

> I have compassion only for those who
> sincerely bewail their doubt, who re-
> gard it as the greatest of misfortunes,
> and who, sparing no effort to escape
> it, make of this inquiry their princi-
> pal and most serious occupation.
>
> Pascal: *Pensées*

NOT SINCE the winds of Erasmianism blew over
the land in the early sixteenth century was the Catholic Church of Spain exposed to such scrutiny and
criticism as from the pen of Miguel de Unamuno. The
Spanish Enlightenment—a pale simulacrum of the
French—had advocated the introduction of the new
experimental sciences into a retrograde university
curriculum still dominated by arid scholasticism, had
sniped at censorship exercised by the Inquisition, and
had even discussed the injuries inflicted on the national economy by the vast, unproductive holdings of
the Church. But rarely did it mount any direct attack
on dogma and doctrine, ritual and ceremony, rarely
did it question the basic concepts of belief.

The nineteenth century secularists, in the main,
sought to relax the hold of priests on education, and
although they put a serious dent into that monopoly,
attacks on "altar and throne" were refuted by such
apologists of tradition as Jaime Balmes, Juan Donoso
Cortés, and especially Marcelino Menéndez y Pelayo
—one of Unamuno's professors at the University of

Madrid—whose prodigious erudition and output were among the most potent intellectual weapons at the service of the conservatives. And the Church had nothing to fear in the twentieth century from Unamuno's younger contemporary and major rival in the field of speculative thought, José Ortega y Gasset, whose contempt for religious concerns was reflected in his total lack of interest.

Unamuno was no village atheist—as the novelist Pío Baroja often tended to be—nor was he a dabbler in novelties *à la* Bouvard and Pécuchet. He was a man of impeccable morals and education, married and with a growing family, a professor of Greek and later also of the history of the Spanish language at Spain's most ancient university, Salamanca, accredited in his perfervid love of the national scene by several lyrical travel books. He had cut his teeth on Hegel and was a student of Kant and Kierkegaard; a voracious reader in several languages, he was steeped in German historicism, and could do battle with the theologians on their own grounds. A champion of religious toleration, he nonetheless defended faith against Spencerian agnosticism; while he despised Voltairean deism, he attacked curialism, institutionalized religion, conditioned religious reflexes, and the alliance of Church and State, with all the strength of his vast knowledge and his gift for jeremiad.

Although he was—and still is, to a certain extent—accused of atheistic leanings, his posture was, in his own terms, more that of the free believer than the free thinker. His love of the mystics, his constant biblical frame of reference, his obsessive preoccupation with the huge question mark of the afterlife, the agonies he suffered over his innate religious disposition at loggerheads with rational analysis, all these placed him in a religious no-man's-land. He looked back with longing upon the spiritual tranquility of his childhood and early adolescence, and repeatedly called himself a medieval man, yet regretted that Spain had not passed through the three R's: Renaissance, Reformation, and Revolution.

If he exalted the person and activity of Loyola, he called the Jesuits "degenerate" sons of the great saint, in the same way that he stood in awe of the Godhead and despised the subtleties of His interpreters. In Kierkegaard and other critics of Christendom as against Christianity, he found confirmation of the interiorization of the God-man nexus, but those who, like Renan, reduced Jesus to a model of righteousness without mystery, he found shallow and unconvincing. Bishops and theologians were middlemen of religion, God was their industry, and agony (conflict) beyond their ken; equally pernicious, however, were the skeptics and materialists who, even as his favorite Wordsworth had said, "murder to dissect." Neither the one nor the other understood that God was *deus absconditus*, speaking only to the heart, to the *esprit de finesse* and not to the *esprit de géométrie*.

He condemned the unthinking "faith of the charcoal-burner," yet fought the cult of logic and reason; unable to conform to strict religious command, his work was nevertheless a long *meditatio mortis*. Above all, once a Socialist, he always stressed, in one form or another, that political meliorism was a *divertissement* to keep man from fully realizing that "the last act is bloody, however fine the rest of the play." It is no wonder that, pursued by the understanding that even the most disinterested acts are selfishly motivated, he turned his eyes heavenward.

Thus Unamuno allowed nothing to stand between

him and his hunger for God, neither the exegesis of proof nor the exegesis of denial, just as in his *Life of Don Quixote and Sancho*, he allowed nothing, not the erudition that had accrued around Cervantes's novel, nor even Cervantes himself, to stand between him and the Spanish Christ. He anathematized all forms of professionalism: the erudition that is "drop-counting" and "word-hunting," the militarism that replaces the noble war of spiritual conflict with the shedding of blood, pedagogy that merchandises culture, systematic theology that coarsens the inwardness of religion.

It cannot therefore be said that Unamuno rejects Christianity; he vigorously rejects, however, the codification of its pristine faith or "pistis" into "gnosis"—into philosophical certainties, infallible hierarchy, empty formulae—and wishes to lead a quasi-independent ecclesiastical structure back to the people from whom it sprang and back to the purposes for which it presumably stood. When the Church moved from faith and hope in an afterlife into a solidified corpus of belief, it made itself vulnerable to refutation, it handed itself over to skeptical, legalistic minds that could bore holes into its walls. The exclusive objective of the Church, according to Don Miguel, was to console the faithful for having been born to die, and any other goals constituted self-betrayal. If Unamuno on occasion called himself a Spanish Protestant, and even suggested the Quaker by his apparel, his goal was to unclog the Church of its excess of form which had led to involuted speculation, wars of words (and bloody wars *over* words) and perhaps most reprehensibly, into worldly ambitions.

"To wish to believe," Unamuno had jotted down in his *Diario* or Journal at the very end of the last century, "is it not the beginning of belief? He who desires and begs for it, does he not already have it, even if he does not realize it?" Later, in his essay "My Religion," one of his most succinct statements on the intentionality, rather than the persuasion, of his belief, he stated:

> As regards religion, there is scarcely a single point I have resolved rationally, and since I have not, I can not communicate any of these points logically, for only what is rational is logical and transmissible. I do have, in my affections, in my heart, in my feelings, a strong tendency toward Christianity, without abiding by any special dogmas of this or that Christian confession. I consider any man who invokes the name of Christ, with respect and love, a Christian, and I feel repugnance for the orthodox, whether Catholics or Protestants (the latter are usually as uncompromising as the former), who deny Christianity to those who do not interpret the Gospel as they do.

Years later, Karl Jaspers would say: ". . . what matters is not our knowledge of God but our attitude towards God." And Paul Tillich affirmed: "The first word, therefore, to be spoken by religion to the people of our time must be a word spoken against religion. It is the word the old Jewish prophets spoke against the priestly and royal and pseudo-prophetic guardians of their natural religion. . . ."

Although Unamuno has not received the proper credit, he is, in this sense, an undeniable if unprogrammatic herald of today's *aggiornamento*, one who infused, furthermore, into radical change a sense of personal crisis and loss.

*   *   *

The Unamuno who would not be bound by the categories of religion, also rejected the laws that distinguished one literary genre from another. For him Spinoza's *Ethics* was just as much the epic of a mind as *The Divine Comedy* was a long theological commentary. Thus, some of Unamuno's finest essays are short stories, and vice-versa, and for the most part, his novels are essays in fiction form where the action is rapidly narrated so that the author can hurry back to bare, stylized dialogue. His most comprehensive work, *The Tragic Sense of Life*, is a long, rambling tapestry of commentaries on quotations pulled out of original context from numberless sources and bent to his needs. Loosely woven, para-professional, so to speak, it is neither an artistic tour-de-force nor a philosophical treatise, but the incandescent confession of a man whose mind is crammed with conflicting information and whose soul is caught in a tug-of-war between traditional Spanish Catholicism and the impact of European rationalism. *The Tragic Sense of Life* is the drama of a spirit longing for the certainties and comforts of a personal and national childhood and inescapably caught in currents from abroad, finding a strange sort of surcease or therapy in bizarre juxtapositions of ideas, alternations of revolt and reverence, holding up to the light every suggestion of an endless spectrum of possibilities. "The comic apprehension," says Kierkegaard, "evokes the contradiction or makes it manifest by having in mind a way out, which is why the contradiction is painless. The tragic apprehension sees the contradiction and despairs of a way out."

Years later, confronted by the fears, loneliness, and anger of exile, Unamuno wrote a kind of codicil to *The Tragic Sense of Life* in a series of essays on *The Agony of Christianity*. Again he conceives of Christianity as the conflict (*agon*) between mind and heart, between letter and spirit, and brings in the tragic chorus—this time far more limited than in the earlier book —of Pascal, the biblical Abishag the Shunammite, and Father Hyacinthe Loyson. Less far-ranging than *The Tragic Sense of Life*, *The Agony of Christianity* is a complex of very personal reactions to random readings and quotations, a moving attempt at propping up flagging courage, in short again a *sui generis* confession.

During the same period he wrote one of his most perplexing books: *Cómo se hace una novela*, or *How to Make a Novel*, which brings to a culmination one of Unamuno's most nagging preoccupations, namely the mystery of personality. If Unamuno was tormented by the uncertainty of where life ends, he was agonizingly aware of the multiple roles he himself had played: teacher, preacher, orator, writer, spiritual *agent provocateur*, father, husband, poet. When he wrote *How to Make a Novel*, he was in self-imposed exile from the Primo de Rivera dictatorship. True, he had been banished to the island of Fuerteventura by the military regime, but on the very day of his escape to France, he had been amnestied. Did he prolong his stay in France out of a deep opposition to the regime, or was he also enjoying the role of proscript? What good was his absence from Spain doing the cause of democracy? Was he dramatizing himself, making of himself a novel, was he making a bid for lasting admiration, was he reenacting the role of the great exiles, Dante, Victor Hugo, Mazzini? And most of all, would he pay for his strange, aberrant, disguised self-satisfaction by death far from family, friends, familiar surroundings? *How to Make a Novel* is a strangely contrived piece of work with shifting focuses, a complex of political invective, self-pity, elaboration on fragments from Mazzini's love letters, and most of all, reflections on how living, even on the most altruistic level, is a series of self-destructive steps.

* * *

Implicit, then, in many of Unamuno's *cris-de-coeur* is doubt over his own sincerity. In one of the entries in his *Diario* of 1897 he had exclaimed: "Simplicity, simplicity! Oh, Lord, grant me simplicity! Let me not play the role of convert, let me not play it out in the arena, but for myself alone!" And later in the same Journal, "Like those poor creatures who show off their sores at the side of the road, there are people, writers, who show off the sores of their souls and present themselves as interesting beings." If his religious outlook was a network of antinomies, the man Unamuno was hard put to gauge the degree of authenticity behind his public performances in word and deed. One of his great metaphors is *intrahistoria*, or "infrahistory," the silent continuity of unspectacular lives, the bedrock over which the cataclysms of history are played out. Was there an Unamuno behind and beneath the public Unamuno of the wide gesture and startling contradictions, or had they become hopelessly confused?

Already at the beginning of his career, as a professor of Greek, he had been plagued by questions as to why he made no contribution to his "speciality." But Unamuno had already conceived of his role as lay preacher, spiritual "whip," *"excitator Hispaniae"* (as Curtius would call him) and not a "scholar." And he lashed out, and would continue to do so, at those who wished to compartmentalize him, relegate him to a pigeonhole. His "Madness of Doctor Montarco" is one of Unamuno's earliest answers to the critics wished to deny him the freedom of being a "whole" man, who wished to confine him to a "party," make of him a "part." The story-essay of Doctor Montarco is Unamuno's catharsis, for the ultimate madness into which the doctor falls is Unamuno's "ex-future," something that might have overtaken him but which he fortunately escaped.

Tía Tula, a treatment of another of Unamuno's favorite themes, that of the woman as virgin mother, again suggests the dilemma of the precarious balance to be maintained between fidelity to self and duty. But if Unamuno had always held that the main function of woman is maternal—to child, lover, husband—now he questions, not the courage of Tula's clinging to her chastity but her refusal to compromise. She had managed to fulfill her need for motherhood while preserving her virginity, but through her stubborn refusal to "sully" herself sexually, she had driven her brother-in-law, the man who had always loved her, to sin. The Church had always proclaimed the superiority of the virginal state over marriage, and had designed the priesthood, the convent, and the monastery for "fathers" and "mothers" who educated and catechized the children of others, but here lay another aspect of the contradiction, or agony, of Christianity: if the spirit of Christianity was purer than the letter, it could nevertheless not perpetuate itself without the word or "logos." If Christianity could not love without the support of Christendom, the creation of human beings for the greater glory of God, could not be brought to be without the "inferior" pull of the flesh. Furthermore, like the great saints—and like Tía Tula, finally—Unamuno understood the pride and self-satisfaction that are inevitable components of virtue, dedication, self-sacrifice, and he puts into the mouth of one of his characters in the play *The Other*, these words: "The criminal must be forgiven his crime, the virtuous man his virtue, the proud man his pride, the humble man his humility."

The Other, another one of Unamuno's strange hybrid works, was born, as the author himself avows "from the obsession . . . the mystery—not the problem—of personality, from the agonizing concern over our identity and individual, personal continuity." The most fertile state of man, Unamuno had often reiterated, is "civil war," war with his fellowmen, conflict within himself, between heart and mind, feeling and conviction, desire and lucidity, between the transcendental dimension of man and his involvement in the world's transactions. To objectify oneself at any given moment—or even to look at oneself in the mirror— is to fracture one's consciousness, to reveal the "other" or "others" which surprise or repel. From among the various elements of one's personality, some are molded spontaneously, others governed by external forces, or temptations, and yet is there a sharp line separating the innate from the conditioned? Indeed, one could scarcely be conditioned unless ambition or histrionic leanings aided and abetted the process. Thus does Unamuno stress one of his most painful recognitions: we cannot be victimized unless we allow ourselves to be victims; and he adds yet another reversal to the many cause-and-effect relationships he had upset all his life: the existence of the child bestows paternity upon the parent: Don Quixote made Cervantes, and Hamlet Shakespeare; the worship of His creatures makes for the existence of God; turning the other cheek incites the brutality of the opponent.

And if Cain had not killed Abel, Abel would have killed Cain. Unamuno had already treated the Cain and Abel theme in other works, principally his novel *Abel Sánchez*, and here in his "mystery" *The Other*, he deliberately blurs the distinctions between the murderer and the murdered. And all efforts on the part of the "logicians" and the "rationalists," Ernesto and Don Juan, are blocked by The Other and even by the *Ama* who had raised the two brothers. And as in Pirandello's *Così è se vi pare*, another claustrophobic charade, we are left without resolution, caught in the mystery, in a deadlock of right and wrong, truth and lies, the spurious and the authentic.

*   *   *

Unamuno had coined the word *nivola* to differentiate his "unfurnished" or naked novel from the realistic tradition he had inherited. Unamuno's *nivola* minimizes the solid outlines of time and space, the specificity of description, and except for his first novel, the documented *Paz en la guerra* (*Peace in War*), 1897, he rejects the comprehensiveness of a Balzac, Zola, or Pérez Galdós, or the detailed canvas of a Flaubert, in favor of the vaulting passions or obsessions of his protagnists. Unamuno considered the objectivism of the great nineteenth century tradition too deliberate, too scientific, too premeditated, and opts for the noumenal character whose suffering, if exacerbated through his contact with others, is consubstantial with himself. The Don Avito of his *Amor y pedagogía* (*Love and Education*) is a foolish determinist who puts his entire faith in the infallibility of scientific laws; the Joaquín Monegro of *Abel Sánchez* is an abcess of *ressentiment* who refuses to be lanced; Aunt Tula is so beset by maternal passions she cannot abide even legitimized sexual relations; Alejandro Gómez of *Nada menos que todo un hombre* (*Every Inch a Man*) is monumentalized masculine pride.

The Novel of Don Sandalio, Chessplayer represents

the *nivola* pursued to its logical end, the *finis terrae* of Unamuno's technique in fiction. For not only is the background a nebulous one, but Unamuno dispenses with the *sine qua non* of narrative, character psychology. Don Sandalio is simply the most impassible of people, the chessplayer, without past or present, except as he concentrates on his game. True, hints come dribbling in from afar to the author of the letters in the novelette, but the latter is so fascinated by the opaque mystery that he steadfastly refuses to penetrate it.

As many have pointed out, the germ of this little work is to be found in the essay of 1910 "Sobre el ajedrez" or "On Chess" and later collected in *Contra esto y aquello* (*Against This and That*), 1912, but philosophically it underlines what was to Unamuno one of life's saddest phenomena: the lack of communication even between people who meet regularly but on neutral grounds, avoiding the friction that gives heat and light. People interact according to preordained patterns or rites, in order to avoid the pain and confusion of entanglement, in much the same way as we detach ourselves from the *cuestión única* (the one basic issue) of immortality by enveloping ourselves in a cocoon of polished manners, or the surrogate religion of art or politics or domesticity—all constituting Kierkegaard's "aesthetic" or ante-penultimate stage. Even those who live on the ethical level—the doctor with his remedies, the lawyer with his hair-splitting, the professor with his research—are shutting off the sight of the abyss no less than the *reductio ad absurdum* of the chessplayer's intense concentration. For Unamuno, as for his spiritual ancestor Kierkegaard, the highest stage on life's way is the religious concern which intersects existence at every point and is the

nub at which all men should meet in ecumenical compassion over the utter tragedy of life truncated by
death.

*   *   *

The full awareness of what it meant to confound
rather than unravel had to encompass for Unamuno
a profound uneasiness and even remorse over spread-
ing the gospel of doubt, over undermining certainties
and complacencies. If he had converted a few, he
had sown dismay among the many; he had suggested
much and consoled little. He had undone the codifica-
tions of religion but could not deny that spirit needs
matter; he was anti-monarchical but unconvinced of
any republican panacea; he adored rural life but affirmed that civilization came from *civis*, city. Did his
paradoxes make of him a Don Quixote or a maverick,
was he a Moses leading his people to the Promised
Land or a Herostratus destroying the temple to achieve
immortal fame?

Saint Manuel Bueno, Martyr is Unamuno's supreme act of contrition, a public statement of regret
for having tried to involve so many in his personal
turmoil, and an expression of the nostalgia the icono-
clast feels for simpler times. In design it is a subtle
mosaic of autobiographical hints, of metaphysical and
political symbols. The protagonist—or "agonist," as
Unamuno preferred—is the priest the young Unamuno had once wanted to be, while his parish, Valverde de Lucerna, is a fantasy of a closely knit community that slumbers under the wings of the dove,
the holiness of its spiritual leader. And it is the mission of the sorrowing, unbelieving priest to protect the
weak, the poor, the disabled and the sinful from perceiving those options which might indeed mitigate
some injustices but which would also cut them off

from the sight—the mirage?—of an ultimate justice.

When Unamuno was writing this poignant novelette, enormous social and political changes were pend-
ing, and even *he* was temporarily caught up in the eu-
phoria. But he understood that once the eternal legiti-
macy of established religion is drastically challenged,
man could be impelled as much by a compulsion for
change as by its benefits, and that the orthodoxy
of prescription could be replaced by the equally tyrannical ban on *all* prescription. If the Church had once
broken asunder over the issue of "filioque," unbounded
pluralism could spawn endless Babels. And if cata-
clysmic changes bring down huge structures, those
who live up high are indeed toppled, but the structures collapse upon the many who live closer to the
street. Organized, programmatic changes can only be
realized if awareness of individual faces can in some
way be blurred, and when Christianity intrudes in
such areas of social reform, it does so only at the risk
of losing its unique, irreplaceable spiritual identity.

Saint Manuel Bueno, Martyr points up the artist
Unamuno at his surest, without flights of rhetoric,
without needless digressions or interpolations. The
biblical rhythms are still there, but subdued to match
the still sadness of the humanity made to die. The
limited cast of characters themselves personify some
of Unamuno's central concepts. Don Manuel is the
reconciliation of the author's two principal antinomies:
he is the nonbeliever who, unlike his creator, will not
use the "truth" to disturb the peace, and who, very
much like his creator, holds onto orthodox morality
while rejecting accepted religion. More than thirty
years earlier Unamuno had asked himself in his Journal, "If you gave yourself over to the ideal of Christian
perfection, would you not end up by professing the

Christian faith?" The answer in *Saint Manuel Bueno, Martyr* is, tragically, no.

The faceless villagers, the eternal mountain and the lake exemplify Unamuno's grandiose, romantic metaphor of the continuity of nature and humanity underlying and feeding recorded history. Angela is what her name suggests, an angel of pity, of compassion toward Don Manuel; yet if she is still another of Unamuno's virgin mothers, the mother to her spiritual father (a variant of Dante's "figlia del tuo figlio") she is also the goad of Don Manuel's conscience, the one who brings up again and again those theological questions which the priest had supposedly rejected.

Lázaro (Lazarus), Don Manuel's confidant, is so named since he had transcended a faith in radical dogma as intransigent as any of the traditional precepts of the Church, and had truly progressed to compassion for humanity mortality. *Taedium vitae*—the *ennui* of the Baudelaire whom Unamuno strangely misunderstood, the *noia* of the Leopardi whom he worshipped—can push men to despair as irresistibly as the exploitation which, in one form or another, shall always be with us, and as Unamuno so perspicaciously perceived, that *taedium vitae* increases in direct proportion as commodities, mobility, discoveries (*l'infini de petitesse* and *l'infini de grandeur*) multiply. "All that is made perfect by progress perishes also by progress," Pascal had asserted.

If, for the greater part of his life, Unamuno had believed opposition to the establishment to be exhilarating, he was also beset by the knowledge that blind faith in dissent is at best ingenuous, at worst enslaving. If he had been for so long the declared enemy of the "faith of the charcoal-burner," he now set Saint Manuel Bueno and his "Joshua," Lazarus, up as de-

fenders of that faith, not so much because he en-
visaged the world as a congeries of small rural com-
munities governed by benevolent and disinterested
despots, but because he was—as always—dissenting
from the new dissent already congealing into a radical establishment. Unamuno, who had always been
"Against This and That," was now denouncing the
tyrannies of Fascism, Communism, incipient Nazism,
the sacred cow of abstract democracy and its hier-
archical officialdom, the new slogans, the many camou-
flages of utopianism. Along with many other men of
goodwill, he saw how the pretense of the "system
for man" could be transformed into "man for the system"; he sounded the warning against dehumaniza-
tion on every level: the mechanization of life, the cult
of technique, stifling urbanization, the faddishness of
sophistication, and above all, the inconceivable cruelty
of sacrificing the present for a problematical bright
future. The propaganda of newspaper and radio, of
parties and cénacles, was not to him in any way a step
forward from the priest using his persuasive powers
upon his flock, and justice, in the hands of legalists,
was not a matter of right over wrong, but frequently
a question of who was most astute.

Unamuno's recoil from these dismal prospects is
crystallized in Blasillo the Fool, the simpleton who is
Don Manuel's ex-future, the one he would like to have
been, but could never more be. If Don Manuel is—by
virtue of his name, his martyrdom, his function as a
pool of healing, perhaps even his "pious fraud"—as-
similated into the figure of Jesus Christ, Blasillo is one
of the children Christ suffered to come unto Him. He
personifies surrender to the pristine faith which the
Church, following its own species of Enlightenment,
had converted into ritual, doctrine, and superstition.

Furthermore, in *Saint Manuel Bueno, Martyr*, the resonances of Dostoevsky's Grand Inquisitor, if muted, are unmistakable. Unamuno, in his work, dares challenge the monolithic notion of "liberty," often a warrant for narcissism and vulgarity. Unamuno understood better than most that "self-determination" and "openness" may degenerate into free-for-all politicking on the collective level, and "doing one's thing" on the personal. If Unamuno's contempt for sexual license smacks of Puritanism, it also sounds a warning against *machismo*, exhibitionism, and self-indulgence. And if religion is the opium of the people, men are in urgent need of that opium to allay the pains of being, in Pascal's terms, "condemned to death." Unlike the Grand Inquisitor, however, Unamuno does not object to Christ's message of freedom of conscience: his objection is to the ease with which individualism may be contrived into banality, where the sense of obligation may be emptied of its indispensable ingredient of self-denial.

If retrograde censorship was to him always reprehensible—he himself had been its victim—the removal of pressures could bring in its wake irresponsibility and even promote aberration. In a word, Unamuno fought the new Manichaeanism which simplistically and dogmatically denies continuity, which brackets the old with the bad and the new with the good. Finally, Unamuno judges that those who live without God and without seeking Him, are unworthiest of all, for as Pascal had pointed out: ". . . there are two kinds of people one can call reasonable; those who serve God with all their heart because they know Him, and those who seek Him with all their heart because they do not know Him."

MARTIN NOZICK

Tía Tula

Prologue

SAINT TERESA TELLS us: "I had one brother almost of my own age. It was he whom I most loved, though I had a great affection for them all, as had they for me. We used to read the lives of saints together. . . . It used to cause us great astonishment when we were told that both pain and glory would last for ever. We would spend long periods talking about this and we liked to repeat again and again, 'For ever—ever—ever!' Through our frequent repetition of these words, it pleased the Lord that in my earliest years I should receive a lasting impression of the way of truth.

"When I saw that it was impossible for me to go to any place where they would put me to death for God's sake, we decided to become hermits, and we used to built hermitages, as well as we could, in an orchard which we had at home. We would make heaps of small stones, but they at once fell down again, so we found no way of accomplishing our desires. But even now it gives me a feeling of devotion to remember how early God granted me what I lost by my own fault. . . .

"I remember that, when my mother died, I was twelve years of age or a little less. When I began to realize what I had lost, I went in my distress to an image of Our Lady and with many tears besought her to be a mother to me. Though I did this in my simplicity, I believe it was of some avail to me; for when-

3

ever I have commended myself to this Sovereign Virgin I have been conscious of her aid; and eventually she has led me back to herself. . . ."

And again, the same Teresa wrote to Don Lorenzo de Cepeda:

"God be praised forever, for the grace he has granted Your Grace in sending you a wife who can give you great relief. My own warm congratulations, for it is to me a source of consolation to think that you have her. I kiss the hands of Doña María, your wife, over and over again. In this house she has me, and many others, as her lady chaplain. We should much like to have her to enjoy, but, if it were through the work to be done hereabouts, then I would rather she take her ease there than see her suffer here."

And in Chapter 11 of her *Life*, Saint Teresa says that she was "fond of books of chivalry" (her own books are books of chivalry, too, *a lo divino*). In one of the sonnets in our Rosary of Sonnets we call her:

> Lady Quixote
> *a lo divino* who put our immortal Spain
> in the saddle, her work never vain:
> only the immortal exists: God or Nought!

It might appear that Saint Teresa differs from Don Quixote in that the Knight (uncle to his immortal niece) made himself ridiculous, a toy and a mockery for mothers and fathers and for queens and drones. But, in all truth, did Saint Teresa avoid or escape ridicule? Was she not mocked? Do not many people nowadays find her impulses quixotic, that is, ridiculous, and her life and work that of an adventuress and knight-errant?

The reader must not think, because of the matter which precedes it, that the following tale is in any

way a commentary on the life of the Spanish saint.
Nothing of the kind! We did not so much as think of
Saint Teresa in conceiving the story, or in unfolding
it; nor of Don Quixote either. It was only later, after
finishing the work, that the parallel, a surprise even
for the mind which conceived the book, struck us, and
it was then we discovered the roots of this novelistic
account. The deeper meaning had escaped our notice
while the story was written. It was not until we ex-
amined our work, as author, that the Quixotic and
Teresian roots became clear. And we realized, too,
that the roots of one and the other, of Don Quixote and
Saint Teresa, are one and the same root.

Is this book, then, a novel of chivalry? The reader
can take it as he likes. . . . To some it may appear to
be a hagiographic novel, the *Life* of a saint. We can
assure the reader that it is, in any case, a novel.

Though it had never occurred to us, a friend of
ours—a Frenchman, to be brief—noted that the in-
spiration (pardon the word!) behind the novel *Mist*
had the same root as Calderón's *Life Is a Dream*. But
in the present case we ourselves noted, after concluding it, that the novel in your hands, reader, sprang
from Quixotic and Teresian roots. Of course, this fact
does not mean that the events related could not have
occurred outside Spain.

* * *

Before putting an end to this Prologue, we should like
to make another observation. To some it will appear
to be a linguistic or philological fine point, though it
is merely a psychological one. Although, in truth, is
psychology anything more than a matter of linguistics
and philology?

Here is my observation. We have *paternal* and

paternity from Latin *pater*, father, and *maternal* and *maternity* from *mater*, mother. Now paternal and maternal are quite different qualities, and paternity and maternity are totally different one from the other, so that one wonders why we do not have, along with *fraternal* and *fraternity* from *frater*, brother, the words *sororal* and *sorority* (apart from the *club*-usage) from *soror*, sister. Latin has *sororius -a -um*, sisterly, the sister's, and the verb *sororiare*, to grow equally and jointly.

It might seem that *sorority* would be the same as *fraternity*, but that would not be the case at all. If in Latin *filia* had a different common name, one with a different root, from that of *filius*, it would be worthwhile distinguishing between the two filialities.

Sorority was the quality possessed by the admirable Antigone, that woman saint of Hellenic paganism, daughter to Oedipus, who suffered martyrdom for love of her brother Polynices and because she confessed she believed that the eternal laws of conscience and consciousness—which govern the eternal world of the dead, which prevail in the world of immortality —are not those promulgated by the despots and tyrants of this earth, such as Creon, her jailer.

When Creon accuses his niece Antigone, in the drama by Sophocles, of having violated the law, the imperial mandate, by performing funeral services for her brother the fratricide, a duel of words between the pair ensues:

ANTIGONE: It is not unnatural to honor others of the same womb. . . .
CREON: Was not the murdered man from the same womb as well?
A: He was of the same blood, by mother and father. . . .

C: How, then, dishonor him?

A: He would not say as much. . . .

C: But the truth is that you honor him in the same way you do the dishonorable man.

A: It was not his servant who died, but my brother.

C: Laying waste the land which the other defended . . .

A: The other world, nevertheless, favors equality before the law. . . .

C: How can it be equal and the same for the villain and the noble?

A: Who knows if these maxims are held sacred down below . . .

May not the fact, perhaps, that, because of Fate's terrifying decree, Antigone was carnal sister to her own father, Oedipus, account for her being able to grasp the nature of eternal law, so that she appeared in the eyes of Creon and the citizens of Thebes to be an anarchist? For with Oedipus, her father, she had carried out as well the office of *sorority*.

Antigone's *sororal* act of burying the unburied corpse of her brother, Polynices, thus sparing the body the royal fury of her uncle, Creon, struck the latter as the deed of an anarchist. "There is no greater evil than anarchy!" the tyrant proclaimed (*Antigone*, line 672). Anarchy? Civilization?

Antigone was an anarchist in the eyes of her uncle, the tyrant Creon, who was himself a model of virility if not of humanity. And Antigone, sister to her father Oedipus and therefore aunt to her brother Polynices, may perhaps represent religious domesticity, domestic religion, the religion of the hearth, as against political and tyrannical civility, civil tyranny; in short, Antigone perhaps represents domestication *vis-à-vis* civilization. Though in all truth, is it possible to become civilized without first having been domesticated? Are civility and civilization possible where domesticity and domestication rest on no firm foundation?

We speak of *patrias*, fatherlands, and, over and above them, we talk of universal fraternity, but it is no linguistic artifice to maintain that they cannot prosper except upon the basis of *matrias*, mother-lands, and the principles of sorority. And we will endure the barbarity and devastation of war and of other calamities so long as the drones, circling the queen in the dance of fecundation and devouring the honey they never made, are allowed to reign in the hive.

And as regards war: the first warlike act, according to what we know as Sacred History, biblical history, was the murder of Abel by his brother Cain. That was a fraternal death, death between brothers, the first act of fraternity. And Genesis tells us that Cain, the fratricide, was the first to build a city: ". . . he builded a city, and called the name of the city, after the name of his son, Enoch" (Gen. 4: 17). And he had begotten this son on his sister. And it must have been in that city, in that *polis*, that civic and political life began; there that civility and civilization began, the end-product, as we have seen, of fratricide. And when, centuries later, Lucan, the Spaniard, called the wars between Caesar and Pompey *plusquam civile*, more than civil (he says this in the first line of the *Pharsalia*), he means that they were *fraternal*. Wars which are "more than civil" are fraternal.

Aristotle called man *zoon politicon*, that is, a civil or city animal (not a "political animal," which is a failure in translation), an animal that tends to live in cities, in clusters of dry vertical husks with dead roots cemented into the ground. There you have a definition of man, especially of the male of the species: a civil, urban, fraternal animal, and . . . a fratricide. Still, must not this civil animal be rendered more acceptable through domestication? And may not the hearth, the true hearth, be found in the roving herder's tent pitched somewhere along the road? Antigone accompanied her father, blind and driven, down the desert tracks, until he disappeared at Colonus. How poor fraternal civility, the civil order of a Cain, if it did not and could not count on domestic sorority! . . .

For domesticity, which is the foundation of civility, goes hand in hand with sisters, with aunts if you will, with spiritual wives, altogether chaste, the likes of Abishag the Shunammite, whose story is told in I Kings 1, a maiden given to David, who was close to death, so that she might sustain him in the sunset of life, ministering to him and warming him in the bed where he slept. Abishag sacrificed her maternity to him, she kept her virginity for him—poor David "knew her not"—and later she caused Solomon, son of David's sin with the adulteress Bathsheba, to slay Adonijah, his half-brother and the son of David and Haggith, because Adonijah sought to take Abishag as his wife, Abishag who had been in effect the last queen to David, so that by taking her as wife Adonijah thought to inherit the kingdom.

But we will leave off talking of Abishag, for we plan to dedicate an entire book to her and her fate, a book which will not be precisely a novel, nor even a "nivel" or *nivola*.

Whoever has read this Prologue so far—and it is of little moment or use for understanding what follows—can go on to meet Tía Tula, Aunt Tula, who,

if she knew of Saint Teresa and Don Quixote, probably did not know about Antigone the Greek or Abishag the Israelite.

In my novel *Abel Sánchez* I attempted to delve into
certain hiding places of the heart and catacombs of
the soul where most mortals fear to tread. Most people
fear that the dead live there and believe it is best not
to pay them any heed even though they, the dead,
govern our lives. This is our heritage from Cain. In
the present novel, on the other hand, I have attempted
to delve into certain other catacombs and hiding
places. And just as there were those who told me
Abel Sánchez was inhuman, so there will be those who
say the same, though in a different sense, of this book.
Abel Sánchez struck some as inhuman because it was
too virile and fraternal. This book will strike them
as too *feminil* and *sororial*. All the same, no one can
deny that men inherit femininity from their mothers
and women virility from their fathers. For does not
the drone have something of the bee about him and
the bee something of the drone? Are there not, if you
will, male bees and female drones?

And that will do, for I must not make a novel of
another novel.

*In Salamanca, city, on the day
of Our Lady's Betrothal, in the year of grace 1920*

I

IT WAS ROSA—and not her sister Gertrudis, who always went out with her—at whom Ramiro directed his eager glances. He enveloped her in them. Or at least that was what he and she believed as they were inexorably drawn to each other.

The two sisters, always together (although that did not mean they were always united), formed an apparently indissoluble pair, one single value. It was the spectacular beauty of the rather provocative Rosa, a flower of the flesh which opened up to the flowery sky in any light and in any sight, which would initially attract attention to the pair. But then it was the tenacious eyes of Gertrudis which held the gaze of whoever looked at them, and it was those same eyes which set the limits. At first glance, some men immediately considered making an overture, but the eyes of Gertrudis mutely rebuked them in advance. "Don't play around with us," she seemed to indicate in silence.

But closer up, the eyes of Gertrudis aroused even deeper longing, an anticipation of pleasure. While her sister Rosa opened herself before every wind, spread open the flower of her flesh to every light and sight, Gertrudis remained a closed coffer, a sealed chest suggesting a secret treasure.

Ramiro, who also wore his soul in the open, in his open gaze, thought he was looking only at Rosa, and he naturally addressed himself to her.

"Do you know that Ramiro has written to me, proposing?" Rosa asked her sister.

"Yes, I saw the letter."

"What? You saw it? Are you spying on me?"

"Could I have possibly missed seeing it? No, I don't spy on you ever, as you well know, and you only suggest such a thing in order to say something. . . ."

"You're right, Tula. Forgive me."

"Yes, once again, because that's the way you are. I don't spy on you, but neither do I conceal anything. I saw the letter. . . ."

"I know, I know. . . ."

"I saw the letter, and I was expecting it."

"Well, and what do you think of Ramiro?"

"I don't know him."

"You don't need to know a man to say what you think of him."

"I would have to know him."

"But you've seen him, you know what you've seen. . . ."

"I can't judge even that without knowing him."

"Don't you have eyes in your head?"

"Perhaps not in that way. I'm short-sighted, you know. . . ."

"Excuses! But he *is* a handsome lad."

"So he seems."

"And charming."

"If he's all that for you, that's good enough."

"But do you think I've already said yes to him?"

"I know you will, eventually. And that's all I need to know."

"That's not the point. He must be made to wait, and even driven a bit crazy. . . ."

"What for?"

"One cannot be too eager."

"That's not the way to do it, Rosa. That kind of coquettish play is unworthy."

"You mean that you . . ."

"Me? He hasn't asked me."

"Supposing he had?"

"There's no point in asking meaningless questions!"

"But let's suppose he *had* asked you. What would you have answered?"

"I didn't say I thought he was handsome, or attractive, and so I would have had to consider the question. . . ."

"And what if in the meantime, another girl appeared. . . ."

"Most likely that's what would happen."

"Well, in that case, dear, you might as well prepare yourself. . . ."

"Yes, to become an aunt."

"What do you mean, aunt?"

"Aunt to your children, Rosa."

"What things you say!" and Rosa's voice broke.

"Come, Rosita. And please forgive me." And she kissed Rosa on the cheek.

"But if you say such things again . . ."

"I won't!"

"So then, what shall I tell him?"

"Tell him Yes!"

"But he'll think I'm too easy. . . ."

"Then tell him No!"

"But, the thing is that . . ."

"Of course. You think he's handsome, and attractive. So tell him Yes, and don't waste your time being coquettish, because that's plain ugly. Tell him Yes. After all, it's not likely you'll do better. Ramiro is well off, he's an only son. . . ."

"I didn't mention anything like that."

"But I'm mentioning it, Rosa, and it's all the same."

"Won't people say, Tula, that I'm rather desperate for a man? . . ."

"They'll merely be saying the obvious."

"Again, Tula? . . ."

"And a hundred times more. You want a man and it's only natural you should have one. If not, why did God make you so pretty?"

"Never mind the flattery!"

"You know well enough that I don't go in for flattery. Whether we like it or not, our destiny leads either to marriage or to a convent. You don't have the vocation to be a nun. God made you to live in the world and to have a home and husband, in short, to be the mother of a family. . . . You won't be left behind to take care of holy images. So tell him Yes."

"What about you?"

"What do you mean, me?"

"Because you, then, later . . ."

"Just let me be."

On the very next day after this conversation, Rosa and Ramiro established what are called "amorous relations."

And Gertrudis felt more alone than ever.

The two sisters, orphaned of both father and mother, lived with a maternal uncle, a priest, ever since they were little girls. The priest had no need to support them, for they had a small inheritance which allowed them to live comfortably, but he did furnish them with good counsel at the meals they took together. For the rest, he left them to their natural instincts. His good counsel came from books, from the same books which served him for his sermons, his rare sermons.

The priest's name was Primitivo, Don Primitivo as he was always called. And he ruminated:

"Why should I meddle in their private lives, meddle with their feelings and inclinations? Best not to talk to them about such things. It only serves to open their eyes too wide. Although . . . did I say open them? Ah! they're already open wide enough. They're women after all. We men don't know anything about that kind of thing. We priests, even less. What the books tell us is beside the point. And as for that little Tula, Tulilla, she scares me! . . . I don't dare, in front of her, I don't dare say anything! She asks such questions! She just looks at me so serious, out of her big melancholy eyes . . . just like my sister's, like my mother's—may God keep them both in His Glory! Eyes in mourning, and they go straight into one's heart. . . . Serious and all, they seem to laugh around the edges. They seem to be saying: 'That's quite enough foolishness, Uncle, no more please!' She's a little devil! I'll never forget the day she insisted on taking her sister and herself to hear me preach. What a bad time I had of it! I did my best to keep my eyes off her, so as not to falter, or stop altogether. But it was no use, her eyes were a magnet. I couldn't avoid them! It was the same with her mother, my sister, and the same with my own mother, her mother, too, may God keep them both in His Glory! I never could preach easily before them, and I told them to stay away. My mother went secretly and sat behind a column so I couldn't see her and she never would say a word later about my sermon. And my sister did the same. But I knew what she was thinking, even though she was such a good Christian, I know well enough! 'Man stuff!'—that's what she thought of my sermons. And this girl, Tula, thinks the same. I'm sure of it. No, I wouldn't dare preach in front of that one. And as for giving her advice . . . Me? Once she used the very same phrase as her mother, it slipped out: 'Man stuff!' She wasn't talking about me, no, granted, but I understand her, I know what she means. . . ."

The poor man felt the most profound respect and admiration for his niece Gertrudis, the young Tula. He was convinced that wisdom, in his family at least, was carried through the female line. He believed that his mother had been the providential intelligence of the house in which he had been reared; that his sister, though only for so brief a time, had been the same in her own house. As regards his niece Rosa, he believed she was safe under the protection and guidance of her sister. "But truly God has made her beautiful, and may He be praised! That girl will either make a great marriage with whomever she wants, or the lads of today have no eyes in their heads."

One day, after Rosa had left the table feigning some indisposition or other, Gertrudis was left alone with her uncle, and she told him:

"I have something serious to tell you, Uncle, something very serious. Very serious . . . very serious . . ." The poor man was startled, and then he wondered if she was not laughing maliciously at him out of the corners of her brooding eyes.

"Yes, very serious."

"Well, then, out with it! We're all alone here and we can talk things over."

"The truth is that Rosa has a suitor."

"Is that all!"

"But it's formal, a regular suitor you understand."

"Of course. So I can marry them, then."

"Naturally!"

"And what do you think of the lad?"

"You haven't asked me yet who he is."

"What difference does it make, since I scarcely know anybody anyway? But what I want to know is what you think of him. Tell me now."

"Well, I don't know him either."

"But don't you know who he is?"

"Yes, I know his name, and I know the family he's from, but . . ."

"That's enough. How does he seem to you?"

"I think he's a good match for Rosa, and I believe they'll come to love each other."

"But don't they love each other already?"

"Do you think, Uncle, that they can begin by loving one another, just like that?"

"So they tell me, my little girl, and they even say it strikes people down like a bolt of lightning."

"That's merely a manner of speaking, Uncle."

"If you say so . . . that's enough for me."

"His name's Ramiro . . . Ramiro Cuadrado. . . ."

"What! The son of Doña Venancia, the widow? Well, I'll be . . . There's nothing more to say."

"Ramiro has been carried away by Rosa's beauty. He's dazzled and has convinced himself that he's in love with her."

"He will be, Tula, Tulilla, he will be."

"That's what I said. He will be. Since he's a man of his word, he will eventually feel great tenderness for the woman to whom he has given his word and to whom he is promised. He's not a man to go back on his word, I believe."

"And what about her?"

"The same will happen to her."

"You know more than Saint Augustine, my girl."

"These are not things one learns, Uncle."

17

"In any case, let them get married! I'll give them my blessing, and that will be an end to it!"

"Or a beginning! But we have to get them married, and soon, before he changes his mind."

"But do you think he might?"

"I'm never certain of men, Uncle."

"And you're certain of women?"

"Let men worry about women. But I will say, without any offense meant to the . . . stronger sex, isn't that what they're called? . . . I will say that constancy, steadfastness, is more natural on our side. . . ."

"If all women were like you, little one, I'd believe you, but . . ."

"But what?"

"You're an exception, Tulilla!"

"More than once I've heard you say that the exception proves the rule."

"Come now, you're confusing me. . . . Well, then, we'll see them married, before he changes his mind . . . or she hers."

Gertrudis' deep eyes darkened. They reflected the shadow of a storm cloud, and if the silence could be heard, the echo of the phrase "or she hers . . ." would have sounded and resounded in the cellar-vaults of her soul.

II

BUT WHAT'S this now? What's troubling Ramiro, and he formally betrothed to Rosa, so soon as he walks into the house, her house? What is this procrastination, this coldness of manner?

"Tula, I simply don't understand! He always seems to be distracted, as if he were thinking of something else—or of some other person, who knows!—or as if he were afraid someone was about to surprise us. And when I approach him, in an offhand way, as if I didn't mean anything special, and try to talk to him about marriage, he acts as if he didn't hear me, as if he were waiting for someone else . . . some other woman perhaps. . . ."

"And that's just because you do speak to him in an offhand way. Talk to him as if you meant it."

"And give him the idea that I'm in a hurry to get married!"

"Let him think so! Isn't it the truth?"

"But do you really think, Tula, that I'm dying to get married?"

"Do you love him?"

"That has nothing to do with it. . . ."

"Do you or don't you love him? Yes or no?"

"Well . . ."

"Do you or don't you?"

Rosa lowered her eyes and then her head. She had flushed red all over, her voice became tremulous, tearful, and she stammered:

"You say such things, Tula. You're like a confessor!"

Gertrudis took one of her sister's hands into hers; with the other she lifted Rosa's head and fixed her dark gaze on her sister and said:

"We live alone, Sister. . . ."

"And Uncle?"

"We live alone, I tell you. We women always live alone. Poor Uncle is a saint, but a saint out of a book, and even though he is a priest, he's a man after all."

"But he hears confession. . . ."

"Perhaps that's why he knows so little. Besides, he forgets all he hears. And that's the way it should be. We live alone, I tell you. And what you should do right now, is to confess, make a confession right here, confess to yourself. I ask you again: Do you love him?"

Poor Rosa began to cry.

"Do you love him?" the implacable voice insisted.

And Rosa finally convinced herself that the question, put to her in a solemn dusky voice out of the far-off distance of ordinary life's simple purity, was her own voice, or perhaps the voice of the mother the two sisters shared.

"Yes, I believe I'll come to love him . . . love him very much." She spoke in a low voice on the verge of sobbing.

"Yes! You'll get to love him very much and he'll love you even more!"

"How do you know that?"

"I know that he will love you."

"Then, why is he so distracted? Why does he avoid talking of our marriage?"

"I'll speak to him about it, Rosa. Leave it to me!"

"You?"

"Yes, I! Is there anything strange about that?"

"But . . ."

"I won't be inhibited the way you're inhibited, by the fear that inhibits you."

"But he'll say that I'm dying to marry him!"

"He won't say that to me. He may tell me that I want you to get married so I can be free to run this place by myself or to make it easier for me to have a suitor. Sheer nonsense in either case. And anyway he can say what he likes. I'll settle the matter with him whatever he says."

Rosa fell into her sister's arms, and Gertrudis added in a low voice:

"And then, later, you must truly love him, do you understand?"

"And why do you tell me that, Tula?"

"Because it's your duty."

The next day, when Ramiro went to visit his betrothed, he found himself alone with the other girl, the sister. He was visibly upset and changed color as he began to speak. Looking into her great dark mournful eyes he felt a rush of blood to his heart.

"Where is Rosa?" he asked, not hearing his own voice.

"Rosa has gone out, and it's my turn to talk to you."

"You?" He found that his lips trembled.

"Yes, me!"

"You're very serious." And he tried to laugh.

"I was born serious, they tell me. Uncle assures me that I inherited my manner from my mother, his sister, and from my grandmother, his mother. I don't know, and I don't care. I do know that I like things to be clear and simple and straightforward and without any deceit."

"Why tell me that now, Tula?"

"Why do you avoid talking about your marriage with my sister? Tell me now, why?"

The poor boy looked downcast and turned red. He had received an unexpected blow.

"You did ask her to accept you, and you were well-intentioned, as the naive would say, weren't you?"

"Tula!"

"Never mind the Tula! You chose her to be your wife and the mother of your children, did you not? . . ."

"But what's all this great hurry about? . . ." And once more he attempted to laugh.

"There's every cause for hurry. Life is short."

"Life is short! And the girl who says so is twenty-two years old!"

"Do you plan to marry Rosa or not?"

"Of course." And he found that his entire body trembled.

"Well, if you plan to marry her, what's the point of putting it off?"

"We're still young. . . ."

"All the better!"

"We must get to know each other. . . ."

"What! What does that 'get to know each other' mean? Do you think you'll know her any better in a year? You'll know her less, much less. . . ."

"And suppose later . . ."

"You didn't think about that when you came into this house!"

"But, Tula . . ."

"Never mind the Tula! Do you love her, yes or no?"

"Do you doubt me, Tula?"

"Never mind the Tula, I told you! Do you love her?"

"Of course I do!"

"Well, you'll love her even more. She'll be a good wife to you. You'll make a fine couple."

"And with your guidance . . ."

"Nothing of the sort! Never mind my guidance! I'll be a good aunt. That's all."

Ramiro appeared to be struggling within himself, searching for words to express his inner turmoil, and finally, with a gesture of desperate resolution, he exclaimed:

"Very well, Gertrudis, I'd like to tell you the whole truth!"

"There is no need, no call for you to tell me any more of the truth. None at all." Gertrudis cut him short, sharply. "You've told me you love Rosa and that you are determined to marry her. You can tell her the rest, the rest of the truth, after you're married to her."

"But there are certain things . . ."

"There is nothing you shouldn't tell your wife. . . ."

"But Tula!"

"Don't call me Tula! I already told you that. If you love her, marry her. And if you don't love her, your presence in this house is a mere intrusion."

These words came from her coldly. Her heart, meanwhile, felt as if it had stopped. The silence which followed was icy. The blood in her body, which seemed to have stopped flowing, suddenly was released and she flushed crimson. In the prophetic silence, she could hear her heart pound.

The next day the wedding was announced.

III

DON PRIMITIVO authorized and blessed the marriage of Ramiro and Rosa. And no one seemed gayer than Gertrudis. Such was her gaiety that many who knew her were somewhat taken aback, and there were even people who found it not quite normal.

The newlyweds went home and, once installed, Rosa began to insist that Gertrudis visit her continually. The latter replied that privacy was a natural need for newlyweds.

"Quite the opposite, Tula, I've never missed you more. It's only now that I realize how much I needed you."

Rosa was constantly embracing and kissing her sister.

"Yes, yes," replied Gertrudis, smiling her serious smile. "Your happiness requires witnesses. Your joy is multiplied when you have witnesses to it."

And so she went from time to time "to keep them company." Sometimes she took a meal with them. Rosa would overwhelm her sister with the greatest tenderness, and then demonstratively caress her husband. He, for his part, seemed embarrassed in the presence of his new sister-in-law.

"Rosa, don't gush so!" Gertrudis would admonish. "You act as if you had invented the idea of marriage."

One day she noticed a dog in the house.

"What's that?"

"A dog, of course. Can't you tell?"

"How did it get here?"

"I found it in the street, abandoned and half-dead. I took pity on it, brought it home and fed it. And here it is." Rosa cuddled the dog in her lap and kissed its muzzle.

"Well, see here, Rosa, I think you'd better give it away, because killing it would be an unnecessary cruelty."

"Why should I give it away? Just listen, Tití, they're telling me to throw you out. Where would you go, you poor little thing?" And she pressed the dog to her breast.

"Come now, don't act like a child. I'll bet your husband shares my opinion."

"Naturally, as soon as you tell it to him . . . Since you're the wise one around here . . ."

"Never mind that. And let the dog go."

"What do you have in mind? Do you think Ramiro might get jealous?"

"I never thought marriage would make you so silly."

When Ramiro learned of the disagreement over the dog, he did not dare to side with either one of the sisters, but merely said the matter was of no importance.

Gertrudis answered:

"No, it's of no importance. Or it's all-important. All this is a kind of child's play in any case, and something worse. For instance, Rosa, would you have gone so far as to have brought to this house the twin doll you had along with me, and set it up in her chair?"

"Of course. She's in the living room right now, wearing her best dress and sitting in one of the better chairs. Do you want to see her?"

Ramiro added: "It's all too true."

"Well, then, you'll get rid of her."

"Oh, all right. I'll put her away. . . ."

"So that your daughters can play with her . . ."

"The things you say, Tula!" And Rosa turned red.

"You're the one who thinks up strange things. Like that dog . . ."

"And what about you, Tula, don't you have your own doll? Or have you given her away, or taken her apart?" Rosa was anxious to put an end to the goading inquisition.

"No, I still have that doll. But she's put away."

"She's so well hidden I could never find her!"

Ramiro spoke, to bridge the gap, without knowing what he was saying:

"Gertrudis keeps her for herself alone."

"God knows why! She's a talisman from my child-hood."

*   *   *

Don Primitivo, for his part, scarcely ever called on the newlyweds at home. "The eleventh command-ment says: never butt in," the good man would say.

The days passed, one like the other, in both houses. Gertrudis had made up her mind to visit her sister as little as possible, but Rosa would come around if so much as two days went by without a visit.

"What's the trouble? Aren't you well? Or are you still annoyed about the dog? Because if you are, I'll get rid of it. . . . Why do you leave me all alone?"

"Alone, Rosa? What about your husband?"

"He goes off to take care of his affairs."

"Perhaps he invents them. . . ."

"What! You mean you think he goes away on pur-pose? Do you know something I don't? Tell me, Tula, for our mother's sake, tell me!"

"No. But it's easy to see you're bored with your happiness and with being alone. But you'll eventually get rid of the dog—otherwise you'll begin to have cravings, woman's hankerings."

"Don't say such things."

"I tell you, you'll begin to have cravings."

And then one day, Rosa came to tell her sister that she had gotten rid of the dog. Gertrudis smiled grave-ly and caressed her like a child. And she asked her in a whisper:

"You were beginning to be afraid of your cravings, weren't you?"

Rosa whispered an assent, and Gertrudis hugged her sister with a warmth which was altogether unex-pected in her.

"Now your marriage is true. You won't be bored any longer, either of you, and your husband will have his time taken up. This is what the two of you were missing. . . ."

"Perhaps it is what you were missing, too. . . . Isn't that true, little sister?"

"Where did you get that idea?"

"Well, even if I'm slow, I've lived with you all my life. . . ."

"That's enough of jokes. . . ."

But from then on, Gertrudis frequented her sister's house more and more.

IV

AT ROSA'S CHILDBED, which was difficult, no one was calmer and more useful than Gertrudis. One would have thought she was a veteran at these things. It was a difficult birth and Rosa was close to death. Then there was some question of whether she or the infant would survive. The doctor spoke of delivering the infant dead or alive.

"Dead? Absolutely not!" Gertrudis was adamant.

"But don't you see," the doctor, too, was adamant, "that even if the child dies, the mother remains and can have more children? If the mother dies, everything is changed. . . ."

It occurred to Gertrudis that there were always other mothers, but she refrained from saying so. She did insist, however:

"A dead child? Absolutely not! Besides, there's a soul to be saved."

The woman in childbed was totally unaware of all this talk. Finally, worn out with the effort, she gave birth to a boy.

Gertrudis picked him up at once, avidly, as if she had been doing it all her life. She washed him and wrapped him in diapers.

The doctor was impressed:

"You are a midwife by nature."

Gertrudis carried the boy to his father, who was crouched in a corner as if overwhelmed with contrition for some sin and awaiting in terror the news of his wife's death.

"Here's your first-born, Ramiro. Look how handsome he is!"

When the new father raised his head, freed of his anguish, he saw only the great dark eyes of his sister-in-law. There was a new light in them; they were darker but also more brilliant than before. And when he went to kiss the bundle of flesh which was presented to him as his child, his own feverish cheek brushed against his sister-in-law's.

She addressed him in an even voice:

"Now you go and thank your wife, and ask for her pardon. Bring her around."

"Ask for her pardon?"

"Exactly. Ask her to pardon you."

"But why?"

"I know why, and she'll know why. And as for this little one, he's my responsibility now. And if I have any strength at all, I'll make a man of him."

As she said this, she pressed the newborn creature against her breast, which moved to her deep emotion.

Ramiro grew dizzy with confusion. He heard a voice within him asking: "Which of the two is the mother?"

Presently, Gertrudis was carefully laying the child alongside Rosa, who seemed to have sunk into an exhausted sleep, her face white as snow. But suddenly she opened her eyes slightly and found herself looking into those of her sister. A tremor of delight ran through the victorious body of the new mother. She half-moaned:

"Tula!"

"I'm here, Rosa, and I'll stay here with you. Now rest. When you can, you'll give this creature your breast to suckle. That will quiet him down. Don't worry about anything else."

"I thought I was dying, Tula. Even now it seems as if I were dreaming in death. I felt so sorry for Ramiro. . . ."

"Quiet now! The doctor said you should not speak much. . . . Poor Ramiro was closer to death than you. Now you can begin to feel good . . . and get ready for the next one!"

The poor mother smiled wanly.

"This one will be called Ramiro, like his father," Gertrudis decreed in a small family council some little time later. "And the other one, the next one, will be a girl, and she shall be called Gertrudis, like me."

"You mean you're already thinking of another one?" exclaimed Don Primitivo. "After your poor sister nearly didn't make it . . ."

"What else is there to do? What else did they get married for? Isn't that the way things are, Ramiro?" Gertrudis's eyes fixed on him.

"The important thing now is for her to get well," said the husband, cowed by that gaze, the sister's eyes.

"It's nothing! A woman quickly recovers from this kind of thing."

"The doctor is right, Niece, when he says that you're a born midwife."

"Every woman, Uncle, is born a mother."

And she spoke with such homely solemnity that Ramiro fell prey to an indefinable uneasiness and a strange sense of guilt. "Do I love my wife as she deserves?" he asked himself.

"Now you can say you have a wife, Ramiro," his sister-in-law told him.

From then on, Gertrudis did not miss going to her sister's house a single day. She dressed and undressed and took care of the child until its mother could do it.

And the mother came quickly around. She had grown even more beautiful than before. She treated her husband with more tenderness than ever. But in the end she accused him of being evasive.

"I feared for your life," he told her, "and I was terrified. I was desperate and filled with remorse."

"Remorse? For what?"

"And if you had died, I'd have shot myself!"

"Come, now, what would be the point of that? 'Man stuff,' Tula would call it. But that's all past, and now I know what it's like."

"But didn't it scare you, teach you a lesson, Rosa?"

"Scare me? Teach me a lesson?" Rosa put her arms around her husband's neck, drew him to her, and whispered passionately: "I want another one, a girl, Ramiro! Now I do love you! Even if you kill me at it!"

Gertrudis meanwhile lulled the baby lest it be affected by its parents' ardor.

The aunt worked almost systematically from the very first at preventing any awareness in the child, even by the remotest gesture or sign, of the passion which brought it into being. She naturally hung a protective medal around its neck, an effigy of the Virgin Mother with the Child in her arms.

Whenever the mother showed signs of impatience in quieting the child she would tell her:

"Give him to me, Rosa, and go take care of your husband."

"But, Tula . . ."

"You've got to take care of the two of them, and I've got only the one."

"You've a way of putting things, Tula. . . ."

"Don't be a child. You're a woman and a mother. And you can thank God that we can share . . . this way."

"Tula . . . Tula."

"Ramiro . . . Ramiro . . . Rosa."

The mother would pout, but she would go to her husband.

And thus the days passed. Until another child was born. A girl.

V

THE GIRL WAS scarcely born when they found Don Primitivo dead. Gertrudis washed and shrouded him with the same care with which she washed and dressed the new babies. Alone with the old man she found herself weeping in a way she had not imagined possible. "I would never have believed I felt so strongly about him," she said aloud. "He was a holy man. He tried to make me believe I was a font of wisdom. And he was such a simple man!"

"He was our true father," she went on later, talking to her sister. "And he never even raised his voice."

"Of course not, since he let us do anything we felt like."

"He knew that his presence was enough to sanctify our desires. He was our father, and he educated us. And the simplicity and innocence of his life was enough to show us the way. . . ."

"That's true," Rosa agreed, her eyes filled with tears. "I've never known a man with his simple goodness."

"It would have been impossible to have been brought up in a purer household than this."

"What do you mean, Tula?"

"He filled our life in silence, almost total silence, hardly speaking to us at all, and he filled it with the cult and veneration of the Holy Virgin Mother, and of our mother, his sister, and of our grandmother, his mother. Do you remember how his voice would break when we said the rosary together at night, just as he got to the Ave Maria for the eternal rest of our mother's soul, and then he would go on to pray for his mother, our grandmother, both women we never knew? He gave us a mother through that rosary, and he showed you how to be a mother."

"And you . . . and you, too, Tula!"

"Me?"

"Yes, he showed you, too. Who else is the real mother of my children?"

"Never mind that, now. . . . A saint lies before us, a silent saint. They tell me that the poor holy women in the church used to cry when he preached even though they didn't understand a single word he was saying. I can understand why. Even his voice was a loving call, a call to loving harmony. . . . And now, the rosary!"

The two sisters knelt at the foot of their uncle's deathbed and said the rosary as they had said it with him through the years, with two Paternosters and Ave Marias for the eternal rest of the souls of their mother and of the man lying there, to which they added another Paternoster and another Ave Maria for the soul of the newly blessed. The soft sweet tongues of the candles as they burned at either side of the corpse shining on the dead man's forehead, as white as the white of their own wax, seemed to accompany them in their prayers, swaying with the rhythm of the words. Deep peace permeated the death chamber. The two sisters rose as a pair from the floor. First Gertrudis and then Rosa kissed the waxlike forehead of the priest, and then they embraced each other, dry-eyed now.

"There's no one left for you now, Rosa, but your husband. So you can love him more. Make him happy and . . . give us more children!"

"And there's no one left for you either. So you'll come live with us, won't you?"

"No, not that!" Gertrudis replied with sudden fire.

"Why not? . . . And you say no in such a way . . ."

"Yes, yes, Sister, I know. Forgive my outburst. Forgive me. . . . Will you forgive me?" Gertrudis seemed about to kneel down, again.

"Come now, Tula, don't be sad. It's not so important. It's only that you have such impulsive . . ."

"I know. But you forgive me, don't you? You will forgive me? . . ."

"You don't have to ask that. But you will come and live with us?"

"Don't insist, Rosa, don't insist. . . ."

"Won't you come? . . . Otherwise you'll be abandoning your niece and nephew, almost your own children. . . ."

"But I haven't left off seeing them for a single day. . . ."

"You'll come? . . ."

"I'll think about it, Rosa, I'll think about it. . . ."

"Well, then, I'll insist no more."

But a few days later she did insist. Gertrudis tried to put her off.

"No, no, I don't want to be in your way."

"In our way? What are you talking about, Tula?"

"A man and woman must have their own home."

"And can't that same home be yours?"

"No, no. Even though you don't realize it, I'd be infringing on your freedom. Isn't that so, Ramiro?"

"No, not at all. I don't see . . . ," the husband stuttered in confusion, as he usually did whenever his sister-in-law addressed him unexpectedly.

"Yes, Rosa, your husband—even though he does not say so—understands well enough that a couple, especially a young couple in full production, needs to be alone. I, the aunt, will come whenever possible to teach the children whatever you don't have time to show them."

And she continued going to their house, sometimes very early, only to find the boy up and about while the parents slept. "If I were to say I'm needed here . . ."

VI

THE THIRD CHILD was due. Rosa lamented her fecundity. "We're going to be loaded with children," she complained. Her sister answered: "What other point was there in getting married?"

The pregnancy proved troublesome for the mother, so that she had to neglect the other children; they were thus thrown upon the care of the aunt, who was delighted to have them. She even managed to take them to her house on more than one occasion, to her solitary house where she lived with the ancient maid who had served Don Primitivo. She kept the children with her closely, and they responded with a blind tenderness for that grave, exacting woman.

Ramiro, always irritable during the last months of his wife's pregnancies, an attitude which disturbed Gertrudis, was now more irritable than ever.

"What a nuisance all this is!"

"A nuisance for you?" the sister asked without raising her eyes from the niece or nephew she held in her lap.

"Yes, for me. I live in a continuous state of alarm, fearful of everything."

"Nonsense! All your fears will prove groundless. Nature is most wise."

"The pitcher goes to the fountain only so many times before it breaks. . . ."

"Ah, my son, everything has its risks and every state of being has its inconveniences!"

Ramiro was astonished to hear himself called "my son" by his sister-in-law, who consistently avoided using his name; for his part, he was happy calling her by the familiar "Tula."

"How right you were, Tula, not to get married!"

"Really?" She raised her eyes and fixed him with her deep glance.

"Yes, really. It's all trouble and care and risk. . . ."

"But tell me, do you know for certain I'm not going to get married?"

"Well, as far as age is concerned, you could, of course. . . ."

"Then what's to stop me?"

"You don't seem to have much interest. . . ."

"Interest in getting married? What kind of interest do I need?"

"Well, the truth is . . ."

"You mean you don't see me hunting for a man, isn't that it?"

"No, that's not it."

"Yes, it is."

"If you were to accept them, there would certainly be no lack of men. . . ."

"But I can't go looking for them. I'm not a man. Women must wait to be chosen. And the truth is that I like to choose for myself, rather than be chosen."

"What's this you're talking about?" Rosa came up and dropped into an armchair, exhausted.

"Nothing much. Your husband's concerns over the advantages and disadvantages of marriage."

"That's no subject for men. They don't know anything about it. It's we women who get married, not you men."

"What do you mean, Rosa?"

"Just come and help me out of this chair now. I find I can't get up so fast. And I can scarcely stand. I'm going to lie down. Goodbye, Tula. I'll leave the children to you."

Ramiro went and helped her up, and she put one

arm around his neck, and leaned her head on him, her right hand in his right hand. They moved off slowly, Rosa, supported by her husband and moaning softly, Gertrudis, a child on each knee, watching her sister's laborious retreat; Rosa resembled a vine encircling its prop. Gertrudis's large eyes, eyes of mourning, gravely serene, filled with tears, and she clasped the two children to her, pressing one to each cheek. The little boy, Ramirín, seeing his aunt, his Aunt Tula, cry, began to cry, too.

"Come, come, don't cry, Ramirín. Let's go play."

The third birth left Rosa in a highly weakened state.

"I have the most awful forebodings, Tula."

"Pay no attention to omens, Rosa."

"It's not a matter of omens. I feel my life running out on me. I've no blood left."

"Your blood will come back to you."

"For the moment anyway I can't nurse the child. And wet nurses terrify me, Tula."

And so they did. In the space of a few days three came and went. The father grew furious and spoke of whipping them. Meanwhile the mother grew weaker.

"Time is running out here!" declared the doctor one day.

Ramiro wandered around the house like a ghost. He was prey to the strangest fears and the most sudden furies. One afternoon he went so far as to tell the sister:

"The trouble is that Rosa does nothing to stay alive. She's getting it into her head that she must die and, of course, that way she'll die. Why don't you try to rouse her and convince her that it's important to live?"

"That's up to you, Son. You're her husband. If you can't rouse her appetite for life, who can? And it's true enough that her main enemy is not the loss of blood, but her fixed idea of dying. Even the children tire her out at once. . . . And as for her soul, she scarcely even asks after its care."

The fact was that Rosa lived on as if in a dream, in constant vertigo, and saw everything through a fog.

One evening she called her sister to her side and, in a faltering voice, thin and feverish, clutching Tula's hand, told her:

"Listen, Tula, I'm dying, and there's no help for it. I leave you my children, three parts of my heart, and I leave you Ramiro, another child. He really is like a child, believe me, a big child with whims, but good all the same, good as can be. He's never made me unhappy, not even once. I leave them to you, Tula."

"Don't worry, Rosa. I know my duty."

"Duty . . . Duty . . ."

"I know my loves. And as long as I live your children will have a mother."

"Thank you, Tula, thank you. I wanted to hear you say that."

"You need have no doubts."

"You mean, then, that my children, those pieces of my heart, will never have a stepmother?"

"What do you mean, Rosa?"

"That you will become his wife, Tula."

"I didn't say that, Rosa! And now, at this moment, I cannot, even out of pity, lie to you. I didn't say I would marry your husband if you were gone. I said that your children would never be without a mother. . . ."

"No, you told me they wouldn't have a stepmother."

"All right, then. They won't have a stepmother!"

"And that can't be for sure unless you marry Ramiro. And I'm not jealous. If he must belong to some other woman, let it be you. Let him be yours. Perhaps . . ."

"But why must he remarry?"

"Ah, Tula, you don't know men! You don't know my husband."

"No, I don't."

"Well, I do."

"Who knows . . ."

The invalid was losing consciousness.

Not long after, she called for her husband. When Ramiro left the room he was beside himself, pale as a ghost.

Death roamed the house of Rosa and Ramiro. While the young mother's life ebbed away in a rosary of blood drops, the search was begun for a new wet nurse for the infant, who was also falling away from hunger. Gertrudis, leaving her sister to sleep in the cradle of her slow agony, frenziedly sought a milk-filled breast for her little nephew.

She worked at deceiving the child's hunger with a bottle as substitute.

"Where's that wet nurse?"

"She can't come until tomorrow, Señorita!"

"Listen, Tula," . . . Ramiro implored.

"Leave me alone! Go to your wife's side. She's dying and may go any moment. Go, now, that's your place, and leave me alone with the child!"

"But, Tula . . ."

"Leave me alone, I've told you. Go and watch her die. Let her enter the other life with your arms around her. Go on! Leave me!"

Ramiro went away. Gertrudis picked up the infant,

who was wailing, and locked herself up in her bedroom. She took out one of her breasts, one of her
virginal breasts, milkless, flushed red as if with fever
and palpitating with her own heartbeat, and pushed
the nipple into the pale rose flower of the infant's
mouth. And the infant wailed even louder as he sucked
with pale lips at the impassioned breast without milk.

"A miracle, Holy Virgin!" Gertrudis moaned while
her eyes became veiled in tears. "A miracle, and no
one will know, no one!"

And she pressed the child to her breast like a mad-
woman.

She heard steps, and then someone trying the door.
She put her breast back into her dress, dried her eyes,
and opened the door. Ramiro stood before her.

"It's finished!"

"May God take her to His glory! . . . Now, Ramiro, we must take care of the . . ."

"Take care? You . . . because without you . . ."

"Very well. Let's begin to raise them."

VII

A N D N O W , now that he was a widower, Ramiro
saw clearly how much he had cared, without realizing
it, for his wife. He sought surcease in the room where
they had lived out their love, and there he relived his
life as husband.

He recalled his courtship, which had been slow-
paced even if not drawn out. Rosa had seemed intent
on making off with his soul, letting it be known that
he would never have her or know her until she became

his totally and forever. It was a courtship carried out under the steady gaze of Gertrudis, who was all soul, and so it was careful and reserved. He well remembered how the presence of Gertrudis, the Aunt Tula of his children, had cowed him and kept him in bounds, so that he never dared attempt the usual liberties of a courtship. And he had weighed his words.

Then the wedding, and the intoxication of the first months, of the honeymoon. Rosa opened herself and her soul to him, but her soul was so simple and transparent that he realized that she never had held anything back from him. He found that his wife lived her life as if it were an offering of herself to him, a gesture of permanent offering, her spirit and sensibilities put out in the open air of the world, totally given over to the moment, in the way that roses live in the field or larks in the sky. And Rosa's spirit was like a reflection from her sister's, like running water is to the sun, for which the water is a hidden font.

Finally, one day, Ramiro saw clearly what he had not seen before. He realized, now that it was all over, that Rosa was not the beauty he had invented, but a rather ordinary mortal, with the tender charm of the ordinary, the sweetness of the humble. She was like good bread, not a perilous exotic potion. Her quiet gaze, her smile, her liveliness personified domestic tranquility. There was a plantlike quality in her silence and tractability; she had taken the light like a plant and converted it into peacefulness; and with a shaded and yet potent force she had imbibed the juice of ordinary common life; her perfume was that of sweet naturalness.

He had a plethora of memories. He recalled how he had pursued her through the large house, when her final capture and his triumph were a matter of long endless kisses. He would gaze into her eyes in silence, and would hold her around and press his ear to her breast to hear her heartbeat, as if it were telling him something.

And he recalled the visits of Gertrudis, with her grave face and great large eyes of mourning in which a muffled voice seemed to say to them: "You're a couple of children who, when I'm not around to watch you, play at being man and wife. This is no way to get ready to raise children. Marriage was instituted to bring grace to a couple and allow them to raise children for heaven."

Children! They were their first great concern. For a month had passed and then another and then several more, and there was neither sign nor signal of fertility in their love. And then it was he wondered if Gertrudis had been right in her tacit disapproval. Was it true after all that they had merely been playing at man and wife, without the strength of faith in duty, without truly desiring the fruit of the benediction of a just love? What troubled him most at the time, he recollected now, was the opinion of others, what they might think; for there might be people who would think that because he had been unable to produce children, he was less of a man than other men. Why could he not do what fools, cripples, and cretins did? He felt wounded in his pride. He would have liked his wife to have given birth to a child at the end of the well-rounded nine months after marriage, a just and fair period. Besides, in those days, people said that having or not having children depended on how much or how little the couple cared for each other, though it was plain to see that there were people deeply in love with each other who still had no children while others who had

married for convenience or money were loaded down
with offspring. But, he thought now of how he had
concocted his own theory to explain all this, and it
was based on his belief that an obvious, conscious
love, one originating in the mind, might be great and
authentic and yet prove sterile, while a secret essential
love, hidden even from the two who felt it, a love felt
by souls and bodies bound entirely together, would always be fertile. Did he not love Rosa sufficiently or
did Rosa not sufficiently love him? He recalled how
he had tried to decipher the mystery while he caressed
her in silence in the darkness of night and while he
recited his own endless litany asking her if she truly
loved *him*. Rosa always answered with an ecstatic af-
firmative. It was all a ritual madness, and he felt
ashamed now of its baseness, especially when he
thought of Gertrudis, Gertrudis with her constant
serenity. He was cured of this sickness by the flower-
ing of love: the arrival of the first child. He had tri-
umphed at last! And with the first fruits came the
first authentic love.

Yes, love. But what do writers on love, amatory
if not amorous writers, know about love? Their only
interest is in arousing their readers. What did these
galley slaves of letters know of love? Or rather, not
of love, but of tenderness. All that business about love
comes from books, Ramiro thought now. The phrase
I love you is heard more often in theatres and in novels, while in real life the phrase should be *I want you*.
Even more meaningful is the love which says nothing.
Neither love nor desire are words big enough to de-
scribe what cannot be said because it is at one with
life itself. Most of your amatory singers know as
much about love as your novena-swallowers and ro-
sary-digesters know about prayer. Prayer is not so

much a recital at certain hours in a certain specific place in a certain posture as it is to vow one's whole soul before and in God. Why, even eating is prayer! And drinking and walking and playing and reading and writing and talking and even sleeping are and should be forms of prayer; and even praying is prayer, can be prayer, and our entire life, thought Ramiro, should be a continuous and muted chorus of "Thy will be done!" and an incessant "Thy kingdom come!" Not the mere words said, or even thought, but lived. Ramiro recalled having heard a holy man, who even had fame as a holy man, speak of prayer in this way once. And he himself had identified it later with love. For it was clear that whoever professed his wife as one might profess Christianity would see, once she was gone, that his entire life's routine, his daily life, had been in her; that he had breathed her in with the thousand nothings of the day, that she was like the air itself, noticed only when missing, when gasping for breath. For Ramiro now struggled to breathe, and the anguish of his bereavement revealed the fullness of the love he had lived and which was now gone.

The beginning of marriage had been lived, indeed, under the sign of desire. He had burned and turned and trembled every time he had touched her, but that was because she was not truly his, not yet him, they were not truly one, yet. Later, when they touched, his hand on her naked flesh, it had become as if he touched himself; he no longer burned, and yet, if her flesh had been cut, he would have felt the hurt. Did he not in a sense feel and suffer the travail of delivery and the birth-pangs along with Rosa?

When, after the suffering of the first birth, he saw her begin to exult, he understood that love is stronger than life or death and that it rises above the discords

of both; he understood that love causes life to die and
death to live, just as now he lived Rosa's death and
died in his own life. The sight of the child serene in
sleep, his lips parted like petals, assured him of the
existence of love made living flesh. Contemplating the
fruit of love, he drew the mother to him over the
cradle, and while the infant slept, Ramiro covered
Rosa with kisses and urged her to have another child.
She demurred and said that once was enough. And
then he had gotten the notion of their having twins
and pleaded for two more. When she was once more
pregnant, he insisted she had grown big enough to
be holding two, at least two. But she held that one
more was enough, for good and all. The second child,
Tulita, came; the mother recuperated from her travail, and Ramiro agreed that she had done enough;
Rosa, who had won over life and over death, smiled
in easy contentment.

And she died! It did not seem possible, but she died.
The terrible day came when the last battle was waged
and lost. Gertrudis was there whenever the care of
the hungry infant permitted her to get away; she dis-
pensed useless medicines, straightened the bed, en-
couraged her sister, gave heart to all. Lying in the
bed where three lives had begun, Rosa was losing her
power of speech; she lost all strength eventually and
merely held her husband's hand. She gazed at her
man, the father of her children, in the way that a voy-
ager on a ship about to lose sight of land looks back at
the last promontory of native coast as it becomes en-
gulfed in the mist of distance, as it grows indistinct
from the sky above it. As she seemed to sink she
stared ever deeper into his eyes, her eyes now gazing
back from the confines of eternity. She seemed to ask
one last desperate question, as she prepared to leave

for the last time, about the purpose of it all, about the hidden sense of life altogether. In the final repose of desperation she seemed to ask the man who had been her life, who had brought life into being along with her, who had brought new mortals to earth, who had drawn three lives from out of her, what purpose had been served. It was an afternoon lived on the edge of the abyss. During the lulls in the final battle, Rosa held her husband's trembling hands in her own feverish fingers, she looked up at him with eyes weary of living; smiling sadly she looked then upon the child sleeping nearby and whispered that he should not be disturbed in his sleep but allowed to dream on as long as possible. And then at last came the final passage, the transit. It was as if, at the very gates of eternal darkness and suspended over the abyss, she clung to him with increased desperation, until he felt he was being dragged along. She tore at her throat with her nails as if to open it, staring at him wildly as if pleading for air; her look plunged into the depths of his soul and then, letting go his hand, she fell back upon the bed where she had conceived and brought forth his three children. The two of them rested, Rosa in death, and Ramiro, his spirit withered, in a bottomless lethargy. The child, too, went on dreaming. It was Gertrudis who, with the infant at her breast, closed her sister's eyes: after which she covered the sleeping child, and brought to it with a kiss the final warmth she had found on its mother's forehead when she had kissed her sister for the last time.

But, in all truth, did Rosa die then? Did she really die altogether? Could she be said to be dead while she lived on in Ramiro? In the night, now solitary, while he slept in that bed of death and of life and love, he sensed her breathing alongside him, felt her

warmth, albeit he felt it as in a void. He would stretch
out his hand and run it over the empty half of the
bed and would clasp . . . nothing. When he sat up
and thought about her, he could think only—and that
was the worst of it—of bookish love, not of life's desire and tenderness. He was chagrined that his virile
feeling, the life of his life and air of his spirit, could
only find expression in abstract maunderings. His sorrow was spiritualized, that is, intellectualized, and it
only took on flesh when Gertrudis was around.

He was also brought around by the small voice
which called for its father. And there she was again,
taking form in another form, the immortal dead wife.
And the same small voice called for its mother. And
the voice of Gertrudis, gravely sweet, would answer,
crying out, "Son!"

No, Rosa, his Rosa, had not died, she could not
possibly have died; the woman and wife was there, as
alive as before and exuding life around her; the woman
and wife could not die.

VIII

GERTRUDIS, WHO HAD moved into her sister's
house on the birth of the third child and had stayed
on during the final illness, told her brother-in-law one
day:

"Ramiro, I'm going to move out of my house for
good."

Ramiro's heart began to pound.

"Yes," she added, "I must come live with you and
take care of the children. Besides, it won't do to leave
that fine rogue of a wet nurse alone here. . . ."

"Thanks be to God, Tula."

"Never mind the Tula, I told you. I'm Gertrudis to you."

"What's the difference?"

"I know the difference."

"Look, Gertrudis . . ."

"Well, now, I'm off to see what the wet nurse is up to."

Gertrudis had a mania about the wet nurse. She would not allow her to nurse the infant in front of the father; and she scolded her for taking out her breast with a roguish air.

"You don't need to keep showing it around here. The child's the one who needs it and who is supposed to see it. It's up to him to decide if you've got enough milk."

Ramiro suffered and Gertrudis could feel him suffer.

"Poor Rosa!" he kept exclaiming.

"The ones who are poor now are the children and it's of them we must think. . . ."

"It's not enough. I can't sleep. I can't rest. Especially at night I'm worn out with solitude. I spend whole nights without sleep."

"Go out after supper, just as you used to do, most especially toward the end of your married life. And don't come home until you're tired. You must go to bed sleepy."

"The point is I feel empty. I feel a void. . . ."

"A void when your children are all around you?"

"Nothing can take her place."

"I agree. . . . Although you men . . ."

"I didn't believe I cared so much. . . ."

"That's normal. The same thing happened to me with my uncle, and then with my sister, your Rosa. I didn't know how much I cared for her until she died. I know it now that I'm taking care of her children, your children. I think we must care for the dead in the persons of the living."

"Isn't it more likely that we care for the living in the dead?"

"Let's not make fine distinctions."

Every morning, after Ramiro was up, Gertrudis would go to his bedroom and throw wide the windows leading onto the balcony. "Man's odors!" And she would avoid being alone with Ramiro, trying always to make sure that one of the children was with her.

Sitting in the armchair where her sister used to sit, she would survey the children at play.

"But I'm a boy, and you're no more than a girl," she heard little Ramirín say, in his piping voice, to his sister one day.

"Ramirín, Ramirín, what are you saying? Are you already a man, become a brute so soon . . . ?"

One day Ramiro called his sister-in-law and told her:

"I've found out your secret."

"What secret?"

"That you were seeing my cousin Ricardo."

"All right. That's true enough. He insisted, hounded me, wouldn't leave me in peace, and finally I felt sorry for him."

"And you'd concealed it all so carefully, made such a secret. . . ."

"What was the point of talking about it?"

"And I know more. . . ."

"What do you know?"

"That you've sent him off."

"That's true, too."

"He himself showed me the letter."

"What? I didn't think he'd go that far. A man, after all! I did right in breaking with him."

Ramiro had in fact been shown a letter from his sister-in-law to his cousin. It read as follows:

My dear Ricardo:

You can't imagine how badly I'm faring, what a difficult time it has been since my sister died. The last few days have been terrible ones, and I have not ceased asking the Virgin Mary and her Son to give me strength to make out my future clearly. You cannot imagine what pain it gives me to tell you that our relationship cannot go on. I cannot marry. My sister continues to plead with me from the other world that I never abandon her children and that I act as their mother. And since I have these children in my care, it is impossible for me to marry. Forgive me, Ricardo, forgive me for God's sake, and consider carefully my reasons for acting in this way. It grieves me greatly, for I know I would have grown to love you and, above all, because I realize how much you love me and how you will suffer. My soul grieves to cause you this sorrow. But you, being good, will understand my duty and the motives for this decision, and you will find another woman, one free of my sacred obligations, and she will be able to make you happier than I could have done. Good-bye, Ricardo. May you find happiness, and give joy to others. You can be sure that I will never ever forget you.

Gertrudis

"And now, despite everything," added Ramiro, "Ricardo wants to see you."

"Am I in hiding?"

"No, but . . ."

"Tell him to come to our house to see me whenever he likes."

"Our house, Gertrudis, our house . . ."

"Yes, ours, and our children's."

"If you wanted . . ."

"Let's not speak of that!" And Gertrudis stood up. Ricardo appeared the very next day.

"Tula, for God's sake . . ." His voice broke.

"Be strong, Ricardo. You're a man."

"But these children already have a father. . . ."

"It's not enough. They don't have a mother . . . or rather, they do have one."

"Ramiro could get married again."

"Get married again? . . . In that case the children will come with me. . . . I promised their mother on her deathbed that they would never have a stepmother."

"What if you were to become the stepmother, Tula?"

"What do you mean?"

"Yes, you. By marrying him, marrying Ramiro."

"Never!"

"Well, that's the only reason I can think of for leaving me."

"Never, I said. I would not risk having some children of my own, that is, of my own flesh and blood, because they would take away from the tenderness I feel for these children. More children, now? No, never. These are enough to bring up well."

"You won't convince anyone, Tula, that you've come to live here for that reason."

"I'm not trying to convince anyone of anything. As far as making you believe me, it should be enough for me to tell you so."

They parted forever.

"What happened?" Ramiro asked later.

"We've separated, agreed to part. It could not have been otherwise."

"And so now you're free. . . ."

"I was already free. I'm still free, and I intend to die free."

"Gertrudis . . . Gertrudis . . ." His voice trembled with entreaty.

"I sent him away because I owe myself, as I've told you, to your children, Rosa's children. . . ."

"And yours . . . don't you also say that?"

"And mine, yes!"

"But if you wanted . . ."

"Don't persist. I've already said that I should not marry you, and even less anyone else."

"Even less? . . ." He breathed deeper.

"Yes, even less."

"How is it that you never became a nun?"

"I don't like to be told what to do. I don't like to take orders."

"Whatever convent you entered you'd soon be the Abbess, the Mother Superior."

"I like giving orders even less. Ramirín!"

The child answered the call. His aunt took hold of him and said: "Let's go play, love."

"But, Tula . . . ," Ramiro began.

"I've already told you," and now she came up to him, keeping hold of the child's hand the while, and whispered, "not to call me Tula, especially in front of the children. They can call me Tula, but not you. Have some consideration for them."

"How have I failed to show them consideration?"

"In allowing your instincts out into the open in front of them . . ."

"But they don't understand. . . ."

"Children understand everything, more than we. And they forget nothing. And if they don't understand now, they'll understand tomorrow. Any one of these things which a child sees or hears is like a seed in his soul, which later grows and gives fruit. And that's enough! *Basta!*"

IX

THE LIFE OF that house became one of unhappy restlessness and of mute battle. She defended herself by means of the children, whom she managed always to have around her, while she urged him to go and seek distraction. For his part, he overdid talking to the children about their poor mother and overwhelmed them with attentions, especially the little girl, whom he devoured with kisses in front of their Tula.

"Not so much! You'll only upset her with all that. Besides, it's not natural. And let them call me Aunt, and not Mamá. And don't go so far. Control yourself."

"Am I not to find consolation with my children?"

"Yes, Son, of course. The first thing is to educate them well."

"So?"

"Overwhelming them with kisses and too many sweets will only make them weak. And then children know, they guess. . . ."

"How is that my fault?"

"Can there be a better home for the children than the one they have right here? This is a true hearth, with a father and mother, pure and chaste, where they can roam at will, go anywhere at any time, a house where not a single door need be locked, a home without mysteries. Could you want anything better?"

But Ramiro kept attempting to be near her, very near her, grazing her. And at the table she had occasion to say once:

"Don't look at me that way. The children can see, you know."

She had the children pray for their mother every night. One night, when their father was present, she asked them for an additional prayer:

"And now, my children, a Paternoster and an Ave Maria for Papá too."

"But Papá isn't dead, Mamá Tula."

"That doesn't matter. He could die. . . ."

"Yes, but you could, too."

"That's true. Another Paternoster and an Ave Maria for me then."

Afterwards, after the children were in bed, she told Ramiro dryly:

"Things cannot go on this way. Unless you can control yourself, I must leave, even though Rosa will never forgive me. . . ."

"But it's just that . . ."

"Never mind. You heard what I said. I won't have you perverting things, even with looks. You're ruining the house where your children's souls should be formed. Remember Rosa. . . ."

"But what do you think men are made of?"

"Of flesh. And they're savage, too."

"What about you? Have you never looked at yourself?"

"Now what are you talking about?" Her face changed color.

"Even if you were not their mother, which by every right you really are, do you believe you have the right to persecute me in this way, with your mere presence? Is it right to reproach me when the whole house is filled with you, with your eyes, with the sound of your voice, with your body which is all soul, a soul which is all body? You're a magnet, and I . . ."

Gertrudis felt as if she were on fire. She lowered her head and said nothing. Her heart was pounding.

Ramiro went on: "Whose fault is it then? Tell me."

"You're right, Ramiro. But if I were to leave, the children would cry like little birds for me, because they do love me. . . ."

"More than they do me," said the father sadly.

"I don't cover them with kisses, nor fondle them so much, and when I do kiss them they know I mean it, and that the kisses are for them and not meant for someone else. . . ."

"And who is to blame, I asked you?"

"All right. . . . Let's wait a year, then. We'll wait a year. Let me have a year to think things out, and you can do the same, and then you'll be sure. . . ."

"A year . . . a year . . ."

"Does it seem so long?"

"And then, at the end of the year . . ."

"Then . . . we'll see. . . ."

"We'll see . . . we'll see. . . ."

"I won't promise any more."

"And if in the course of the year . . ."

"What? If you do something foolish . . ."

"What do you mean by something foolish?"

"Falling in love with someone else and getting married again."

"I'll never do that!"

"You say that easily enough. Too quickly!"

"Never, I said."

"Men find it easy to swear, to make promises."

"And if I did, who'd be to blame?"

"To blame?"

"Yes, to blame."

"It would only mean that . . ."

"That what?"

"That you never did love her, that you don't love her as she did you, as she would have loved you if she were a widow instead of you a widower. . . ."

"No, it would mean something else altogether, and it's not . . ."

"That's enough. Ramirín, come here! Come, quick!"

And that was the way that particular battle was suspended. Gertrudis continued with her job of educating the children.

She did not allow the girl to learn the usual girl-things: needlework and sewing and such.

"Women's work? Proper to her sex? Nothing of the sort. No 'studies proper to her sex.' A woman's work is to make men and women, not dress them."

One day, when Ramirín used a vulgar expression which he had picked up in the street and his father was about to reproach the boy, Gertrudis stopped him, saying in a low voice: "No, let him be. We should pretend we didn't hear. There must be a whole world which is not even to be condemned in this house."

And once when she heard a young woman say she was being left without a man, and was fit only to dress the images in church, she added: "Or to dress the souls of children!"

"Tulita is my girl," Ramirín announced one day.

"Don't talk foolish. Tulita is your sister."

"Can't she be my sister and my girl too?"

"No."

"Well what does it mean to be a sister?"

"A sister is a . . . to be a sister means . . ."

"To live in the same house," the little sister herself put in.

Another day the little girl came home in tears. She had been bitten by a bee on a finger. Tula immediately put the finger in her own mouth and began to suck on it; she had read that the venom from certain snakebites could be extracted in this manner. Shortly after, the children, with their father leading the chorus, loudly announced that they wouldn't leave a single bee alive in the garden, but would kill them one and all.

"No, you won't," exclaimed Gertrudis. "Nobody is going to kill bees."

"Why not?" asked Ramirín. "Because of their honey?"

"No one is to bother them, I said."

"But they're not mothers, you know, Gertrudis," said Ramiro.

"I know that. I know that well enough. I read about bees in one of your books. I know about these bees, the ones that sting and make the honey; I know about the queen and I know about the drones."

"Drones, that's us. The men."

"Of course!"

"Well, listen. I have some news for you. I'm going to enter politics. I'm being backed as a candidate for provincial deputy."

"Really?" Gertrudis was delighted and unable to hide it.

"Does it please you that much?"

"Everything that makes you happy, that takes your mind off . . ."

"There are only eleven months to go, Gertrudis. . . ."

"For what? The election?"

"The election, yes!"

X

A FIERCE STORM was blowing up in the closed soul of Gertrudis. Her head was in conflict with her heart, and both were at war with something even more deep-seated, something in the nature of the marrow of her spiritual bones.

Alone, while Ramiro was away from the house, she would pick up Ramirín, the child of Rosa and Ramiro, the child she called son, and press him to her virgin's breast, filled with anguish and confusion. And she would sometimes find herself gazing at her dead sister's portrait, the one who had been and still was her sister, and would half ask her if she had really meant that she, Gertrudis, should follow her, take her place, with Ramiro. "Yes, she did tell me that I should be the mother, and his other wife. But she could not have wanted that, no, she could not have. . . . I, at least, in her place, would not have, could not have, wanted that. . . . Another woman? No! Not even after my death! And not even by my sister! . . . Another woman's, no! He can only belong to one. No, she could not have wanted such a thing. She would not have wanted her own shadow to lie between her man, the father of her children, and myself. . . . She could not have! For if he were with me, beside me, close to me, flesh to flesh, who would know if it were she he was with? In mind and memory, so that I would be merely a recollection of her, something worse than a memory of the other woman! No, what she asked me to do was to prevent her children from having a stepmother. And I will prevent it! And I would not prevent it by handing myself over to Ramiro, giving him my body, not only my soul, marrying him. . . . Then I would be a stepmother. And all the more if he gave me children of my own flesh and blood. . . ." The idea of children of her own flesh made Gertrudis shudder in the marrow of her spiritual bones. She was all maternity, all mother, but all maternity of spirit.

And she closeted herself in her room, in her stark room, to cry before the image of the Most Holy Virgin Mother, to cry as she whispered, "The fruit of thy womb. . . ."

Once, while she pressed Ramirín to her breast, the child said:

"Why are you crying, Mamita?" That was the word she had taught him to use in addressing her.

"I'm not crying. . . ."

"Yes, you are. . . ."

"Do you see me crying?"

"No, but I can feel you crying. . . . You're crying. . . ."

"It's because I'm thinking of your mother."

"But, don't you say that you are our mother?"

"Yes, but I was thinking of the other one, Mamá Rosa."

"Oh, yes, the one that died . . . the one that belonged to Papá . . ."

"Yes, the one that belonged to Papá!"

"And why does Papá tell us not to call you Mamá, but Aunt, Aunt Tula, little Aunt Tula, and you tell us to call you Mamá and not Aunt, not little Aunt Tula? . . ."

"But . . . is that what he tells you?"

"Yes, he told us you're not our Mamá yet, that you're only our Aunt now."

"Not yet your Mamá?"

"Yes, he told us you're not our Mamá yet, but that you will be. . . . Yes, that you will be our Mamá after a few months have passed. . . ."

Gertrudis thought to herself: "Then I would be your stepmother." But she did not dare repeat her guilty thought aloud.

"Look now, don't pay any attention to these things, my son. . . ."

When Ramiro came home. Gertrudis took him aside and said severely:

"Don't go about telling your children such things. Don't tell them I'm not yet their mother, only Aunt Tula, but that I will become their mother. That's a way of perverting them, of making them look at things they shouldn't see. And if you do it so as to influence me through them . . ."

"You told me that you wanted a year. . . ."

"If you tell the boy those things so that he will influence me, think of the role you ask him to play, the role of a . . ."

"That's enough of that!"

"Words don't frighten me. But I won't use it. And you can think of Rosa, your first . . . love."

"Tula!"

"No more! And don't look around for a stepmother for your children. They already have a mother."

XI

"WITH THIS situation, it's time to get away," Gertrudis thought to herself, as she suggested to Ramiro that they all spend the summer in some coastal town. She favored a place with a mountain behind it, one

which would dominate the sea and in turn be dominated by it. She wished to avoid anything fashionable,
but still she wanted a place where Ramiro would be
free to go his own way, find fellow cardplayers and
the like, for she feared the kind of solitude which
might throw the two of them constantly together.

At the place finally chosen, they went for long
walks every day, climbing the mountain for views of
the sea through the stands of madroño trees. They
always went out together: Gertrudis and Ramiro and
Ramirín and Rosa and Elvira. She would never have
gone out alone with Ramiro, even there, where no
one knew them; or rather, even less there than elsewhere. She would seek out a tree trunk fallen near the
footpath by way of rustic bench and they would contemplate the sea, the two of them, while the children
played nearby, the nearer the better as far as Gertrudis was concerned. She kicked up a small fuss one
day when Ramiro tried to make her sit amid the mountain grass:

"No, not on the ground! I won't sit on the bare
ground, especially not with you, and in front of the
children. . . ."

"But it's perfectly clean . . . and besides, there's
grass. . . ."

"No, I won't sit there under any conditions. It's
not pleasant. In fact it's worse than unpleasant. . . ."

Seated together on a tree trunk, gazing out to sea,
they would talk endless small talk, for as soon as the
man would try to stray into areas of conversation
which by tacit agreement were out-of-bounds, the
woman was ready with a loud call for "Ramirín!" or
"Rosita!" or "Elvira!" But when she spoke to him
vaguely about the sea, her words reached the man
enveloped in the vague sight and sound of the waves,

as if she were singing a lullaby written for the soul. In fact she was rocking the cradle of his passion to lull it to sleep. And she would gaze out to sea and never at him. And yet, she saw, reflected back at her in some mysterious way, the look of the man upon her. The pure sea was joining together their contemplative gazes and their souls.

Sometimes they walked in the woods, among the chestnut trees, and then she would need to be doubly vigilant. She must watch him and watch over the children. And first she would look for a fallen tree to serve by way of rustic seat.

She thought to accustom him to family life in the purity of the countryside, tire him with light and open air, so that he might fall asleep to the sound of the cricket and not dream any dreams at all and wake to the song of the rooster and the early comings and goings of the country people and the seamen.

Mornings they would join the summer colony at a small nearby beach. The children would splash in the water and afterwards play at deviating the flow of a small stream which straggled through the sand into the sea at this point, and their father would sometimes join them at their games.

But Gertrudis began to see that her plans were going awry; she had miscalculated, and she grew even more fearful. Ramiro fled the company of cardplayers and the like among the summer colony and seemed more than ever intent on finding opportunities to be by her side in solitude. And the little house where they all lived was more like a tent for wandering gypsies. And the countryside itself, far from lulling, not merely the man's passion, but his desire, excited it further. Even she, the stern Gertrudis, grew vaguely restless. Life offered itself more nakedly among the fields, in the woods, in the folds of the mountain. And the animals, domesticated and raised by man as they were, surrounded them in all their naturalness. Gertrudis was confounded to watch with what close attention the children followed the actions and play in the barnyard. No, the country set no example for purity. The only purity available was to be found in sinking one's gaze in the sea. And then, even the sea . . . The sea breeze could be like a goad.

"How beautiful it is!" exclaimed Gertrudis one afternoon at sunset as they were sitting by the sea.

She was looking at a full moon, its paleness shot through with red, emerging from among the waves like a gigantic solitary flower in the mirage of a desert.

"Why is it that poets mention the moon so often?" asked Ramiro. "And its light, which affects romantics and lovers?"

"I don't know," said Tula, "but perhaps because it is the only land—it is land, after all—which we've come to realize we'll never reach. It's the inaccessible land. The sun is different. The sun rejects us out of hand. We like to sunbathe, but we know full well that the sun is uninhabitable, that we'd burn up in it, while we dream that we could live on the moon in eternal peace and twilight, without any storms; for it never seems to change. But we feel we can't get there. . . . It's that intangible . . ."

"And the moon always shows us the same face . . . such a sad and serious face. . . . Well, not always exactly the same face, because it covers itself up little by little until it's all dark; and then again sometimes it's like a sickle. . . ."

"Yes," continued Gertrudis, as if she had not been listening at all to the pointed commentary of her companion, although the truth was just the opposite, "it always shows the same face because it is constant and faithful. We don't know how it may be on the other side, of course . . . even what its other side may be. . . ."

"And that adds to the mystery."

"Perhaps . . . perhaps . . . I can understand that somebody would want to go to the moon—the impossible!—in order to see the other side, see what it's like . . . to know and explore its other face. . . ."

"The dark side . . ."

"Dark? I don't think so! When the side we see is illuminated, the other must be in darkness. Unless I'm wrong, the other side is lit, at full moon, when this side grows dark, when we have a new moon on this side. . . ."

"Full moon on the other side? For whom?"

"What do you mean 'For whom'?"

"Yes, who sees it?"

"It's enough that heaven sees it. Or do you think God made the moon merely to give us light at night on earth? Or for us to talk such nonsense?"

"All right, Tula, listen. . . ."

"Rosita!"

And she stopped him from commenting further on the intangibility and fullness of the moon.

When she spoke to him of returning to the city, he was quick to accept the idea. The brief season in the country, between the mountain and the sea, had not served his purpose in any way either. He, too, told himself that he had made a mistake, for she seemed even surer of herself here than at home; here she seemed to cloak herself with the mountain, muffle herself with the woods, and even the sea seemed to serve her as shield; she seemed as intangible as the moon. "And meanwhile," he told himself, "the salt-filled air filtering through the sunlight rouses one's blood. . . . And she seems to be restless, suspicious. She's on guard. One would almost say she doesn't sleep. . . ."

For her part Gertrudis was thinking: "No, purity is not a feature of the countryside. Purity is in a cell, in the cloister and in the city. Purity is found among people who live in vertical husks the better to isolate themselves. The city is a monastery, a convent for recluses. Out here, the earth on which they lie down to sleep unites them and the animals, which are like so many more serpents in paradise. . . . It's time to go back to the city!"

Her own convent, her hearth, her own cell was in the city. She could lull her brother-in-law better back there. Oh! If she could only say of him what Saint Teresa said in a letter (Gertrudis was a great reader of Saint Teresa) about her own brother-in-law, Don Juan de Ovalle, the husband of her sister Doña Juana de Ahumada: "He is by condition very childlike in things. . . ." How could she make *her* brother-in-law be like a child?

XII

AT LENGTH Gertrudis was no longer able to cope with her solitude and she determined to take her trouble and anguish to Father Alvarez, her confessor—though not her spiritual director. For she had always avoided being directed, especially by a man. She had formed her own norms of moral conduct, her own religious convictions and beliefs, from what she had heard around her and from what she read, all of which she interpreted in her own manner. Her poor uncle, Don Primitivo, the ingenuous priest who had raised the two sisters and taught them the catechism of Christian doctrine, had always felt profound respect for the intelligence of his niece Tula, whom he also admired.

"If you were to become a nun," he used to tell her, "you would go far. You'd become another St. Teresa. . . . What things you say!" Or again he might say: "It seems to me that what you're saying, Tulilla, smacks of heresy. . . . I don't know of course, I don't know now, because it doesn't seem possible that your guardian angel would inspire you to heresy, and yet what you're saying smacks of . . . I just don't know . . ." And she would answer: "Yes, Uncle, it's only something that occurred to me, but, now that you tell me it sounds like heresy, I won't think about it any more." But who can set limits and barriers to thought?

Gertrudis had always felt she was alone. That is, alone as far as being helped is concerned, because when it came to her helping others she certainly was not left alone. She was like, say, an orphan loaded with children. She was the staff for all those around her, but should she chance to weaken, if her mind should let her wander from the path she was on, if her heart were to fail her, who would be her support? Who would be her staff? For the truth was that she, so endowed with the highest of passions and feelings, with the sentiment of maternity, had no filial feeling.

And she would ask herself: "Is that not a manifestation of pride?"

And thus she found herself unable to support her

solitude and decided to go with her anguish to Father Alvarez. And she told the priest about Ramiro, about his declaration of love and his proposed one-year waiting period, and even how he had told the children not to call her mother yet, and of her own reasons for maintaining the house and hearth as it was. And she explained that she did not wish to give herself to any man whosoever, but to keep herself free to dedicate all her efforts to raising Rosa's children.

"But I find your brother-in-law's conduct quite normal," said the good father of souls.

"It's not a question now of my brother-in-law, Father, but of me. And I assume he hasn't come to you, too, in search of support. . . ."

"No, no, my child, no!"

"Of course they do say that the confection of marriages is a speciality of the confessional, and that you priests are also marriage-brokers. . . ."

"All I want to say at this point is that it's only natural that your brother-in-law, a young, strong widower, should want to remarry, and further, that it's even more natural and even exemplary that he should want another mother for his children. . . ."

"Another? He already has one!"

"Yes, but . . . And if this one should leave . . . ?"

"Leave? Me? I'm not going anywhere. I'm as tied to these children as their flesh-and-blood mother would be, were she alive."

"And then, there's the matter of people talking about you in that house. . . ."

"I don't care what they say or what they talk about. . . ."

"And what if you do what you do precisely because of what they say, to give them something to talk about? You must examine yourself and see if you don't desire to affront other people, defy them all. . . ."

"And what if that were the case?"

"That would surely be sinful. But, in fact, there's another question here."

"What question?"

"The question of whether you love him or not. That's the question. Do you love him, yes or no?"

"To be my husband . . . no!"

"Do you reject him then?"

"Reject him . . . no!"

"And if when he chose your sister, he had instead chosen you . . ."

"Father! Father!" There was grieving in her voice.

"Yes, we must follow along that vein. . . ."

"Father, that's not a sin! . . ."

"But now it's a matter of spiritual direction, of our taking counsel together. . . . And yes, it might be a sin; perhaps it is a sin. . . . Perhaps we have here an old case of jealousy. . . ."

"Father!"

"We must look further into this aspect. Perhaps you have not yet forgiven him."

"I've told you, Father, that I do love him, but not to be my husband. I love him as I would a brother, someone more than a brother, as the father of my children; for these children, his children, are mine from the innermost part of me, from my heart. But to be my husband, no. I cannot take my sister's place in his bed. . . . And more than all else, I cannot foist a stepmother on my children. . . ."

"A stepmother?"

"Yes, a stepmother. If I were to marry him, the father of the children of my heart, I would become a stepmother to those same children. Even more so if

I were to have children of my own flesh and blood with
him. Such a thing now . . . no, never!"

" 'Such a thing now,' you say?"

"Yes, now that I have the children of my heart . . .
my children . . ."

"But think of him, of your brother-in-law, in his
situation. . . ."

"Think of him?"

"Yes, exactly! Don't you feel any compassion toward him?"

"Yes, I do. And that's why I help him and encourage him. He's like another one of my children."

"You help him . . . and you encourage him. . . ."

"Yes, I help him be a father and encourage him."

"To be a father . . . a father . . . But he's also a
man. . . ."

"And I'm a woman!"

"He's weak. . . ."

"Am I strong?"

"More than necessary."

"More than necessary? And shouldn't a woman be
strong?"

"But the danger is that strength, daughter, sometimes may turn into hardness, cruelty. And you are
hard with him, very hard. You say you don't love him
as a husband? What difference does that make! That's
not necessary for marrying a man. Often a woman
must marry a man out of compassion, so as not to
leave him all alone, in order to save him, to save his
soul. . . ."

"But I don't leave him all alone. . . ."

"Yes, yes, you do. And I think you understand me
without my explaining it any further, without my
making it any clearer to you. . . ."

"Yes, yes, I understand you, but I don't want to.

He's not alone. It's me who's alone! Alone . . . alone
. . . always alone . . ."

"Well, you know the saying, 'It is better to marry
than to burn. . . .' "

"But I don't burn. . . ."

"Weren't you complaining about solitude?"

"I don't burn in solitude. It's not the kind of
solitude of which you're speaking, Father. That's not
it. I don't burn. . . ."

"And what if he burns?"

"Let him cool himself in the care and affection of
his children."

"Very well. But you understand what I'm driving
at?"

"Only too well."

"And if you don't, I'd like to add that your brother-
in-law is in danger, and if he falls, part of the blame
will be yours."

"Mine?"

"Of course! Clearly so."

"I don't see it so clearly. But since I'm not a
man . . ."

"You've said that one of the things you feared from
marrying him was having children by him. Isn't that
so?"

"Yes, that's true. If we were to have children, I
would be, willy-nilly, a stepmother to the children
left me by my sister."

"But marriage was not instituted solely for the
sake of children."

" 'To marry is to give grace to the married couple
and allow them to raise children for heaven.' "

" 'To give grace to the married couple' . . . Do you
understand that?"

"Barely . . ."

"So that they may live in grace, free of sin."

"Now I understand it even less."

"Well, then, it's meant to be a remedy against sensuality."

"What! What's that? How?"

"Now why do you get excited like that? . . . Why are you suddenly upset?"

"What is the remedy against sensuality? Marriage or the woman?"

"Both . . . The woman. And the man."

"Not at all, Father! No! Not at all! I'm not a remedy against anything! I will not be a remedy! What is the meaning of taking me for a remedy? And a remedy—against that! No. I'm more than that. . . ."

"But the point is . . ."

"No, there's nothing for you to say now. If he did not have any children by my sister, I would perhaps have married him in order to have children . . . to have them with him, yes. . . . But to be a remedy! And against that! Me a remedy? No!"

"And what if, before he made overtures to your sister, he had sought you instead. . . ."

"Me? Before? When he first met us? . . . Father, there is no more to say. We don't understand each other. We talk different languages. I don't understand your language and you don't understand mine."

Saying this, she stood up from beside the confessional. She found it difficult to walk away. Her legs hurt from kneeling so long. And her soul hurt. The joints of her soul ached, and she felt her solitude more deeply than ever. "No, he doesn't understand me at all. He's a man, after all! . . . Still, do I understand myself? Can I possibly? Do I love him or don't I? Isn't it a matter of pride? Is my solitude like the sad solitary passion of the ermine which won't jump into the muddy river to save its mate because it's afraid of getting dirty? . . . I don't know . . . I don't know. . . ."

XIII

O f a s u d d e n Gertrudis realized that her brother-in-law had changed. He seemed to have become another man altogether. And he seemed to be possessed of a secret. He was out of the house a good deal. But it was not his absences that were noteworthy, but rather his secretive and evasive conduct at home. By dint of patience and sharpsighted observation, Gertrudis at length deciphered the looks passed between master and serving-girl as those of a knowledgeable intimacy.

The serving-girl, Manuela, was nineteen and had come to them from the Orphanage. She was a pale, fragile girl, with a feverish look in her eyes, docile of manner, scant of words, soft-spoken and melancholy. Without knowing why, she trembled before Gertrudis, whom she called "Señora." Ramiro tried to make her use the proper "Señorita," denoting Gertrudis' unmarried state as "Miss."

"No, call me as you have been doing. Never mind the 'Señorita.'"

The girl was frightened or cowed in the presence of Gertrudis. And she avoided the children and scarcely ventured to speak to them at all. For their part, their indifference to her verged on aversion. They even went so far as to make mock of her, mimicking her way of talking, which caused poor Manuela to blush furiously. "The strange thing is," thought Gertrudis, "that despite everything she obviously does not want to leave. . . . She's as durable as a she-cat." And shortly, Gertrudis found out why she stayed.

For one day she came upon Manuela as she emerged from Ramiro's room (the Señorito's room: for the girl addressed the master by that title, even though he was no bachelor). The poor girl was all afire and breathless. They exchanged looks, and the girl gave way and lowered her eyes. And then came the day when Ramirín asked his aunt:

"Tell me, Mamá Tula, is Manuela our sister too?"

"All men and women are brothers and sisters, as I've told you."

"Yes, but is she like one of us, living together?"

"No, because although she lives here, this isn't her house."

"And which is her house?"

"Her house? You don't need to know. And why do you ask?"

"Well, I saw Papá kissing her. . . ."

That night, after they had put the children to bed, Gertrudis told Ramiro:

"We must have a talk. . . ."

"There are still eight months to go. . . ."

"Eight months?"

"Wasn't it four months ago you asked for a year?"

"That's not the question now. It's more serious than that."

Ramiro turned pale.

"More serious?"

"Yes. It has to do with your children, with their upbringing. And it has to do with that poor girl from the Orphanage, whom you're apparently taking advantage of. . . ."

"If I were, whose fault would it be?"

"You dare ask? You mean you'd like to blame me?"

"Of course!"

"Then, listen to me, Ramiro. The year's wait is over, there'll be no more waiting. It can't be. I'm leaving. And whatever the law may say about it, I'm taking the children with me. I mean, they'll go with me."

"Gertrudis! Have you gone mad?"

"It's you who's gone mad."

"What did you want of me?"

"Nothing. It's either her or me. Either you put that girl out of the house or I leave."

There was an anguished pause, a dreadful silence.

"I can't turn her out, Gertrudis. Where would she go? Back to the Orphanage?"

"She can be a servant in some other house."

"I can't turn her out, I cannot . . . ," and Ramiro broke down.

"Poor Ramiro!" she murmured, and covered his hand with hers. "I'm sorry for you."

"Now you're sorry. Now . . ."

"Yes, I'm sorry. . . . I'd be willing to do anything, whatever. . . ."

"Gertrudis! Tula!"

"But you said you couldn't turn her out. . . ."

"It's true. I can't." And once more he broke down.

"What does that mean? Is it that she wouldn't be going alone, by herself?"

"No, it wouldn't be just one, not just herself."

"Eight months' time, is it?"

"I'm lost, Tula, lost!"

"No, it's she who's lost, the foundling, the little orphan, the homeless girl."

"Yes, that's true, it's true. . . ."

"But don't grieve so, there's an easy solution to it all. . . ."

"A solution? An easy solution?" Ramiro dared look her in the face.

"Yes. You need only marry her."

These simple words struck Ramiro like a lightning bolt.

"Marry the maid! Marry the serving-girl! Marry the foundling, the orphan! And you're the one to tell me that!"

"Who else is there to tell you? Who but the real mother of your children now?"

"And you want me to give them a stepmother?"

"No, not ever! I'm here to continue being their only mother. But you should be the father to your new child, and give the child a mother, too. That little orphan has the right to be a mother. And now she has the duty to be one, and the right to have her child and the father of her child."

"But Gertrudis . . ."

"Marry her! I tell you that . . . and Rosa tells you that. Yes." Her somber voice resounded like a bell. "Through me, your wife Rosa tells you to marry the foundling. . . . Manuela!" She called the girl.

"Señora!" The voice of the serving-girl answered weakly, in a kind of wail. She had been sitting crouched by the fire, within range of their voices, hearing it all. And now she could not move. Gertrudis called her again, and again she answered, "Señora!" But again she did not move.

"Come here, or I'll go and get you!"

"For God's sake!" Ramiro exclaimed.

The girl appeared, covering her tearful face with her hands.

"Take your hands off your face and look at us!"

"No, Señora, no!"

"Yes, look at us. Here's your master, Ramiro, who

asks your forgiveness for what he has done to you."

"No, it's I who want to be forgiven, and to you I . . ."

"He's asking your forgiveness and will marry you. . . ."

"But, Señora! . . ." the poor girl exclaimed at the same time that Ramiro cried: "But Gertrudis" . . . !

"Mind what I said. He's to marry you. That's the way Rosa will have it. You can't be left in that state. Because you're already . . . Isn't that right?"

"I think so, Señora. But I . . ."

"Don't cry like that, and never mind the wild vows. I know it's not your fault. . . ."

"But everything could be arranged. . . ."

"Manuela here knows well enough that I never planned to abandon her. . . . I'll find her a place. . . ."

"Yes, Señora, that's it. I'd be happy enough, I'd be content. . . ."

"Not at all. You shouldn't be content with whatever you were going to say. Or rather, Ramiro here can't be content with that. . . . You, you were brought up in the Orphanage, weren't you?"

"Yes, Señora."

"Well, your child will not be raised there. The child has the right to a father, his own father. And he'll have him. And now go . . . go to your room and leave us alone."

Alone with Ramiro she said:

"I assume you will not hesitate now for a moment."

"But what you're doing is all madness, Gertrudis!"

"What you were thinking of doing was madness, or worse than madness, it was dishonor and infamy."

"At least consult Father Alvarez."

"I don't need to. I've already consulted Rosa."

"But surely she asked you not to allow a step-mother for her children. . . ."

"Her children? And yours!"

"Yes, of course, our children. . . ."

"And I'll see they don't have a stepmother. I'll continue to be their mother, the mother of our children. But the child by that girl . . ."

"No one will stop her from being a mother. . . ."

"Yes, you would, if you didn't marry her. That way she wouldn't be a mother. . . ."

"Well, she . . ."

"What of it? Just because she never knew her mother, there's no reason you should prevent her from being a proper mother."

"But please realize that this girl . . ."

"It's you who should have realized . . ."

"This is madness . . . a piece of madness. . . ."

"The piece of madness came before. And now you can think it over: if you don't do what you should, I'll be the one to create a scandal. The whole world will know about it."

"Gertrudis!"

"Marry her! And that's an end to it!"

XIV

A PROFOUND melancholy settled upon the house once Ramiro had married the foundling, who became more of a servant than ever, while Gertrudis became more than ever the mistress. And Gertrudis saw to it that the newly married pair came into contact with the children less than ever, and the children were kept to a minimal awareness of their father's intimate relationship with the girl. But it proved necessary to find another maid, and then the new developments had to be explained to the children.

But how explain to them that the former maid was now seated at the dining-room table and ate with the people of the house? For Gertrudis insisted she be found a place.

"Please, Señora," Manuela pled, "don't put me to shame. . . . To make me sit at table with the master and mistress . . . and with the children . . . and to address the Señorito in the familiar . . . oh, I can't do that ever!"

"Address him any way you like, but the children, of whom you're so frightened, must see that you're one of the family. Once that's understood, they won't catch you out unawares. They won't have to creep about and you won't either. You can conceal your-selves more naturally. You were pretty obvious be-fore; when you tried to hide from them, you gave yourselves away."

Manuela began to suffer a difficult pregnancy. She was too fragile to carry it off well. Gertrudis sug-gested she keep her condition from the children's notice.

Ramiro lived in resigned despair. And he submitted to the will of Gertrudis more completely than ever. He would say:

"Yes, I understand now, there was no way out. And yet . . ."

"Do you regret it?" Gertrudis asked.

"Not getting married, no. But getting remarried, yes!"

"It's no longer the time to think about that. You've got to face up to life now!"

"Ah, if you had only cared, Tula, only want-ed . . . !"

"I gave you a year's grace. Were you capable of honoring it?"

"And if I had, in the way you wanted, what would have happened at the end of the year? Tell me. You never did promise me anything."

"Even if I had promised you something, it would have been the same. No, it would have been worse. In our circumstances, my making you a promise, even my asking you for more time, would have made things worse."

"But supposing I had kept the truce, the way you wanted me to keep it, tell me, what would you have done?"

"I don't know."

"You don't know, Tula, you don't know . . . !"

"No, I don't know, I tell you."

"But your feelings . . ."

"You'd best think of your wife now. I don't know if she can manage this burden you've put upon her. She's such a poor little thing! And she's so frightened. . . . She's still all a-fright at being your wife and the mistress of the house."

When the delivery came, Gertrudis went through the same self-sacrifice she had shown at all her sister's deliveries. She was the first to pick up the newborn, a tiny stunted creature; she wrapped it up and brought it to its father.

"Here you have him, he's yours."

"Poor little creature!" Ramiro was confounded at the sight of the little roll of suffering flesh; he felt infinitely sorry for its scant existence.

"Well, he's yours anyway. Another child come to us."

"Come to us? To you, too?"

"Yes, to me, too. I certainly am not going to act

like a stepmother to this one, after I've made sure the others don't have a stepmother."

And in all truth she did not draw any distinction between the children.

"You're a saint, Gertrudis. But a saint who has forced people into sin."

"Don't say that. I'm a sinner who strives to make saints, saints of your children, of you and your wife."

"My wife! . . ."

"Yes, your wife, the mother of your children. Why do you treat her with that kind of benevolent aversion, as if she were a burden to you?"

"What do you want me to do, fall in love with her?"

"Weren't you in love when you seduced her?"

"With whom, with her?"

"Oh, I know you weren't, I know. . . . But the poor girl deserves some love."

"But she's the least bit of woman possible, she's really nothing at all, there's nothing there!"

"You're wrong. She's more than you think. There's more to her than you know. Though the truth is you don't really know her yet."

"She's no more than a slave. . . ."

"That may be. But you ought to set her free. . . . She's frightened. . . . She was born frightened. . . . And you took advantage of her fright."

"I don't know. I don't recall how it happened. . . ."

"That's the way men are. You don't know what you're doing, nor do you give it a thought. You do everything without thinking. . . ."

"It's very often worse to think things over and then do nothing. . . ."

"Why do you say that?"

"Oh, for no reason, no reason at all . . ."

"Doubtless you believe that I do nothing but think?"

"No, I didn't say that. . . ."

"Yes, you believe I'm no more than thought. . . ."

XV

A N D   T H E N   O N C E again, poor Manuela, the girl from the Orphanage, found she was pregnant. And once again, Ramiro was in a temper.

"As if I didn't have enough with the others . . ."

"What do you want me to do!" exclaimed the victim.

"After all, this is the way you wanted it," Gertrudis concluded.

And then, talking to him alone, Gertrudis reproached him again for his compassionate disdain, his benevolent aversion for his new wife, who bore her pregnancies even worse than the first wife.

"I'm afraid for her," said Don Juan, the doctor, a widower himself, who came to the house more and more often.

"Do you think she's running a risk?" asked Gertrudis.

"The poor girl is in bad shape. She has a case of advanced tuberculosis. She'll last, no doubt, until childbed, for Nature is very wise, but then . . ."

"Nature, nothing! The Holy Virgin Mother!" Gertrudis interrupted.

"Just as you wish. I surrender, as always, to your superior opinion. But as I was saying, Nature, or the Virgin, for it's all one to me . . ."

"No. The Virgin is Grace. . . ."

"All right. For Nature, or the Virgin, or Grace, or whatever, sees to it that the mother lasts until the new being is brought into the world. The innocent creature serves the poor mother by way of a shield against death."

"And then?"

"Then? You'll probably have to raise the child yourself, availing yourself of a wet nurse, of course. One more child. You have four now, you'll be burdened with five then."

"With all God sends me."

"And then, most probably, I don't exactly know when, Don Ramiro will once again be free," and he gazed fixedly at Gertrudis through his gray eyes.

"And ready to get married again, for the third time," she added, acting the innocent.

"That would really be quite heroic!"

"Well, you cannot be very heroic yourself, since you remain a widower, and a widower without children."

"Ah, Doña Gertrudis, if I could only speak!"

"You'd best keep quiet."

"I won't say a word."

The doctor took her hand in his, held it a while, patting it with his free hand, and said with a sigh:

"Every man is a whole world, Gertrudis."

"And every woman a moon, isn't that the way it is, Don Juan?"

"Every woman can be a whole heaven."

Gertrudis thought the man was paying court in Platonic fashion.

The entire household was concerned with and concentrated on Manuela and her care, when, of a sudden, Ramiro fell ill. The immediate diagnosis was pneumonia. The poor orphan girl was in a daze.

"Leave all this to me, Manuela. You take care of yourself and of what you're carrying. Don't worry about waiting on your husband. You'll only get worse. . . ."

"But I should . . ."

"You should take care of your part of it, of what's yours."

"And isn't my husband mine?"

"No, not now. The child who's coming is yours now."

Ramiro got worse.

"I'm afraid of complications. His heart," declared Don Juan. "His heart is weak. Naturally, after all his troubles and disappointments."

"But will he die, Don Juan?" Gertrudis asked, overcome.

"Anything can happen. . . ."

"Save him, Don Juan, save him, in whatever way. . . ."

"There's nothing I'd like better!"

"Oh, what a disaster! What a disaster!" For the first time Gertrudis, as she began to sit down, fainted.

She was at last brought around and the doctor continued:

"It is truly a terrible thing! To leave four children —what am I saying?—five children with the one coming—and that girl widow, in her condition! . . ."

"That's the least of it, Don Juan, because I can handle those children all my self. . . . But, what a disaster!"

The doctor went off, saying to himself: "She was counting on having her brother-in-law free again. . . .

Every person is an entire world, and some people are several worlds. What a woman! What strength! What sagacity! And what eyes! What a body! She radiates fire."

One afternoon, when his fever had abated and he was able to speak more or less clearly, Ramiro called for Gertrudis, entreated her to lock the door, and told her:

"I'm dying, Tula, I know I'm dying. My heart is failing. There's nothing to do about it. The injections don't work. There's no hope for me now. . . ."

"Don't think such thoughts, Ramiro."

But she, too, thought he was dying.

"I'm dying, and it's time, Tula, to tell you the truth, the entire truth. It was you who married me to Rosa."

"You couldn't make up your mind and you procrastinated. . . ."

"Do you know why?"

"Yes, I know, Ramiro."

"At first, when I began paying attention to you two, it was Rosa who stood out; she was the one to be seen at a distance; but when I got closer, when I began to visit your house, it was you I saw, only you; you were the only one to be seen up close. At a distance, she put you in the shade; close up, you put her in the shade."

"Don't talk against my sister now, the mother of your children. . . ."

"The mother of my children is you. You're the mother of my children. You!"

"Think of Rosa, now, Ramiro, only of her."

"Because I'll soon be with her . . . isn't that it?"

"Who knows? . . . Concentrate on living, on your children. . . ."

"My children have their mother. You."

"And think of Manuela, poor Manuela. . . ."

"That one year's grace, Tula, that fatal time."

Gertrudis could no longer contain her tears.

"Tula!" The sick man let out a piercing cry and opened his arms wide.

"Yes, Ramiro, yes!" She fell into his arms and embraced him passionately. Their mouths came together and they clung to each other, sobbing.

"Do you forgive me, Tula?"

"No, Ramiro, it's you who must forgive me."

"Forgive you?"

"Yes, you must forgive me. You spoke once of saints who make sinners. I've been possessed by an inhuman idea of virtue. . . . And when you picked out my sister instead of me, I did what I did, what I had to do. And then—I have to confess it to you —men, all men, even you, Ramiro, have always frightened me. I've never been able to see beyond the brute, beyond the beast in man. Male children, yes, but the grown man . . . I've always fled from men. . . ."

"You had good reason, Tula."

"Now, you must rest, for all this talk and these feelings could harm you."

She covered him up, tucking his arms under the covers, kissed him on the forehead as if he were a child—and he was a child for her at that moment— and she left him. Once she was alone she considered: "And suppose he gets well? Suppose he doesn't die? Now that the secret between us is out in the open? What of poor Manuela? I'll have to leave! Where shall I go? And if Manuela should die and he again be free?" Gertrudis hurried off to be with Manuela, who was in a bad way at that moment.

The following day, she brought the children to

their father's bedside. He had already received the last rites and was near death. Gertrudis lifted up the children one by one and had them kiss their father. Then she brought Manuela, whom she had to support, and who seemed on the point of passing out from anguish, to such a degree that Gertrudis had to take her away and put her to bed. Not long afterwards, with his hand clutching one of her hands, Ramiro whispered a last "Goodbye, my Tula!" and died. Gertrudis, the Aunt, emptied her heart of all its anguish, sobbed herself dry, over the lifeless body of her Ramiro, the father of her children.

XVI

EXCEPT FOR THE sovereign of the house, there was scarcely any sign of prostration at Ramiro's death. The children were still too young to understand what had happened. And Manuela, a widow almost without knowing it, had put all her life and will into struggling, in the manner of a plant, for the other life she carried within her in her womb, even while she wailed, like a wounded beast, that she wished to die. Gertrudis took charge of everything.

She closed the dead man's eyes. "Is he looking at me still?" she wondered. She dressed him for the grave, covering him, as she had her uncle the priest, with a habit over the clothes in which he had died and which she left unchanged. Then, worn out with an old exhaustion, with the fatigue of years, she broke down over the body and, putting her mouth to the cold mouth of the corpse, she meditated on their lives, which was all of her life. Only the wailing of one of the children, of the youngest, the first child of the orphan-girl, brought her around. She tore herself away from the dead man to hurry to the side of the living, of the infant whom she picked up, quieted, and caressed.

Manuela was sinking.

"Señora, I won't be able to get through this time. This birth will cost me my life."

And so it happened. She gave birth to a girl, but she herself began bleeding to death. The child itself was born enveloped in blood. And Gertrudis was forced to overcome the repugnance she felt at the sight of blood, especially when it was black and coagulated. It had always been a great struggle for her to overcome her disgust. Once, when her sister Rosa had an attack of vomiting just before her death, Gertrudis had fled in horror. She had fled not from fear but from disgust.

Manuela died, her mind filled with misty figures out of the shadows of the Orphanage, her eyes fixed on the eyes of Gertrudis.

Gertrudis had told her, toward the end: "Don't despair for your children. I'll live long enough to see to it that they can take care of themselves in the world. If not, I'll leave them in the care of their brothers and sister. I'll take special care of this last baby for whom you've given your life, poor little love. I shall be its mother and father."

"Thank you, thank you! God will reward you! You are a true saint!"

The poor girl tried to kiss Gertrudis' hand, but the latter bent over instead and kissed the new mother's head, and then she put her cheek to the other's lips. The little orphan repeated her litany of gratitude as if it were some lesson learned in childhood. And then she died as she had lived, a submissive, patient animal, or perhaps more a household utensil.

And it was this most natural of deaths which most deeply affected Gertrudis, who had assisted at three others already. It was the sense of enigma which struck her most in this death. There was a void growing in her soul, and it was this death—more than that of her uncle, her sister, or that of Ramiro—which seemed to make the void more tangible. This simple death seemed to confirm the other three, seemed to cast a certain light on them.

"The other three died. This girl was killed! . . . She was killed, and it was we who killed her. And wasn't it I who killed her most? Wasn't it I who brought her to this? And yet, did the poor thing ever really live? Could she have lived? Was she ever really born? She was a foundling, exposed on the steps of the Orphanage, and wasn't her death another *exposition*? Wasn't her marriage the same, and she exposed to it? Have we not thrown her into the whirlpool of eternity so that she may land in the Orphanage of Glory? May she not be an orphan and a foundling there too?" Such were the solitary thoughts of Gertrudis following the girl's death.

And Gertrudis was obsessed by the thought of how Rosa might receive her, alongside her Ramiro, in the afterworld. The good priest who had been their uncle and had raised them, had accomplished his mission on earth, protecting them by his presence. Her sister Rosa had gotten her wish, satisfied her desire, and left the children she wanted to have. And Ramiro? Yes, he too had made his way, though upstream and with his back to the guiding star, and he had suffered, but

nobly, and he had sinned and purged his sin. But this
poor girl had not really even suffered, nor sinned, but
had been sinned against or on, and she had died an
orphan! . . . "Eve died an orphan, too," it occurred
to Gertrudis. But then she thought: "No, Eve had God
as father! But as mother? No, Eve never knew a
mother. . . . *There's* an explanation for original sin!
. . . And Eve died an orphan of humanity." The idea
of Eve recalled to her mind the account in Genesis
which she had just read, of how the Lord God had
breathed the breath of life into man's nostrils, and now
she imagined that He took life away in an analogous
manner. And then she imagined further that the poor
foundling, whose sense of life she could not understand, had her life taken away from her by a kiss from
the Lord God, who put His infinite and invisible lips,
which are closed to form the blue sky, to the poor girl's
lips, blue with death, and sucked her breath away.

And so Gertrudis was left with her five children,
having to contend with wet nurses for the youngest.

The eldest, Ramirín, was the living image of his
father in his appearance and gestures, and so from the
first his aunt determined to curb in him the tendencies
and inclinations she had observed to be most prejudi-
cial in the father. "I must be on guard against the
time when the man, the male, begins to be aroused in
him, and raise him so that he will be able to choose
calmly and carefully." The trouble was that the boy
was not in very good health, so that his development
was beset with difficulties and even pain.

All five of them would have to be well placed in life
and brought up in reverence for their lost parents.

And what of the poor children of the foundling
girl? "Those children are mine, too," thought Ger-

trudis, "as much mine as the others, as those of my sister, even more mine. For these are the children of my sin. Are they really mine, though, and not rather his? No, of my sin! They are the children of my sin! Poor girl!" And she found herself most concerned with the smallest, the new girl.

XVII

GERTRUDIS WAS growing more and more irritated at the insinuations made by the doctor, Don Juan. His visits had become ever more frequent; he was in constant attendance on the children and, though she complained of no indisposition or illness at all, he insisted on treating her as a patient. One day she told him point-blank that she was thinking of changing doctors.

"How so, Gertrudis?"

"It's quite obvious. I've noticed certain oddities which strike me as signs of a premature old age, not to say dotage. And we need a doctor with his head firmly in place."

"Very well. If that is what you think, the time has come for me to speak clearly, if you will allow . . ."

"Say whatever you like, Don Juan. But do so in the knowledge that they will be the last words you speak in this house."

"Who knows! . . ."

"Come now."

"I'm a widower and childless, as you know, Gertrudis. And I adore children."

"Then remarry."

"I'm getting to that."

"Ah, and you want my advice?"

"I want more than advice."

"You want me to find you a bride?"

"As I was saying, I'm a doctor who never had any children with my wife, who was a widow already. And worse, we lost the one child she brought me from a previous marriage. I still miss the little lad! And worse, I know, from positive proof and all the evidence, that I never will have any children of my own. In fact I can't have any. Now of course that doesn't make me feel any less a man, any less a man than any other man. You understand me, Gertrudis?"

"I'd like not to understand you, Don Juan."

"To conclude. I believe that these children, your nephews and niece, and even perhaps the other two . . ."

"They're as much nephews and nieces of mine as the others, in fact they're all more like my own children."

"Well, then, I wanted to say that these children of yours, since you consider them yours, could use a father, one who is not badly off, and even moderately rich."

"Is that all?"

"Yes, I'd say they actually *need* a father."

"They're well enough off with Our Father who art in heaven."

"And with a mother, yourself, who is the earthly representative of the Most Holy Mother, is that it?"

"Whatever you say, Don Juan, since it's the last you're going to say in this house."

"You mean that . . ."

"That all this business about your need for children and your inability to have them . . . did I understand you correctly, Don Juan?"

"Perfectly. And incidentally, the last fact is a secret between the two of us."

"I won't be the one to stand in the way of your getting married again. And that account of yours, I was saying, has convinced me that you're not so much looking for children to adopt—which would be a simple matter for you, especially if you were to get married —as you are looking for me, and that you'd look for me even if I were all alone and we had to live without any children whatever. Have I understood you, Don Juan? And do you understand me?"

"It's true enough, Gertrudis, that even if you were all alone, I'd still want to marry you, if you wanted to get married, of course. I'm quite plain-spoken, quite plain-spoken, and I'll admit it's you who attracts me. But in that case we'd have to adopt children however it was done, even if we had to take them out of the Orphanage. For I've noticed, I've seen that you're crazy about children, just like I am, and that you need them and dote on them."

"But you've never seen, and neither has anyone else, any evidence of my being, or having been, incapable of producing children. No one can say I'm barren or sterile. And now: don't ever set foot in this house again!"

"Gertrudis! But why?"

"Because you're a gross and vulgar man!"

That was their final exchange.

But then, after she had thrown him out in such fashion, she began to feel sorry for him. She felt a disdainful pity, a pitying disdain for the poor man. "Was I not too hard on him?" she asked herself. "He annoyed me no end, of course, and the way he looked at me was worse than what he said, but I should have treated him a bit better. He probably needs some help, he needs a 'remedy,' but not the one he wants; something more radical, something 'heroic.' "

She soon learned that Don Juan had found a "remedy." And what she learned made her ask if in reality he had been seeking the warmth of a home after all, and she was taken with a suspicion which roused her wrath even more. "Oh, so what he needed was a housekeeper! A woman to take care of him, to lay his clean clothes out for him on the bed, to see that his dinner is made. . . . That's worse than the other, worse than the 'remedy' even. When a woman is not a 'remedy,' she's a domestic animal, and sometimes she's both at once. These men! . . . It's either filth or folly, lewdness or laziness! And still they tell us that Christianity redeemed our lot, women's lot!" As she said this she thought of her good uncle, and she crossed herself and added: "No, I won't say that again. I won't even think it! . . ."

But who is to put limits to thought once it has bitten into the fruit of the knowledge of evil? "In the end, Christianity, despite the Magdalen, is a man's religion," Gertrudis told herself. "All males: the Father, the Son, and the Holy Ghost! . . . Yet what about the Mother? Oh, the religion of the Mother is summed up in the phrase 'Behold the handmaid of the Lord; be it unto me according to thy word,' and in her asking her Son to provide some wine for a wedding feast, the wine which inebriates and causes sorrow to be drowned in pleasure, all so that the Son can say to her, 'Woman, what have I to do with thee? mine hour is not yet come.' What have I to do with thee! . . . And to call her *woman* rather than *mother*. . . ." And

Gertrudis crossed herself again, this time tremulously. And that was because her Guardian Devil—or so she thought—was whispering: "A man after all!"

XVIII

THE YEARS WENT by serenely. The fact that all the children were now orphans lent an almost spiritual quality to the house: nothing was lacking, nothing was needed, and there were no material obstacles or considerations. There was no reason even to think of the days to come. And the departed father and the two mothers lived on, in sweeter empery, than when their flesh-and-blood bodies occupied their place. They had provided Gertrudis with the elements with which to build the future. And Gertrudis recalled them continuously: "Your mother, you know, can see you!" and "Your father is watching everything!" Such expressions were constant, and Gertrudis placed portraits of the three absent parents in such wise that they could still preside over the house they had inhabited.

And yet the children gradually began to forget them. Only in the words of Mamá Tula, as they called her, did their parents exist at all. The visual images in the mind of Ramirín, the eldest, began to fade, and to mingle with the images evoked by the words of the aunt. His parents became a creation of Tula's.

Gertrudis was particularly intent on avoiding any idea of difference between the two sets of children. She strove to prevent any notion among them that they were separated because of the two separate mothers, or that they were merely half-brothers and sisters. But the facts were impossible to deny. She was tempted at first to say that the two mothers, Rosa and Manuela, were like herself, mothers to them all, but she realized that there would be no way of sustaining such a myth. Moreover, she was a fanatical believer in the truth, and so she did not attempt any lie.

In her mind, love of truth was confounded with love of purity. She despised the popular accounts which abused the innocence of children by telling them they are brought into the world by storks or bought at a children's shop in Paris. "A stupid way to waste money!" a boy from a large family had replied when he was told that a friend of his was to be brought a little brother from the Parisian store. "A stupid way to waste time," Gertrudis had echoed. To her, lies were all a waste.

One day, Manuela's son came home and said: "They told me that my mother was my father's maid, that she was the maid to the mother of my brothers and sister."

In her most serious voice and in front of them all, Aunt Tula answered:

"All of you are brothers and sisters, you're all children of the same mother and the same father, and that's me."

"But haven't you told us, Mamita, that we had another mother?"

"You did, but now I'm your mother. So there! And don't let's discuss it any further, or ever again!"

But she was totally unable to hide her preferences, her favorites among the children. First of all, there was the first-born, Ramirín, who had been conceived while his father was still suffering from having had to elect between the two sisters and then having been forced by Gertrudis to marry Rosa. Her other favorite was Manolita, the pale bud of a fragile rose, who seemed always in danger of being carried off by some early frost or conversely by some early blast of heat.

As concerned Ramirín, Gertrudis was subject to a diabolic temptation. A voice would well up in her, from some unknown depth of herself, and sibilantly whisper, in a humble yet clearly devilish insinuation, that perhaps, when the boy was conceived, his father's mind was on Gertrudis, that he was dreaming of her, and not of Rosa. Gertrudis would cross herself, doubly, on her forehead and on her breast, for she had no way of stopping her sudden thought. And as regards Manolita, the daughter born from the death of the foundling, she was tempted by the notion that if she had not insisted on Ramiro's remarrying, if she had not obliged him to redeem his sin and his victim, this pale bud of a fragile rose would not exist.

And what a struggle it was to nurse the girl! The boy had been nursed by his mother, who, submissive as a domestic animal and obedient to natural instinct, made no attempt to deny the infant her breast, even though she was in a weakened condition. So it had been with the husband that Gertrudis had had to contend, for in view of the mother's obvious weakness, he had begun looking for a wet nurse; and Gertrudis, who had forced him to marry Manuela, now insisted on the mother's feeding the child. "There is no milk like mother's milk," she had reiterated. Her brother-in-law had retorted: "Yes, but she's so exhausted that mother and baby would both be in danger, and the baby would be poorly fed." To which the sovereign lady had replied implacably:

"Words! Excuses! Any woman who can take nourishment, can give her baby nourishment. And Nature always lends a helping hand. And as far as the baby is concerned, I repeat that the best milk is mother's milk, as long as it's not contaminated." And then, lowering her voice: "I assume you haven't contaminated your wife's bloodstream." And Ramiro found himself speechless and had given in. And the argument was settled once and for all one day when Ramiro made a final attempt to relieve his faltering wife of her burden, to remove the sucker from the shoot; the sovereign of the house then took him aside and said: "Why such insistence? It would appear that the child is in your way. . . ."

"How could the child be in my way! I don't understand. What do you mean?"

"You don't understand, but I do!"

"You'd best explain. . . ."

"Explain? Well then, you remember that savage Pascualón who kept your farm at Majadalaprieta and how he . . ."

"Yes, how he accepted the death of his son so calmly. . . ."

"Exactly."

"And what does that have to do with me? For heaven's sake, Tula! . . ."

"His attitude outraged me. And I determined to find out the root of that evil. . . ."

"Always the same mania . . ."

"True. My poor uncle told me I was like Eve, bent on the knowledge of good and evil."

"And you discovered . . . ?"

"That that . . . man . . ."

"Out with it!"

"That that man . . . The child was in his way when it came to using his wife! Do you understand me?"

"What a barbarian!"

And so, in short, Ramiro admitted defeat, and Manuela went on nursing the first child, the boy, for as long as Gertrudis decreed.

Now, with the mother and father both gone, Gertrudis was faced with the problem of nursing the little girl, the daughter of the dead foundling. Necessarily she had to hand the infant over to a rented mother, a mercenary breast. The simple fact horrified her. She even went so far as to imagine that a hired wet nurse, especially if she were single, might well have contaminated blood and therefore contaminated milk. She also feared that a wet nurse was in a position to take advantage of her position. "If she's unmarried, that's bad, because she can go back to her boyfriend, or worse, somebody else. And if she's married, and leaves her own infant to go and suckle another, that's awful too." In fact, she was shocked by the idea of a mother selling the maternal substance secreted from herself in order to keep her own children alive, barely alive perhaps; the maternal instinct was aroused and outraged in Gertrudis. And thus she was engaged in a constant duel with the wet nurses, whom she changed with grim regularity. How terrible not to be able to give suck herself! In the end, she turned to the artificial solution.

And she made an art of it! She made an art of the bottle. And she turned it into poetry. The ritual became more deeply natural than blind instinct would have been. It all became a cult, a ritual sacrifice, almost a sacrament. In short, the nursing bottle, an industrial artifice, became for Gertrudis the symbol and instrument of a religious rite. She cleansed the bottles, boiled the nipples, sterilized the milk with all the ardor and care of a high-priestess performing a religious rite. And when she placed the rubber nipple in the infant's mouth, her own mammae came alive. And the infant touched the hand that held the bottle.

And Gertrudis would lie down to sleep the night with the child, lending it the warmth of her body, against which she kept the bottle for use during the night should the child call for it. She even came to imagine that the heat of her body, fired at times with the fever of virginal maternity, of maternal virginity, lent that industrialized milk a maternal virtue, and even that she transmitted to it, in some mysterious manner, the fervor of the dreams which had flourished in that solitary bed. And when she nursed the baby in the dark night from that device, with no one else around, she would take out one of her own barren breasts, barren but swollen with blood, and put it within range of the baby's hands, so that it might touch it, lay its hand on it perhaps, as it sucked the milk of life. She vaguely thought the infant might feel some satisfaction, some sweet illusion, from this play. It was her own dream, of course. And what was she dreaming? She herself did not know.

When, as happened occasionally, the infant spit up on the bed, always spotless as a Eucharistic plate, Gertrudis felt uneasy. She had a morbid passion for purity, and with it, a mystic veneration of cleanliness, and on such occasions as this sense was violated, she suffered and had to struggle with herself. She understood well enough that life was impossible without taint, that stains from the baby were innocent nothings, but nevertheless she was shaken. And then she would hug the creature to her breast, silently asking forgiveness for her baseless suspicion of its purity.

XIX

APART FROM THIS maternal preoccupation with the poor infant left by the death of Manuela, a labor which involved a mystic and expiatory cult, and the necessary care of all the other children without distinction (she worked at avoiding a show of preference), Gertrudis was particularly intent on watching Ramirín. She guided his footsteps and studied him for signs of his father, whom he physically much resembled. "That's the way Ramiro probably was at his age," she might say, and she would rummage among old papers to find childhood pictures of her brother-in-law and compare them to his son. Her obsessive aim was to make of the boy what she would have made of the father had she been in charge of the latter's upbringing when he first set out upon life's roads. She thought to preserve him from the mistakes his father had made, in her eyes, so that he might avoid all impulsive choice, base his will on a solid fundament of "perfect love, in the light of an appropriate illumination." It was her judgment that one must look to heaven rather than to earth when one planted a sapling or a shoot: more important than the humus in the ground were the rays of light which came from above, for a sapling springing out of a rock in the full light of the sun will grow better than one planted in putrifying leafmold along shaded slopes. Light was purity.

Gertrudis went over all the boy's lessons with him. In this way she also satisfied an old urge to know, an instinct which had led her pious uncle to call her another Eve. One of the things she studied, and the one she found of most interest, was geometry. She would never have believed that a subject which most people found dry should have encompassed such unknown areas of light and purity! Years later, when Ramirín was grown and his aunt's flesh had turned to dust in the dust of the ground, deprived forever of the light of the sun, he told of how on one specially radiant spring day, she had taught him most ardently that there could be only five—and no more than five—regular polyhedrons: three formed of triangles, the tetrahedron of four, the octahedron of eight, and the icosahedron of twenty; one of squares, the cube, of six; and one of pentagons, the dodecahedron, of twelve. "Don't you see how clear it all is?" she had asked. "Only five, you understand, and no more. Isn't that lovely! And it can't be any other way, it must be just that way!" And she had illustrated the lesson with five white pasteboard models; she had made them with her own blessed hands, and had made them of an unearthly white. She had been quite good with her hands, her nephew recalled. And she had been carried away that day, he remembered, as if she herself had discovered the law of the five regular polyhedrons. Poor Aunt Tula! And he remembered how, when a drop of grease had soiled one of those geometric models, she had made another in its place, saying that the demonstration could not be made "clear" if it were done with a soiled model. In her eyes, geometry was light and purity.

By the same token, she detested anatomy and physiology, which she refused to teach. "That's all swill. And none of it is clear, or certain."

And she watched over the boy for signs of puberty. She planned to guide him through his earliest sentimental adventures, for she wanted his first love to be the one and only. Yet she wondered: "Is there really such a thing as a first love?" And the answer eluded her.

It was her nephew's being alone that she most feared, for she feared all solitude unless it was in the light of day. Solitude should mean the holy solitary sun; it was also the Virgin of La Soledad, when the Virgin was left in solitude because her Son, the sun of her soul, was taken from her. She saw to it that the boy did not lock himself into his room, and was never alone for long. She deemed certain forms of solitary company the worst form of company. And she did not wish him to spend time reading. "He should not read too much," she warned herself, "nor study prints." She was less afraid of live nature than of dead nature, of nature painted; less afraid, for his sake, of life and people, than of life and people reproduced in print. "Death seeks out dead matter," she thought.

Gertrudis went to the same confessor as Rami-rín, to the same Father Alvarez, now become the boy's spiritual director; she proposed to direct the spiritual director as regards her nephew's direction, in short, to act as the true director herself. So that even when she made her own confession, she spoke more about the boy, whom she called her eldest, than she did about herself. Until Father Alvarez told her: "Look now, you're here to confess your own faults, not those of others." To which she replied: "But that boy is my fault. . . ."

Then, when she thought she observed certain ascetic tendencies in the boy, perhaps even a bent toward mysticism, she went running to Father Alvarez.

"We simply can't have that, Father!"

"But supposing God were to call him along that path. . . ."

"No, no. He doesn't call him down that path at all. I know better than you, and certainly better than he. . . . It's nothing more than . . . than sensuality beginning to awake in him."

"But Señora . . ."

"Yes, that and sadness. He's melancholy, and that's not a sign of a religious vocation. For it can't be remorse! What would he be remorseful about? . . ."

"The ways of God, Señora . . ."

"The ways of God are clear. And all this is obscure. You must drive it from him. He was born to be a father, and I to be a grandmother!"

"Here we go again!"

"Yes, here we go again!"

"And how you do labor under the weight of your obsession! Why not get rid of that weight. . . . A hundred times now you've told me you had stifled that notion, that bad thought. . . ."

"I cannot, Father, I cannot! But they must not know. My children—for they are my children, my true children—must not know. Let them not find out, Father. They must not even guess. . . ."

"Calm down, Señora. For God's sake be calm! And forget your apprehensions . . . temptations of the Devil, as I've told you a hundred times. . . . Be yourself. The Aunt Tula we all know and admire . . . yes, admire!"

"No, Father, no! You know better. I'm someone else. . . ."

"But you must get the better of that someone else. . . ."

"Yes. But there are days when I want to get all the children together, his children, my children. . . ."

"Yours, that's right, yours!"

"Yes, I'm 'Mother,' just as you're . . . 'Father!'"

"Now we'll have none of that, Señora, none of that. . . . Leave off. . . ."

"Yes, get them all together and tell them that my entire life has been a lie, a mistake, a failure. . . ."

"You're slandering yourself, Señora. That's not you. You're the other woman, the one we all know, Aunt Tula. . . ."

"I ruined him, Father. I made him fall twice. Once with my sister, and then again with another woman . . ."

"Fall?"

"Yes, fall! And it was due to pride!"

"No. It was due to love. True love . . ."

"Self-love, Father." And she began to cry.

XX

GERTRUDIS MANAGED to lead her nephew away from his ascetic inclinations. And then she began to watch for the appearance of his first love.

"Take your time, Son, look around, and don't rush into anything. For once you've compromised a girl, you cannot just leave her. . . ."

"But Mamá, it's not a matter of compromising anyone. . . . First it's necessary to experiment, try one's luck. . . ."

"Nothing of the sort. No experimenting. And no need for courtship, or the like. It has to be serious. . . ."

The fact was that Tula had already made her own selection and proposed to carry Ramirín along to his destiny as chosen by her: Caridad was the girl's name.

"You seem to have made up your mind. Carita has got your eye," she told the boy one day.

The boy shrugged.

"And she has her eye on you, if I'm not mistaken."

"And you have your eye on both of us, or I'm the one who's mistaken. . . ."

"Me? It's your affair, Son. . . ."

But she thrust one upon the other. And she got her way. And then she proposed to marry them off at once.

"She can come and live with us. We'll all live together. There's room enough for everyone. . . . One more daughter!"

And when she had brought Carita into the house, as her nephew's wife, the girl at once became her confidant. And she immediately set about delving into what she did not know of her nephew's private life.

She insisted the new wife use the familiar in addressing her from the very first, and even that she call her Mother. She began to have her take care of little Manolita, made her pay special attention to the mild and timid Manolita.

"I want you to take the very best care, Caridad, of this little innocent, for she's the best and most fragile child ever was. . . . She's my opus."

"She scarcely seems to speak . . . and she can't be heard in the house. . . . She seems too bashful to let herself be seen. . . ."

"Yes, that's the way she is. I've done everything to give her courage, but unless she's stuck to me, hanging onto my skirts, she acts lost. Of course, she was raised on a bottle, not nursed at all!"

"In any case she's obedient and helpful—but she scarcely ever speaks! . . . And then, I've never heard her laugh. . . ."

"Once in a while . . . when she's alone with me. . . . Because she's altogether different then, another Manolita. . . . She comes to life. And I try to encourage her, and console her. And then she says to me: 'Don't worry, Mamita, that's the way I am. . . . Besides, I'm not sad.' That's what she tells me."

"Well, she seems sad. . . ."

"Yes, it's true she does, but I've begun to feel she really isn't, because, well, for instance, take me for example, what do you think, Carita, do I seem happy or sad?"

"You, Aunt . . ."

"Now why do you call me Aunt?"

"Well, you, Mamá, you . . . I don't know whether you're sad or happy, but I think you're happy. . . ."

"You think I'm happy? Well, then, that's good enough!"

"In any case, you make me happy. . . ."

"And that's what God bids us do in this world, make others happy."

"But in order to make other people happy, it's necessary to be happy oneself."

"Or not . . ."

"How not?"

"Nothing gives more happiness than a ray of sunlight, especially if it strikes the green foliage of a tree, and the sun's rays are neither happy nor sad, and who knows . . . perhaps a ray's own fire consumes it. . . . A ray of sunlight brings joy because it is pure, and everything pure is joyous. . . . And poor Manolita should bring happiness because she's pure. . . ."

"Yes, that's obvious. And then those great eyes, which are like . . ."

"They're like two calm pools among green foliage. . . . I've often watched them, close up . . . and

I don't know where she got such eyes. They're not her mother's, for she had the eyes of a tubercular, clouded with fever. . . . And they're not her father's eyes, which were like . . ."

"Do you know whose eyes they're like?"

"Whose?" and her own question sent a shiver through Gertrudis.

"Yours! . . ."

"Perhaps . . . maybe . . . I've never seen my own eyes close up, and I can't see into them . . . but it could be. . . . Perhaps. Anyway I have taught her to look. . . ."

XXI

WHAT WAS THE matter with poor Gertrudis, and why did she feel she was being consumed? Doubtless she had accomplished her mission in the world. She would leave behind her eldest nephew, Ramiro, her "other Ramiro," already through the most difficult passage and launched in his own ship, the other children secure in his care. She would leave a hearth with a fire burning and people to keep the fire going. Now she felt herself disintegrating. She suffered frequent fainting spells, and sometimes, for days at a time, she would see the entire world as through a fog, as if everything were behind smoke. And she dreamed more than she had ever dreamed. She dreamed what might have been . . . if Ramiro had left Rosa for her sake. But she would conclude that nothing would really have been any different. The truth was that she had passed through the world without ever having been in it. Father Alvarez got to thinking that Gertrudis was acting queer before her time, that her strong intelligence was weakening and her robust constitution too. And he strove to defend her against her old manias and temptations.

One day Caridad whispered to Tula: "Mother!" And Tula, seeing the girl all red and flustered, asked: "What! Is it time?" And the girl whispered: "Yes, it's time." And Tula: "Are you sure?" And the girl: "Altogether sure! Otherwise I wouldn't have said anything." And, in the midst of her joy, Tula felt as if an icy sword suddenly went through her heart. She had nothing further to do in the world but wait for the grandchild, the grandchild of her Ramiro and her Rosa, her grandchild, and then be off to give both of them the good news. Around the house, she scarcely did more than take care of Caridad, who was the one who made the place live for her now. She was even beginning to forget about Manolita, her opus, and the poor girl knew it: she sensed that the expected arrival was relegating her to the shadows.

Gertrudis would call Caridad to her side whenever the occasion presented itself—and she was always waiting for the occasion—and ask her about what she felt:

"Do you feel anything, Daughter, do you feel life yet?"

"Sometimes . . ."

"Isn't the child in a hurry to get out? To come into the sunlight? Because in there, in darkness, even though it must be nice and warm and quiet . . . He must be impatient, shoving a bit. If he waits too long I won't see him. . . . Or if I hurry a little . . ."

"Mother! Don't say such things. . . ."

" 'Don't say, don't say' . . . But, Daughter, I feel I'm disintegrating. . . . I'm no good for anything any more. . . . I see everything through a fog . . . as in a dream. If I didn't know already, I couldn't say whether your hair was blonde or black. . . ."

And Gertrudis would gently stroke the girl's splendid blonde hair. And then, as if she had just seen with her finger-ends: "Blonde, blonde like the sun . . ."

And she would insist: "Don't forget: if it's a boy, he'll be Ramiro, and if it's a girl . . . Rosa. . . ."

"No, mother. Gertrudis, Tula, like Mamá Tula."

"Tula! Well, all right . . . But it would be better if you had twins. One a boy and the other a girl . . ."

"Mother, for heaven's sake!"

"What, do you think that would be too much for you?"

"I . . . don't know. . . . I don't know anything about that, Mother, but . . ."

"Yes. That would be perfect. Twins . . . a boy and a girl who lay in a close embrace before they knew anything at all about the world, when they didn't even know they existed, arms around each other in the warmth of their mother's womb. . . . Heaven must be like that. . . ."

"What things you say, Mamá Tula!"

"I've spent my whole life dreaming, you see. . . ."

And then, while Gertrudis dreamt on, holding onto her latest hope, as if she would carry it by way of viaticum on her last journey back to mother earth, her littlest and last, Manolita, fell seriously ill. "Ah, it's all my fault," Gertrudis lamented. "Dreaming of the twins to come, I've neglected the poor little chick. Just when she needed me to give her warmth, she must have been exposed to some blast of cold. . . ."

And she felt her strength coming back as if by some miracle. Her mind cleared and she began to take over the care of the patient.

"But Mother, let me take care of her," Caridad told her. "We can all take care of her . . . Rosita and Elvira and me, we'll take turns."

"No, you can't do it, and you shouldn't. Your obligation is to the life you're carrying. You can't take care of this child and let your own go. You might lose what you have. . . . And though Rosita and Elvira are her sisters well enough and love her as a sister, they simply don't understand. And even though the poor little child is satisfied with anything, she can't get along without me. . . . Even a glass of water will do her more good if I give it to her. I'm the only one who can fix her pillow so that her head won't hurt and she won't have bad dreams. . . ."

"Yes, that's true. . . ."

"Of course, since I was the one who nursed her! . . . And I must be the one to take care of her now."

In short, Gertrudis came to life again. The luminous strength of her heroic days returned. Her pulse-beat no longer wavered, her legs no longer trembled under her. When she held the glass with its portion of medicine and helped the patient to take it, poor Manolita's feverish hands took strength from the strong firm hands of Gertrudis, and a kind of current brought to the invalid a sweet remembrance of splendor, even though all memory in her seemed to have grown dim. And when Aunt Tula sat beside her in bed, the sick girl was comforted merely by looking upon her in silence.

"Am I going to die, Mamá?"

"Die? No, my little swallow, no! You must live. . . ."

"As long as you do . . ."

"And then, and then? . . ."

"Then, afterwards . . . No. What for?"

"But young girls should live. . . ."

"What for?"

"Why . . . in order to live . . . In order to get married, to raise a family . . ."

"But you didn't marry, Mamita. . . ."

"No, I didn't marry, but it was the same as if I had. . . . And you must live so as to take care of your brother. . . ."

"That's true. To take care of my brother, of my brothers and sisters."

"Yes, of all of them . . ."

"But, people say I'm no good for anything . . ."

"Who says so, Daughter?"

"They don't say it, it's true they don't say it, but they think it. . . ."

"And how do you know they think it?"

"Well . . . I know they do! And besides, it's true . . . because I'm really no good for anything, and when you die I'd have nothing in the world to do. . . . If you died, I'd die of cold. . . ."

"Come, come now, cover yourself up and don't say such things. . . . And now I'm going to get your medicine ready. . . ."

And she went off to hide her tears and kneel before the image of the Virgin of La Soledad and plead: "My life for hers, Mother, my life for hers! I feel I'm going, my dead are calling me. And she wants to go with me, to cling to me, to cover herself with the earth, and hide below, where there's no sunlight, and she wants me to give her some warmth or other. . . . My life for hers, Mother, my life for hers! Don't let that curtain of dark earth fall so soon and cover those eyes they say are mine, faultless eyes I gave her . . .

yes, I. . . . Don't let her die. . . . Save her, Mother, even if I must go without seeing the child who is to come! . . ."

And her wish was granted.

The sick girl began to recover. Her color, her pale rose colors, returned to her cheeks. Once again she saw the sunlight playing on the garden green. And, Aunt Tula fell ill with a bronchopneumonia which had developed during Manolita's convalescence. Then it was the girl who felt a sudden access of strength, a flow of energy welling up in her. Now it was her turn to take care of the woman who had given her life.

The household as a whole was astounded with the new Manolita.

"You must tell Manolita," Gertrudis said to Caridad, "not to exert herself so, for she must still be weak. . . . And you mustn't either, of course. You owe yourself to your own, you know that. . . . Rosita and Elvira are quite sufficient . . . Especially since all their efforts will have been in vain. . . . For I've done my work. . . ."

"But Mother . . ."

"There's nothing more to be said. And don't let that little dove of God waste away. . . ."

"But she's grown so strong. . . . I would never have believed . . ."

"Oh, and she was so sure she was going to die, and she wanted to. . . . And I was afraid she would. She seemed so weak! . . . Of course, she never knew her father, who was mortally wounded when he conceived her. . . . And as for her poor mother, I think she was half-dead all her life, lived half-dead. . . . But the little girl has been resurrected!"

"Absolutely! When she saw you in danger, she came to life."

"Of course, since she's my daughter!"

"She's more, isn't she?"

"Yes, more! I'd like to proclaim it, now that I'm on the threshold of eternity. She's more. You and she!"

"She and I?"

"Yes. Because my blood doesn't run in your veins. Her blood is Ramiro's, not mine, but I made her, she's my opus! And I married you to my son."

"I know. . . ."

"Yes, just as I married her father to her mother, my sister, and then I married him to Manolita's mother. . . ."

"I know. . . . I know. . . ."

"I know that you know, but not everything. . . ."

"No, not everything . . ."

"I don't either. . . . Or at least I don't want to know. There are several things I don't want to know when I leave the world. . . . There are things which only taint one when they are known. Original sin . . . The Virgin Mother was born without original sin. . . ."

"Still, some people say she knew everything. . . ."

"No, she didn't know everything. She didn't have any knowledge of evil . . . which is a knowledge. . . ."

"Well, Mother, don't talk any more or you'll only do yourself harm. . . ."

"It's worse if I don't talk, because then I begin to go over and over the ground, to fret, fret, fret. . . ."

XXII

AUNT TULA COULD no longer hold out. Her spirit seemed about to take flight, as if it were a bird in a cage beginning to fall apart. Like a bird leaving a known place for an unknown place, she felt pangs of doubt while at the same time longing to soar above the clouds. She would not get to see the grandchild. Did she feel regret? She dreamed that she would see the child from above: "I'll know whether it's a girl or a boy, and I'll know the child better than I would here, for I'll see it better and more clearly than I would here below. . . ."

The final fever kept her prostrate in bed. She could scarce distinguish between "her children" except by the sound of their footfalls; she recognized Caridad and Manolita most readily, of course. Caridad's footfalls sounded to her like those of a creature heavy with burgeoning, and Tula even thought she could scent "ripeness." Manolita's walk, on the other hand, she knew by its lightness, like that of a bird which swoops across the ground so closely that it is difficult to say whether it runs or flies. "When she comes in," murmured Tula, "I seem to hear the sudden silence of wings folded and fallen."

She chose to take a final leave of Manolita first of all. She stretched an arm out of the bed as if to give the girl her blessing; placing her hand on the girl's head, which was bent with tearfulness, she said:

"Tell me my sweet pigeon, do you still want to die? Tell me the truth!"

"If I could die instead of . . ."

"Instead of me, is that it? No! You must not want to die at all. . . . You have your brother to think of . . . Your brothers, and sisters. . . . You were close to death, but I think that nearness cured you. Isn't that so? Tell me the truth, as if you were in a confessional. I want to tell our family. . . ."

"I no longer think of such things . . . of such foolish things."

"They weren't exactly foolish. . . . But, now that you mention foolishness, bring me your little doll. Because I know you've still got it, haven't you? Bring it here, so I can say goodbye to her, too, and she can say goodbye to me as well. . . . Do you remember?"

"Yes, Mother, I remember."

"What do you remember?"

"I remember when she fell into the orchard close and Elvira called me silly because I cried so much, and she said it was no use crying. . . ."

"That's right. I remember too. What else? What else do you remember?"

"I remember the story you told us then. . . ."

"Tell it to me now. . . ."

"It was about a little girl whose doll fell into a dry well, and she couldn't get down there to get it out, and so she cried and cried so much that the well filled with her tears and the doll floated up. . . ."

"And what did Elvira say to that? . . . I can't remember. . . ."

"Yes, yes, you must remember. . . ."

"Well, what did she say?"

"She said that the little girl must have dried up, then, from crying so much, and died. . . ."

"And what did I say?"

"For heaven's sake, Mother . . ."

"Well, then, don't tell me, little pigeon. And come now, don't cry. Your tears won't fill up the well I'm falling into and I won't come floating up. . . ."

"If that could only be. . . ."

"Ah, yes! If that could only be, I'd hug you and take you with me. . . . But we all have to wait, to wait our turn. . . . Take care of your brothers and sisters. I'm leaving them to you, you know. You can make them think I'm still here. . . ."

"I'll do all I can. . . ."

"Don't let them realize I'm gone. . . . And I'll help you from there. . . ."

"I'll pray to you, Mother. . . ."

"Pray to the Virgin, child, to the Virgin. . . ."

"I'll pray to you every night, Mother, before I go to sleep. . . ."

"All right, but don't cry now. . . ."

"But I'm not crying, don't you see I'm not crying?"

"It's not a bad thing to cry after one has seen something awful, to wash away such sights. . . . But you've never seen anything awful, you mustn't see such things. . . ."

"If I did, I'd shut my eyes. . . ."

"No, no, that way you'd see the most awful things. . . . Just pray for your father, and your mother, and me. . . . Don't forget your mother. . . ."

"I won't forget her. . . ."

"But since you never knew her . . ."

"I do know her!"

"I mean your other mother, the one who brought you into the world."

"Yes, I know her because of you. I *know* her!"

"Poor little thing! She never knew her own mother. . . ."

"You were like her mother!"

"Come now, don't cry anymore. . . ."

"But I'm not crying!" And Manolita ran one hand

across her eyes, while the hand which held the medicine trembled.

"And now bring me your doll. I want to see her. And, yes, over there in that little chest, the one you know . . . yes, that one . . . here's the key . . . in one of the corners, where no one, except me, and sometimes you, ever touched anything, next to the pictures, you know, there's another doll . . . Mine . . . the one I had as a child . . . my first love. . . . Was it really the first? Anyway, bring it to me. . . . But don't let anyone know . . . they'd say we were foolish, too. Because we're the foolish ones, all right. . . . Bring me the two dolls, so I can say goodbye to them, and later we can pretend we're serious and say goodbye to the others. . . . Leave me now, because a bad thought is getting the better of me." And she crossed herself.

The bad thought which was getting the better of her came in the form of a diabolic whisper out of the depths of her sorrowful leave-taking, and told her: "Dolls, all of them!"

XXIII

THEN SHE SUMMONED the others, Caridad among them.

"This is the last fever I'll have. It's the beginning of the fire of Purgatory. . . ."

"What things you say, Mother. . . ."

"The fires of Purgatory . . . Because Hell has no fire. . . . Hell is all ice, nothing but ice. I'm burning up, my flesh is burning. . . . But I'm only sorry I won't see the child to come, and that I'll never know him, or her . . . all those still to be. . . ."

"Come, Mother. . . ."

"Come, yourself, Carita, don't be bashful now. I simply wanted to tell them there what the new child was like. . . . Come, don't cry now. . . . The three of them are calling me. . . ."

"Don't say such things. . . ."

"Do you want me to tell you things to make you laugh? Manolita and I have already said all the silly things between us. We're the foolish ones around here, the pair of us, and now it's up to all of us to take leave like they do in books. . . ."

"Please don't say any more! You mustn't talk. The doctor told us not to let you talk too much."

"Ah, it's you, Ramiro! The man of the house! . . . The doctor, you say? What does the doctor know about it? Don't pay any attention to him. . . . Besides, it's better to live an hour of talk than two days of silence. Now is the time to talk. Besides, it will distract me, and I won't have to think about everything."

"You know well enough that Father Alvarez said it was precisely now that you had to think about everything. . . ."

"Ah, you're here, too, Elvira! Elvira the Wise. So it's Father Alvarez you're going to quote me, Father Alvarez of the Remedy? And what does Father Alvarez know about it? Another doctor! Another man! Besides, I don't have anything of my own to think about. Anything that's mine is yours. My things are yours . . . and theirs. Those who have gone before me and are calling . . . I'm not really alive or dead now. . . . I was never really alive . . . or dead, before.

. . . What are you muttering, Enriquín? You think I'm raving. . . ."

"No, I didn't say that. . . ."

"Surely you did. I heard you whispering to Rosita. . . . Don't you know I can hear even the rustle of Manolita's wings in the still air? And what if I am raving? . . ."

"You should be resting. . . ."

"Rest, rest . . . there'll be plenty of time for me to rest!"

"Don't uncover yourself like that. . . ."

"I'm burning up! . . . And remember Caridad, you must name the girl Tula, like me, and the boy, Ramiro. . . . Because I'm sure there are two, a boy and a girl, arms around each other in the warmth . . ."

No one spoke, but when the dying woman heard the sound of muffled crying, she went on:

"Well, now, we must all take courage! And you must all think, think of what you will do, think well and long, so that you will never have to be sorry for what you did and, even more, what you didn't do. . . . And if you ever see someone you love fallen into the mire, even into a cesspool, jump in to help him, to save his life, even at the risk of drowning yourself. . . . Don't let him drown. Better if you both drown. . . . Better to drown in a common sewer, together, than to let a person drown without trying to help. Better to be that person's remedy. Yes, his remedy! Better to die in a sewer! That doesn't matter. . . . And you can't skim across the top of a sewer to lend help— because we don't have wings. Or we have the wings of a chicken and can't fly. And besides, even wings would get soiled flying low enough over a sewer to help someone sinking there, they'd be splashed by the drowning one's thrashing about. . . . Anyway, we don't have wings. At best only chicken wings. . . . We're none of us angels, even if we will be in the next life . . . where there's no muck and no blood! There's muck enough in Purgatory, burning muck to clean and burn away . . . yes, burn away. . . . In Purgatory, all those who wouldn't cleanse themselves with muck in life will be cleansed with burning muck, burning dung, and they'll be washed in filth. . . . It's all I have to say. . . . Don't be afraid of corruption. . . . And pray for me, ask the Virgin to forgive me."

She had no further strength, or consciousness. Even when she came around, she could no longer gather her thoughts together. And her final agony began gently enough. She began to sink, to sink like a late autumn afternoon shot through with the last rays of sunlight and extinguishing itself in the quiet waters of a river-bend, in which the foliage of poplars, colored red too, is reflected along with the dying light.

XXIV

DID AUNT TULA really die? No, for she began to live a new life in the family, a quickened life of never-ending familiarity, an eternal life of familiarity. Now she was Aunt to her children, her nieces and nephews, no longer Mother, nor Mamá, nor Aunt Tula, but simply *Aunt*, the Aunt. It was an invocation, that name, a true religious invocation, as if she had been canonized as a household saint. Manolita herself, the one who was most her daughter and the heir to her spirit, the depository of her tradition, invoked her only as Aunt.

And the Aunt kept the family together and maintained its unity. If hidden divisions, defensive and offensive alliances, which had been hidden during her lifetime, came to the fore at her death, they were divisions and alliances she herself had provoked; they came from the very life of the family she had created; and she had nurtured its basic and culminating unity over and above the natural dissensions.

Two bands came into being. On the one side, Rosa's eldest daughter, Rosita, seemed to feel close to Caridad, her sister-in-law, rather than to her brother, Ramiro. On the other side, Rosa's second daughter, Elvira, felt a reciprocated affinity for Enrique, her stepbrother, son of the foundling. Ramiro and Manolita remained outside either alliance. For his part, Ramiro lived, or rather he let himself live, attentive to his child and the child's possible future, and busied himself with his own affairs. Manolita devoted herself to the veneration of the *Aunt* and the tradition of the hearth.

In her way, Manolita was preparing herself to serve as the family link between four potential families, the four families which would evolve from the present hearth. With the death of the Aunt, she had come into her own. She conserved and nurtured in herself all she could of Tula, of her spirit and her knowledge. She cultivated the other's manner of speech, the short pointed sentences and judgments; sometimes she merely repeated things she had heard the Aunt say; she held to the same doctrine, practiced the same manner and even the same gestures. "Another Aunt!" her brothers and sisters would mutter, not always kindly. Manolita kept the keys to the private coffers which held the trinkets and papers of the departed Aunt, and there she kept the childhood dolls that had be-

longed to both of them, and the letters, and Don
Primitivo's prayerbook and breviary; and she was the
family historian, the one who knew the events and
stories of the forebears by heart. She knew what there
was to know about Don Primitivo, who was not even
of her own blood; about the first Ramiro's mother;
about Rosa; about her own mother Manuela, the
foundling from the Orphanage, though in her case
it was not a matter of remembered words or deeds,
but of silences and passions. The young Manolita
was the history of the house. She bore in herself the
spiritual eternity of the family. She was the heir to
its soul, the family made spirit through the Aunt.

Inheritance? In a hive, the spirit of the bees, the
beelike tradition, the art of extracting honey from
flowers and the construction of the honeycomb, *bee-
ity* and *bee-ness*, one and all are transmitted by inheritance—and, nevertheless, none of it is transmitted
by flesh and fluid. Carnality is perpetuated by drones
and queens, neither of which can be said to work, nor
do they know how to construct honeycombs, nor make
honey, nor care for larvae, and, not knowing these
things, they cannot transmit this knowledge, through
their flesh and fluid, to their brood. The tradition of
the art of the bees, of the construction of the comb
and the elaboration of honey and wax is, therefore, col-
lateral and not lineal, found not in the transmission of
flesh but of spirit, and it is owing to the aunts, to
those bees which neither fecundate the eggs nor lay
them. And all this was a bit of knowledge which
Manolita had gotten from the Aunt, who had somehow been drawn to the observation of bees in early
youth and had gone on to look into the matter, for
what she found out had made a deep impression on
her, and she had pondered it all—and even dreamed

of it. And one of the most telling words, one with esoteric overtones, and one which Manolita had gotten from the Aunt, and which she used now, applying it to her brothers whenever they bared their most masculine instincts, was to call them "drones!" She would use the word in phrases like: "Be quiet, drone!" The word itself held for her, as it had for the Aunt, a set of resounding implications. And the males who were her brothers took her meaning.

The alliance between Elvira, the first Ramiro's daughter, the girl who had cost Ramiro's first wife, Rosa, her life, and Enrique, the son of Ramiro's transgression with the foundling girl, was a close one. The half-brother and the half-sister (the mother of the former having been the latter's stepmother to boot) were closer to each other than any of the other five were to one another. They went about whispering secrets. And this obvious or apparent conspiracy made Manolita uneasy. It was not that the brother who had shared the same womb, her uterine brother, was closer to a sister born from another woman, it was not that, for she felt no such attraction for either one, and was quite satified to have it so. But this relationship, which she found more than fraternal, repelled her.

"I think it's about time," she told them once, "that one of you fell in love. I'd like to see you find a girlfriend, Enrique, or have someone court you, Elvira. . . ."

"What for?" replied Elvira.

"So you'd stop forever going about arm in arm, pawing each other and whispering into each other's ears and hanging onto each other. . . ."

"Oh, in that case we'd probably hang onto each other even more," Enrique replied.

"How would that be possible?"

"Because she'd be wanting to tell me her boyfriend's secrets, isn't that so, Elvira? And of course I would want to tell her about my girl! . . ."

"Yes, yes, exactly," Elvira burst out, seeming about to clap her hands.

"Oh, that's beautiful! So the two of you would be laughing at the other's boyfriend and girlfriend. A pretty spectacle!"

"Well, now, you tell us, and what would Aunt be saying to that?" and Elvira stared provocatively into Manolita's eyes.

"She'd say that you shouldn't fool with things that are sacred, and she'd call you infantile. . . ."

"Well and good, but why don't you repeat what Aunt used to quote from the Gospels about it being necessary to become like a child in order to enter into the kingdom of heaven . . . ?" Enrique countered.

"Like a child, yes! But not like an infant!"

"What's the fine line of distinction, now, between a child and an infant? . . ."

"Why, in the manner of playing games."

"How does an infant play?"

"An infant plays at being a grown-up. Children are not like grown-ups, not like men or women, but like angels. I remember Aunt telling me that there are languages in which the word child is never either masculine or feminine but always neuter. . . ."

"Of course, in German to go no further. And in German *das Mädchen* is also neuter. . . ."

"Well, this *Mädchen* here," interjected Manolita, attempting unsuccessfully to cover her words with a smile, "is not neuter. . . ."

"Of course I'm not neuter," echoed Elvira, "what an idea!"

"Anyway, you can leave off the infantilism. . . ."

"Yes, none of that. But being childlike is all right, isn't that so?"

"Exactly."

"And how will we know?"

"That's enough of that. What's the use? Certain things only become more obscure the more one talks. . . ."

"Very well, little Aunt," exclaimed Elvira, embracing Manolita and giving her a kiss, "don't be mad at us. . . ."

"No, I won't even get mad at you for calling me Aunt. . . ."

"I didn't mean anything by that. . . ."

"I know. But that's dangerous. What you might mean comes out later. . . ."

Enrique made a face at his full-sister and, clasping the other one, the half-sister, under the arm, took her away with him.

Manolita watched them go. And she wondered: "Are they really only infants? Yes, yes, that's what it amounts to. But did I do well in talking to them as I did?" And she invoked the Aunt: "Did I do the right thing, Aunt?" And she went on: "The meaning of things becomes clear only later, the intention behind it all. . . . But perhaps I'm the one who forces a meaning on everything, provides an intention, me and my far-fetched remonstrances. Perhaps I give them ideas they never had. . . . But still, no! They shouldn't be playing games like that! Because of course, they *are* playing. . . . I only hope he finds a girlfriend soon. And she a boyfriend."

XXV

THE OTHER ALLIANCE in the family was made up, not of Rosita and Ramiro, as might be expected, but of Rosita and Ramiro's wife Caridad, sisters-in-law. In all truth it was Rosita who sought out Caridad, mostly to complain, to pour out her apprehensions and suspicions. In short, their "alliance" was based on Rosita's complaints. The latter considered herself badly used, misunderstood. She seemed to think she was ignored, and so she went about with a sad and worried expression, in the hope, apparently, that someone would ask her what the trouble was. Since no one asked, she suffered all the more. Of them all, Manolita took the least interest in Rosita's imaginary troubles. To herself she observed: "If she really has something wrong, and not just a desire to be fussed over and given special attention, she'll come out with it!" And the sad Rosita went on worrying.

And she would seek out Caridad, her sister-in-law, and chant a litany of complaints against Caridad's husband, her own brother, accusing him of being self-centered, for example. And the wife would listen patiently, not knowing what to say.

"I just don't know, Manolita, what to do about Rosita," Caridad told her other sister-in-law. "She's forever complaining about her brother, who happens to be my husband. She says he's self-centered and haughty and thoughtless and . . ."

"Let her talk, and—agree with her!"

"What do you mean? Should I give her wings so she can float away on fancy?"

"No, you can clip her wings instead."

126

"I don't understand. Besides what she says is not true. Ramiro is none of those things!"

"I know that very well. I know he has defects like all men. . . ."

"And like all women."

"Of course. Only his defects are those of a man. . . ."

"You mean those of a drone! That's what you mean."

"As you will. His defects are those of a man, or since you insist, those of a drone. . . ."

"What about my defects?"

"Your defects, Caridad? Yours are those of a queen, a queen bee!"

"Oh, that's very good! Not even Aunt ever went that far! . . ."

"Ramiro's defects, now, are not those mentioned by Rosa, he's none of those things. . . ."

"In that case, why should I let her go on talking and even agree with her, as you suggest?"

"Because in that way you'll throw her off, upset her plans, you'll see. I know her well enough. . . ."

One morning, the three chanced to be together and Rosita began her attack:

ROSITA: A fine hour your husband chose to come home last night! (When speaking of Ramiro to his wife, Rosita never called him "my brother," but always "your husband.")

CARIDAD: What was wrong with it?

MANOLITA: And what were you doing awake at such an hour, Rosita?

ROSITA: He woke me up.

MANOLITA: He did, did he?

CARIDAD: Well, he didn't manage to wake me. . . .

ROSITA: Such indifference!

MANOLITA: Caridad sleeps easy in this house, and she has every reason to. She's quite right.

ROSITA: Quite right? Quite right? I don't understand. . . .

MANOLITA: Well, I do. But you seem to find some pleasure in all this, and that's a dangerous game, and very ugly. . . .

CARIDAD: Please, Manolita!

ROSITA: Let her go on, let the Aunt speak. . . .

MANOLITA: You sound more like the Aunt than anyone else around here. . . .

ROSITA: Me? I'm the Aunt here?

MANOLITA: Yes, you, Rosa. But why are you trying to make your sister jealous?

CARIDAD: I'm sure Rosita isn't trying to make me jealous, Manolita. . . .

MANOLITA: I know what I'm saying, Caridad.

ROSITA: Yes, she's surely the one here who knows what she's saying. . . .

MANOLITA: We all know what we're saying but, besides, I know what I mean. Do you understand me, Rosa?

ROSITA: The Aunt's refrain . . .

MANOLITA: That may be. And I'm telling you that you're capable of marrying the worst possible husband in order to provoke him into giving you cause for jealousy. You'd rather do that than give him cause for jealousy yourself.

ROSITA: Marry? Me marry? I haven't the slightest desire. . . .

MANOLITA: I know what you say about marriage and all, but I don't know what you think. . . . I know you say you won't get married and you don't want a boyfriend. . . . And I know you're thinking about whether you should or shouldn't enter a convent. . . .

128

CARIDAD: And how do you know that, Manolita?

MANOLITA: Ah, but do you all think I don't know your secrets. . . . I know about them precisely because they *are* secrets. . . .

ROSITA: Well, and supposing I *was* thinking of entering a convent, what's so strange about that? What's wrong with that? What's wrong in serving God?

MANOLITA: There's nothing wrong in serving God of course. . . . But the fact is that if you entered a convent it wouldn't be to serve God. . . .

ROSITA: No? Then what would it be for?

MANOLITA: So as not to serve men . . . or women either . . .

CARIDAD: For God's sake, Manuela, the things you say . . .

ROSITA: Yes, what things she says and does, and I do and say mine . . . But where did you ever hear, Sister, that one can't serve men from a convent?

MANOLITA: No doubt, by praying for them . . .

ROSITA: Of course, praying God to free them from temptation . . .

MANOLITA: But I think you'd be more likely to pray "Lead me not into temptation" rather than "Lead us not into temptation. . . ."

ROSITA: Of course I'd enter a convent to avoid temptation. . . .

MANOLITA: But haven't you just tried to lead Caridad, your own sister, into temptation? Or perhaps you don't believe that was a temptation. Weren't you trying to lead her into temptation?

CARIDAD: No, Manolita, Rosa wasn't trying to do anything of the sort. . . . Besides, she knows I'm not jealous, that I'm not going to be jealous, that I'm not capable of jealousy. . . .

ROSITA: Let her go on, Caridad. Let the little bee
sting away. . . .

MANOLITA: It smarts, does it? Well, scratch away
then, Daughter!

ROSITA: Oh, now I'm "Daughter" am I?

MANOLITA: And Sister. Always.

ROSITA: And tell me little Sister, little bee, did you
not ever think of entering the comb of a convent, a
beehive? . . .

MANOLITA: One can make honey and wax in the
world.

ROSITA: And one can sting. . . .

MANOLITA: Exactly! One can sting!

ROSITA: In short, you're going to be an aunt, just
like Aunt Tula. . . .

MANOLITA: I don't know what I'm going to be, but
if I were to follow the Aunt's example, I wouldn't be
following such a bad path, would I? Or do you think
she was on the wrong road after all? Surely you
wouldn't want to forget everything she taught us. And
certainly she never tried to divide this house against
itself, or sow discord of any kind. Would she ever
have come out against anything any of us did?

CARIDAD: For heaven's sake, Manolita! Out of respect
for the memory of Aunt Tula, please say no more. . . .
And please, Rosita, don't cry like that. . . . Come,
don't bury your head in your hands, let's see your
face. . . . Come, come, stop crying. . . .

Manolita put her hand on her stepsister Rosita's
shoulder to soothe her and, in a voice from another
world, the eternal world of the immortal family, said:

"Forgive me, Sister, I went too far! . . . I was hurt
by what you were trying to do. I feared for the in-
tegrity of the family. I think I spoke as Aunt Tula

130

might have done at such a time. . . . Forgive me for doing so!"

Rosita let her head fall on her sister's breast. She hid her face in the younger girl's bosom and spoke between sobs:

"It's you who must forgive me, Sister! . . . No, not Sister, Mother . . . my Mother . . . Aunt! Aunt!"

"Aunt Tula is the one who will forgive us, and unite us, and guide us all!" exclaimed Manolita.

Saint Manuel Bueno, Martyr

If in this life only we have hope in Christ,
we are of all men most miserable.

Saint Paul: i Cor. 15:19

NOW THAT the bishop of the diocese of Renada, to which this my beloved village of Valverde de Lucerna belongs, is said to be urging the process of beatification of our Don Manuel, or rather, Saint Manuel Bueno, who was parish priest here, I want to put in writing, by way of confession (although to what end only God, and not I can say), all that I know and remember about that matriarchal man who pervaded the most secret life of my soul, who was my true spiritual father, the father of my spirit, the spirit of myself, Angela Carballino.

The other, my flesh-and-blood temporal father, I scarcely knew, for he died when I was still very young. I know he came to Valverde de Lucerna from elsewhere—he was a stranger to the place—and that he settled here when he married my mother. He had brought a number of books with him: *Don Quixote*, some classical plays, some novels, a few histories, the *Bertoldo*, a veritable grab bag. These books (practically the only ones in the entire village), set me daydreaming, and I was devoured by my daydreams. My dear mother told me very little about the words or the deeds of my father. For the words and deeds of Don Manuel, whom she worshiped, of whom she was enamored, in common with all the rest of the village—in an exquisitely chaste manner, of course— had obliterated all memory of the words and deeds of her husband whom she fervently commended to God, as she said her daily rosary.

I remember Don Manuel as if it were yesterday, from the time when I was a girl of ten, just before

I was taken to the convent school in the cathedral city of Renada. At that time Don Manuel, our saint, must have been about thirty-seven years old. He was tall, slim; he carried himself erect, his head the way our Buitre Peak carries its crest, and his eyes had all the blue depth of our lake. As he walked he commanded all eyes, and not only the eyes but the hearts of all; gazing round at us he seemed to look through our flesh as through glass and penetrate our hearts. We all loved him, especially the children. And the things he said to us! The villagers could scent the odor of sanctity, they were intoxicated with it.

It was at this time that my brother Lázaro, who was in America, from where he regularly sent us money with which we lived in decent comfort, had my mother send me to the convent school, so that my education might be completed outside the village; he suggested this move despite the fact that he had no special fondness for the nuns. "But, since, as far as I know," he wrote us, "there are no lay schools there yet—especially not for young ladies—we will have to make use of the ones that do exist. The important thing is for Angelita to receive some polish and not be forced to continue among village girls." And so I entered the convent school. At one point I even thought of becoming a teacher; but pedagogy soon palled.

At school I met girls from the city and I made friends with some of them. But I still kept in touch with people in our village, and I received frequent news from them and sometimes a visit. And the fame of the parish priest even reached the school, for he was beginning to be talked of in the cathedral city. And the nuns never tired of asking me about him.

Ever since I was a child I had been endowed, I don't really know why, with a large degree of curiosity and uneasiness, due in part at least to that jumble of books which my father had collected, and at school these qualities were stimulated, especially in the course of a friendship I developed with a girl who grew excessively attached to me. At times she suggested that we enter the same convent together, swearing to an everlasting "sisterhood"—and even that we seal the oath in blood. At other times she talked to me, with half-closed eyes, of sweethearts and marriage adventures. Strangely enough, I have never heard anything of her since, nor of what became of her, despite the fact that whenever our Don Manuel was mentioned, or when my mother wrote me something about him in her letters—which happened in almost every letter—and I read it to her, the girl would cry out ecstatically: "What a lucky girl you are to be able to live near a saint like that, a living saint, of flesh and blood, and to be able to kiss his hand; when you go back to your village write to me a lot and tell me lots of things about him."

I spent five years at school, five years which have now evanesced in memory like a dream at dawn, and when I was fifteen I returned to my own Valverde de Lucerna. By now everything there revolved around Don Manuel: Don Manuel, the lake, and the mountain. I arrived home anxious to know him, to place myself in his care, and hopeful that he would set me on my path in life.

It was rumored that he had entered the seminary to become a priest so that he might thus look after the children of a recently widowed sister and provide for them in place of their father; that in the seminary his keen mind and his talents had distinguished him and that he had subsequently turned down opportunities of a brilliant career in the Church because he wanted to remain exclusively a part of his Valverde de Lucerna, of his remote village which lay like a brooch between the lake and the mountain reflected in it.

How he loved his people! He spent his life salvaging wrecked marriages, forcing unruly children to submit to their parents, or reconciling parents to their children, and, above all, he consoled the embittered and weary in spirit and helped everyone to die well.

I recall, among other incidents, the occasion when the unfortunate daughter of old Aunt Rabona returned to our town. She had been living in the city and lost her virtue there; now she returned unmarried and abandoned, and she brought back a little son. Don Manuel did not rest until he had persuaded an old sweetheart, Perote by name, to marry the poor girl and, moreover, to legitimize the infant with his own name. Don Manuel told Perote:

"Come now, give this poor waif a father, for he hasn't got one except in heaven."

"But, Don Manuel, it's not my fault . . . !"

"Who knows, my son, who knows . . . ! And in any case, it's not a question of guilt."

And today, poor old Perote, inspired on that occasion to saintliness by Don Manuel, and now a paralytic and invalid, has the support and consolation of his life in the son he accepted as his own when the boy was not his at all.

On Midsummer's Night, the shortest night of the year, it was, and still is, a local custom here for all the old crones, and a lot of old men, who thought they were possessed or bewitched—they were, in fact, hysterical for the most part, and in some cases epileptics—to flock to the lake. Don Manuel undertook to fulfill the same function as the lake, to serve as a pool of healing, to treat his people and even, if possible, to cure them. And such was the effect of his presence, of his gaze, and above all of his voice—his miraculous voice!—and the infinitely sweet authority of his words, that he actually did achieve some remarkable cures. Whereupon his fame increased, drawing all the sick of the environs to our lake and our priest. And yet, once, when a mother came to ask for a miracle on behalf of her son, he answered her with a sad smile:

"Ah, but I don't have my bishop's permission to perform miracles."

He was particularly interested in seeing that all the villagers kept themselves clean. If he chanced upon someone with a torn garment he would say: "Go and see the sacristan, and let him mend that tear." The sacristan was a tailor. And when, on the first day of the year, everyone went to congratulate the priest on his saint's day—his holy patron was Our Lord Jesus Himself—it was Don Manuel's wish that everyone should appear in a new shirt, and those that had none received the present of a new one from Don Manuel himself.

He treated everyone with the greatest kindness; if he favored anyone, it was the most unfortunate, and especially those who rebelled. There was a congenital idiot in the village, the fool Blasillo, and it was toward him that Don Manuel chose to show the greatest love and concern; as a consequence he succeeded in miraculously teaching him things which had appeared beyond the idiot's comprehension. The fact was that

the embers of understanding feebly glowing in the
idiot were kindled whenever, like a pitiable monkey,
he imitated his Don Manuel.

The marvel of the man was his voice; a divine voice
which brought one close to weeping. Whenever he
officiated at Solemn High Mass and intoned the Pref-
ace, a tremor ran through the congregation and all
who heard his voice were moved to the depths of their
being. The sound of his chanting, overflowing the
church, went on to float over the lake and settle at
the foot of the mountain. And when on Good Friday
he chanted, "My God, my God, why hast Thou forsaken me?" a profound shudder swept through the
multitude, like the lash of the northeast wind across
the waters of the lake. It was as if these people heard
Our Lord Jesus Christ Himself, as if the voice sprang
from the ancient crucifix, at the foot of which genera-
tions of mothers had offered up their sorrows. And
it happened that on one occasion when his mother
heard him, she was unable to contain herself, and
cried out to him right in the church, "My son!" And
the entire congregation was visibly affected, tears
pouring down every cheek. It was as if the mother's
cry had issued from the half-open lips of the Mater
Dolorosa—her heart transfixed by seven swords—
which stood in one of the side chapels. Afterwards,
the fool Blasillo went about piteously repeating, like
an echo, "My God, my God, why hast Thou forsaken me?" with such effect that everyone who heard
him was moved to tears, to the great satisfaction of
the fool, who prided himself on this triumph of imita-
tion.

The priest's effect on people was such that no one
ever dared to tell him a lie, and everyone confessed
to him without need of a confessional. So true was this

that one day, after a revolting crime had been committed in a neighboring village, the judge—a dull fellow who badly misunderstood Don Manuel—called on the priest and said:

"Let's see if *you*, Don Manuel, can get this bandit to admit the truth."

"So that *you* may punish him afterwards?" asked the saintly man. "No, Judge, no; I will not extract from any man a truth which could be the death of him. That is a matter between him and his God. . . . Human justice is none of my affair. 'Judge not that ye be not judged,' said Our Lord."

"But the fact is, Father, that I, a judge . . ."

"I understand. You, Judge, must render unto Caesar that which is Caesar's, while I shall render unto God that which is God's."

And, as Don Manuel departed, he gazed at the suspected criminal and said:

"Make sure, only, that God forgives you, for that is all that matters."

Everyone in the village went to Mass, even if it were only to hear him and see him at the altar, where he appeared to be transfigured, his countenance lit from within. He introduced one holy practice into popular worship; it consisted in assembling the whole town inside the church, men and women, old and young, about a thousand souls; there we recited the Creed, in unison, so that it sounded like a single voice: "I believe in God, the Father almighty, creator of heaven and earth . . ." and all the rest. It was not a chorus, but a single voice, all the voices blending into one forming a kind of mountain, whose peak, lost at times in the clouds, was Don Manuel. As we reached the section "I believe in the resurrection of the flesh and eternal life," Don Manuel's voice was submerged, drowned in the voice of the populace as in a lake. In truth, he was silent. And I could hear the bells of the city which is said hereabouts to be at the bottom of the lake—bells which are said also to be audible on Midsummer's Night—the bells of the city which is submerged in the spiritual lake of our people. I was hearing the voice of our dead, resurrected in us by the communion of saints. Later, when I had learned the secret of our saint, I understood that it was as if a caravan crossing the desert lost its leader as they approached the goal of their trek, whereupon his people lifted him up on their shoulders to bring his lifeless body into the promised land.

When it came to dying themselves, most of the villagers refused to die unless they were holding onto Don Manuel's hand, as if to an anchor chain.

In his sermons he never inveighed against unbelievers, Freemasons, liberals, or heretics. What for, when there were none in the village? Nor did it occur to him to speak out against the wickedness of the press. On the other hand, one of his most frequent themes was the sinfulness of gossip. As he himself forgave everything and everyone, he would not accept the existence of forked tongues.

"Envy," he liked to repeat, "is nurtured by those who prefer to think they are envied, and most persecutions are the result of a persecution complex rather than of an impulse to persecute."

"But Don Manuel, just listen to what that fellow was trying to tell me. . . ."

"We should concern ourselves less with what people are trying to tell us than with what they tell us without trying. . . ."

His life was active rather than contemplative, and he constantly fled from idleness, even from leisure. Whenever he heard it said that idleness was the mother of all vices, he added: "And also of the greatest vice of them all, which is to think idly." Once I asked him what he meant and he answered: "Thinking idly is thinking as a substitute for doing, or thinking too much about what is already done instead of about what must be done. What's done is done and over with, and one must go on to something else, for there is nothing worse than remorse without possible solution." Action! Action! Even in those early days I had already begun to realize that Don Manuel fled from being left to think in solitude, and I sensed that some obsession haunted him.

And so it was that he was always busy, sometimes even busy looking for things to do. He wrote very little on his own, so that he scarcely left us anything in writing, not even notes; on the other hand, he acted as scribe for everyone else, especially composing letters for mothers to their absent children.

He also worked with his hands, pitching in to help with some of the village tasks. At threshing time he reported to the threshing floor to flail and winnow, meanwhile teaching and entertaining the workers by turn. Sometimes he took the place of a worker who had fallen sick. One bitter winter's day he came upon a child half-dead with cold. The child's father had sent him into the woods to bring back a calf that had strayed.

"Listen," he said to the child, "you go home and get warm, and tell your father that I am bringing back the calf." On the way back with the animal he ran into the father, who had come out to meet him, thoroughly ashamed of himself.

In winter he chopped wood for the poor. When a certain magnificent walnut tree died—"that matriarchal walnut," he called it, a tree under whose shade he had played as a boy and whose nuts he had eaten for so many years—he asked for the trunk, carried it to his house and, after he had cut six planks from it, which he kept at the foot of his bed, he made firewood of the rest to warm the poor. He also was in the habit of making handballs for the boys and many toys for the younger children.

Often he used to accompany the doctor on his rounds, and stressed the importance of following the doctor's orders. Most of all he was interested in maternity cases and the care of children; it was his opinion that the old wives' sayings "from the cradle to heaven" and the other one about "little angels belong in heaven" were nothing short of blasphemy. The death of a child moved him deeply.

"A stillborn child, or one who dies soon after birth are, like suicides, the most terrible mystery to me," I once heard him say. "Like a child crucified!"

And once, when a man had taken his own life and the father of the suicide, an outsider, asked Don Manuel if his son could be buried in consecrated ground, the priest answered:

"Most certainly, for at the last moment, in the very last throes, he must surely have repented. There is no doubt of it whatsoever in my mind."

Often he would visit the local school too, to help the teacher, to teach alongside him—and not only the catechism. The simple truth was that he fled relentlessly from idleness and from solitude. He went so far in this desire of his to mingle with the villagers, especially the young people and the children, that he even attended the village dances. And more than once he played the drum to keep time for the boys and girls dancing; this kind of activity, which in another priest would have seemed like a grotesque mockery of his calling, in him somehow took on the appearance of a divine office. When the Angelus rang out, he would put down the drum and sticks, take off his hat (all the others doing the same) and pray: "The angel of the Lord declared unto Mary: Hail Mary . . ." And afterwards: "Now let us rest until tomorrow."

"The most important thing," he would say, "is for the people to be happy; everyone must be happy just to be alive. To be satisfied with life is of first importance. No one should want to die until it is God's will."

"I want to die now," a recently widowed woman once told him, "I want to follow my husband. . . ."

"But why?" he asked. "Stay here and pray God for his soul."

Once he commented at a wedding: "Ah, if I could only change all the water in our lake into wine, into a gentle little wine which, no matter how much of it one drank, would always make one joyful without making one drunk . . . or, if it made one drunk, would make one joyfully tipsy."

One day a band of poor circus people came through the village. Their leader—who arrived with a gravely ill and pregnant wife and three children to help him —played the clown. While he was in the village square making all the children, and even some of the adults, laugh with glee, his wife suddenly fell desperately ill and had to leave; she went off accompanied by a look of anguish from the clown and a

howl of laughter from the children. Don Manuel hurried after her, and a little later, in a corner of the
inn's stable, he helped her give up her soul in a state
of grace. When the performance was over and the
villagers and the clown learned of the tragedy, they
came to the inn, and there the poor, bereaved clown,
in a voice overcome with tears, said to Don Manuel, as
he took his hand and kissed it: "They are quite right,
Father, when they say you are a saint." Don Manuel
took the clown's hand in his and replied in front of
everyone:

"It is you who are the saint, good clown. I watched
you at your work and understood that you do it not
only to provide bread for your own children, but also
to give joy to the children of others. And I tell you
now that your wife, the mother of your children,
whom I sent to God while you worked to give joy, is
at rest in the Lord, and that you will join her there,
and that the angels, whom you will make laugh with
happiness in heaven, will reward you with their
laughter."

And everyone present wept, children and adults
alike, as much from sorrow as from a mysterious joy
in which all sorrow was drowned. Later, recalling
that solemn hour, I came to realize that the imperturba-
ble happiness of Don Manuel was merely the temporal, earthly form of an infinite, eternal sadness
which the priest concealed from the eyes and ears of
the world with heroic saintliness.

His constant activity, his ceaseless intervention in the
tasks and diversions of his flock, had the appearance
of a flight from himself, a flight from solitude. He
confirmed this suspicion: "I have a fear of solitude,"

he would say. And still, from time to time he would go off by himself, along the shores of the lake, to the ruins of the abbey where the souls of pious Cistercians seem still to repose, although history has long since buried them in oblivion. There, the cell of the so-called Father-Captain can still be found, and it is said that the drops of blood spattered on the walls as he flagellated himself can still be seen. What thoughts occupied our Don Manuel as he walked there? I remember a conversation we held once when I asked him, as he was speaking of the abbey, why it had never occurred to him to enter a monastery, and he answered me:

"It is not at all because my sister is a widow and I have her children and herself to support—for God looks after the poor—but rather because I simply was not born to be a hermit, an anchorite; the solitude would crush my soul; and, as far as a monastery is concerned, my monastery is Valverde de Lucerna. I was not meant to live alone, or die alone. I was meant to live for my village, and die for it too. How should I save my soul if I were not to save the soul of my village as well?"

"But there have been saints who were hermits, solitaries . . . ," I said.

"Yes, the Lord gave them the grace of solitude which He has denied me, and I must resign myself. I must not throw away my village to win my soul. God made me that way. I would not be able, alone, to carry the cross of birth. . . ."

I trust that these recollections, which keep my faith alive, will portray our Don Manuel as he was when I, a young girl of almost sixteen, returned from the con-

vent of Renada to our "monastery of Valverde de Lucerna," to kneel once more at the feet of our "abbot."

"Well, here is Simona's daughter," he said as soon
as he saw me, "quite a young woman, and knowing
French, and how to play the piano, and embroider,
and heaven knows what else besides! Now you must
get ready to give us a family. And your brother Lázaro, when is he coming back? Is he still in the New
World?"

"Yes, Father, he is still in America."

"The New World! And we in the Old. Well, then,
when you write to him, tell him from me, on behalf of
the parish priest, that I should like to know when he
is returning from the New World to the Old, to bring
us the latest from over there. And tell him that he
will find the lake and the mountain as he left them."

When I first went to him for confession, I became
so confused that I could not enunciate a word. I recited the "Forgive me, Father, for I have sinned," in
a stammer, almost sobbing. And he, observing this,
said:

"Good heavens, my dear, what are you afraid of, or
of whom are you afraid? Certainly you're not trembling under the weight of your sins, nor in fear of
God. No, you're trembling because of me, isn't that
so?"

At this point I burst into tears.

"What have they been telling you about me? What
fairy tales? Was it your mother, perhaps? Come,
come, please be calm: you must imagine you are talking to your brother. . . ."

At this I plucked up courage and began to tell him
of my anxieties, doubts, and sorrows.

"Bah! Where did you read all this, Miss Bluestock-
ing? All this is literary nonsense. Don't believe every-

thing you read just yet, not even Saint Teresa. If you want to amuse yourself, read the *Bertoldo*, as your father before you did."

I came away from my first confession to that holy man deeply consoled. The initial fear—simple fright more than respect—with which I had approached him, turned into a profound pity. I was at that time a very young woman, almost a girl still; and yet, I was beginning to be a woman, in my innermost being I felt the maternal instinct, and when I found myself in the confessional at the side of the saintly priest, I sensed a kind of unspoken confession on his part in the soft murmur of his voice. And I remembered how when he had chanted in the church the words of Jesus Christ: "My God, my God, why hast Thou forsaken me?" his own mother had cried out in the congregation: "My son!"; and I could hear the cry that had rent the silence of the temple. And I went to him again for confession—and to comfort him.

Another time in the confessional I told him of a doubt which assailed me, and he responded:

"As to that, you know what the catechism says. Don't question me about it, for I am ignorant; in Holy Mother Church there are learned doctors of theology who will know how to answer you."

"But you are the learned doctor here."

"Me? A learned doctor? Not even in my dreams! I, my little theologian, am only a poor country priest. And those questions, . . . do you know who whispers them into your ear? Well . . . the Devil does!"

Then, making bold, I asked him point-blank:

"And suppose he were to whisper these questions to you?"

"Who? To me? The Devil? No, we don't even know each other, my child, we haven't even met."

"But if he did whisper them? . . ."

"I wouldn't pay any attention. And that's enough of that; let's get on, for there are some sick people, some really sick people, waiting for me."

I went away thinking, I don't know why, that our Don Manuel, so famous for curing the bedeviled, didn't really believe in the Devil. As I started home, I ran into the fool Blasillo, who had probably been hovering around outside; as soon as he saw me, and by way of treating me to a display of his virtuosity, he began repeating—and in what a manner!—"My God, my God, why hast Thou forsaken me?" I arrived home utterly saddened and locked myself in my room to cry, until finally my mother arrived.

"With all these confessions, Angelita, you will end up going off to a nunnery."

"Don't worry, Mother," I answered her. "I have plenty to do here; the village is my convent."

"Until you marry."

"I don't intend to," I rejoined.

The next time I saw Don Manuel I asked him, looking him straight in the eye:

"Is there really a Hell, Don Manuel?"

And he, without altering his expression, answered:

"For you, my child, no."

"For others, then?"

"Does it matter to you, if you are not to go there?"

"It matters to me for the others. Is there a Hell?"

"Believe in Heaven, the Heaven we can see. Look at it there"—and he pointed to the heavens above the mountain, and then down into the lake, to the reflection.

"But we are supposed to believe in Hell as well as in Heaven," I said.

"Yes, that's true. We must believe everything that

our Holy Mother Church believes and teaches, our Holy Mother Church, Catholic, Apostolic, and Roman. And now, that's enough of that!"

I thought I read a deep sadness in his eyes, eyes as blue as the waters of the lake.

Those years went by as if in a dream. Within me, a reflected image of Don Manuel was unconsciously taking form. He was an ordinary enough man in many ways, as everyday as the daily bread we asked for in our Paternoster. I helped him whenever I could with his tasks, visiting his sick, our sick, the girls at school, and helping, too, with the church linen and the vestments; I served in the role, as he said, of his deaconess. Once I was invited to the city for a few days by an old schoolfriend, but I had to hurry back home, for the city stifled me—something was missing, I was thirsty for a sight of the waters of the lake, hungry for a sight of the peaks of the mountain; and even more, I missed my Don Manuel, as if he were calling me, as if he were endangered by my being so far away, as if he were in need of me. I began to feel a kind of maternal affection for my spiritual father; I longed to help him bear the cross of birth.

My twenty-fourth birthday was approaching when my brother Lázaro came back from America with the small fortune he had saved up. He came back to Valverde de Lucerna with the intention of taking me and my mother to live in a city, perhaps even in Madrid.

"In the country," he said, "in these villages, a person becomes dull, brutalized, and spiritually impoverished." And he added: "Civilization is the very opposite of everything countrified. The idiocy of country life! No, that's not for us; I didn't have you sent away to school so that afterwards you might go to waste here, among these ignorant peasants."

I said nothing, though I was ready to oppose any idea of moving. But our mother, already past sixty, took a firm stand from the start: "Change pastures at my age?" she demurred at once. A little later she made it quite clear that she could not live away from her lake, her mountain, and above all, her Don Manuel.

"You are both of you like those cats that get attached to houses," my brother kept saying.

When he realized the extent of the sway exercised over the entire village—especially over my mother and myself—by the saintly priest, my brother began to resent him. He saw in this situation an example of the obscurantist theocracy which, according to him, smothered Spain. And he began to spout the old anticlerical commonplaces, to which he added antireligious and "progressive" propaganda brought back from the New World.

"In this Spain of useless, easy-going men, the priests manipulate the women, and the women manipulate the men. Not to mention the idiocy of the country, and this feudal backwater!"

"Feudal," to him, meant something frightful. "Feudal" and "medieval" were the epithets he employed to condemn something out of hand.

The absolute failure of his diatribes to move us and their lack of effect upon the village—where they were listened to with respectful indifference—disconcerted him no end. "The man does not exist who could move these clods." But he soon began to understand—for he was an intelligent man, and therefore a good one—the kind of influence exercised over the village by Don Manuel, and he came to appreciate the effect of the priest's work in the village.

"This priest is not like the rest of them," he announced. "He is, in fact, a saint."

"How do you know what the rest of them are like?" I asked him, and he replied:

"I can imagine."

Even so, he did not set foot inside the church nor did he miss an opportunity to parade his lack of belief—though he always exempted Don Manuel from his scornful accusations. In the village, an unconscious expectancy began to build up, the anticipation of a kind of duel between my brother Lázaro and Don Manuel—in short, it was expected that Don Manuel would convert my brother. No one doubted but that in the end the priest would bring him into the fold. On his side, Lázaro was eager (he told me so himself, later) to go and hear Don Manuel, to see and hear him in the church, to get to know him and to talk with him, so that he might learn the secret of his spiritual sway over our souls. And he let himself be coaxed to this end, so that finally—"out of curiosity," as he said— he went to hear the preacher.

"Now, this is something else again," he told me as soon as he came back from hearing Don Manuel for the first time. "He's not like the others; still, he doesn't fool me, he's too intelligent to believe everything he has to teach."

"You mean you think he's a hypocrite?"

"A hypocrite . . . no! But he has to live by his job."

As for me, my brother was determined I should read the books he brought me, and others which he urged me to buy.

"So your brother Lázaro wants you to read," Don Manuel declared. "Well, read, my child, read and make him happy. I know you will only read worthy books. Read, even if you only read novels; they are as good as histories which claim to be 'true.' You are better off reading than concerning yourself with village gossip and old wives' tales. Above all, though, you will do well to read some devotional books which will bring you contentment in life, a quiet, gentle contentment, and peace."

And he, did he enjoy such contentment?

It was about this time that our mother fell mortally sick and died. In her last days her one wish was that Don Manuel should convert Lázaro, whom she hoped to see again in heaven, in some little corner among the stars from where they could see the lake and the mountain of Valverde de Lucerna. She felt she was going there now, to see God.

"You are not going anywhere," Don Manuel kept telling her; "you are staying right here. Your body will remain here, in this earth, and your soul also, in this house, watching and listening to your children though they will not see or hear you."

"But, Father," she said, "I am going to see God."

"God, my daughter, is all around us, and you will see Him from here, right from here. And all of us see in Him, and He in all of us."

"God bless you," I whispered to him.

"The peace in which your mother dies will be her eternal life," he told me.

And, turning to my brother Lázaro: "Her heaven is to go on seeing you, and it is at this moment that she must be saved. Tell her you will pray for her."

"But . . ."

"But what? . . . Tell her you will pray for her, to whom you owe your life. And I know that once you promise her, you *will* pray, and I know that once you pray . . ."

My brother, with tears in his eyes, went up to our dying mother and gave her his solemn promise to pray for her.

"And I, in heaven will pray for you, for all of you," my mother replied. And then, kissing the crucifix and fixing her eyes on Don Manuel, she gave up her soul to God.

"Into Thy hands I commend my spirit," prayed the priest.

My brother and I stayed on in the house alone. What had happened at the time of my mother's death had established a bond between Lázaro and Don Manuel. The latter seemed even to neglect some of his charges, his patients, and his other needy to look after my brother. In the afternoons, they would go for a walk together, beside the lake or toward the ivy-covered ruins of the old Cistercian abbey.

"He's an extraordinary man," Lázaro told me. "You know the story they tell of how there is a city at the bottom of the lake, submerged beneath the water, and that on Midsummer's Night at midnight the sound of its church bells can be heard. . . ."

"Yes, a city 'feudal and medieval' . . ."

"And I believe," he went on, "that at the bottom of Don Manuel's soul there is a city, submerged and drowned, and that sometimes the sound of its bells can be heard. . . ."

"Yes. . . . And this city submerged in Don Manuel's soul, and perhaps—why not?—in yours as well, is certainly the cemetery of the souls of our ancestors, the ancestors of our Valverde de Lucerna . . . 'feudal and medieval'!"

Eventually my brother began going to Mass. He went regularly to hear Don Manuel. When it became known that he was prepared to comply with his annual duty of receiving Communion, that he would receive Communion when the others did, an inner joy ran through the town, which felt that by this act he was restored to his people. The rejoicing was so simple and honest, that Lázaro never did feel that he had been "vanquished" or "overcome."

The day of his Communion arrived; of Communion before and with the entire village. When my brother's turn came, I saw Don Manuel—white as the January snow on the mountain, and moving like the surface of the lake when it is stirred by the northeast wind—come up to him with the holy wafer in his hand, trembling violently as he reached out to Lázaro's mouth; at that moment the priest shook so that the wafer dropped to the ground. My brother himself recovered it and placed it in his mouth. The people saw the tears on Don Manuel's cheeks, and everyone wept, saying: "How he loves him!" And then, because it was dawn, a cock crowed.

On returning home I shut myself in with my brother; alone with him I put my arms around his neck and kissed him.

"Lázaro, Lázaro, what joy you have given us all today; the entire village, the living and the dead, especially our mother. Did you see how Don Manuel wept for joy? What joy you have given us all!"

"That's why I did it," he answered me.

"Is that why? Just to give us pleasure? Surely you

did it for your own sake, because you were converted."

And then Lázaro, my brother, grew as pale and tremulous as Don Manuel when he was giving Communion, and bade me sit down, in the chair where our mother used to sit. He took a deep breath, and, in the intimate tone of a family confession, he told me:

"Angelita, it is time for me to tell you the truth, the absolute truth, and I shall tell it, because I must, because I cannot and ought not to conceal it from you, and because sooner or later, you are bound to find it out anyway, if only halfway—which would be worse."

Thereupon, serenely and tranquilly, in a subdued voice, he recounted a tale that cast me into a lake of sorrow. He told me how Don Manuel had begged him, particularly during the walks to the ruins of the old Cistercian abbey, to set a good example, to avoid scandalizing the townspeople, to take part in the religious life of the community, to feign belief even if he did not feel any, to conceal his own ideas—all this without attempting in any way to catechize him, to instruct him in religion, or to effect a true conversion.

"But is it possible?" I asked in consternation.

"Very possible and absolutely true. When I said to him: 'Is it really you, the priest, who suggests that I pretend?' he replied, hesitatingly: 'Pretend? Not at all! It would not be pretending. "Dip your fingers in holy water, and you will end by believing," as someone said.' And I, gazing into his eyes, asked him: 'And you, by celebrating the Mass, have you ended up by believing?' He looked away and stared out at the lake, until his eyes filled with tears. And it was in this way that I came to understand his secret."

"Lázaro!" I moaned.

At that moment the fool Blasillo came along our

street, crying out his: "My God, my God, why hast Thou forsaken me?" And Lázaro shuddered, as if he had heard the voice of Don Manuel, or even that of Christ.

"It was then," my brother at length continued, "that I really understood his motives and his saintliness; for a saint he is, Sister, a true saint. In trying to convert me to his holy cause—for it is a holy cause, a most holy cause—he was not attempting to score a triumph, but rather was doing it to protect the peace, the happiness, the illusions, perhaps, of his flock. I understood that if he thus deceives them—if it *is* deceit—it is not for his own advantage. I submitted to his logic —and that was my conversion. And I shall never forget the day on which I said to him: 'But, Don Manuel, the truth, the truth, above all!'; and he, all a-tremble, whispered in my ear—though we were all alone in the middle of the countryside—'The truth? The truth, Lázaro, is perhaps something so unbearable, so terrible, something so deadly, that simple people could not live with it!'

" 'And why do you allow me a glimpse of it now, here, as if we were in the confessional?' I asked. And he said: 'Because if I did not, I would be so tormented by it, so tormented that I would finally shout it in the middle of the Plaza, which I must never, never, never do. . . . I am put here to give life to the souls of my charges, to make them happy, to make them dream they are immortal—and not to destroy them. The important thing is that they live undisturbed, in concord with one another—and with the truth, with my truth, they could not live at all. Let them live. That is what the Church does, it lets them live. As for true religion, all religions are true insofar as they give spiritual life to the people who profess them, insofar as they console them for having been born only to die. And for each race the truest religion is their own, the religion that made them. . . . And mine? Mine consists in consoling myself by consoling others, even though the consolation I give them is not ever mine.' I shall never forget his words."

"But then this Communion of yours has been a sacrilege," I dared interrupt, regretting my words as soon as I said them.

"Sacrilege? What about the priest who gave it to me? And his Masses?"

"What martyrdom!" I exclaimed.

"And now," said my brother, "there is one more person to console the people."

"To deceive them, you mean?" I said.

"Not at all," he replied, "but rather to confirm them in their faith."

"And they, the people, do you think they really believe?"

"As to that, I know nothing! . . . They probably believe without trying, from force of habit, tradition. The important thing is not to stir them up. To let them live on the thin diet of their emotions rather than acquiring the torments of luxury. Blessed are the poor in spirit!"

"So that is what you have learned from Don Manuel. . . . And tell me, do you feel you have carried out your promise to our mother on her deathbed, when you promised to pray for her?"

"Do you think I could fail her? What do you take me for, Sister? Do you think I would go back on my word, my solemn promise made at the hour of death to a mother?"

"I don't know. . . . You might have wanted to deceive her so she could die in peace."

"The fact is, though, that if I had not lived up to my promise, I would be totally miserable."

"And . . ."

"I have carried out my promise and I have never neglected for a single day to pray for her."

"Only for her?"

"Well, for whom else?"

"For yourself! And now, for Don Manuel."

We parted and each went to his room, I to weep through the night, praying for the conversion of my brother and of Don Manuel. And Lázaro, to what purpose, I know not.

From that day on I was nervous about finding myself alone with Don Manuel, whom I continued to help in his pious works. And he seemed to sense my inner state and to guess at its cause. When at last I approached him in the confessional's penitential tribunal (who was the judge, and who the offender?) the two of us, he and I, bowed our heads in silence and began to weep. It was Don Manuel who finally broke the silence, with a voice that seemed to issue from a tomb:

"Angelita, you have the same faith you had when you were ten, don't you? You believe, don't you?"

"Yes, I believe, Father."

"Then go on believing. And if doubts come to torment you, suppress them utterly, even to yourself. The main thing is to live. . . ."

I summoned up my courage, and dared to ask, trembling:

"But, Father, do you believe?"

For a brief moment he hesitated, and then, taking hold of himself, he said:

"I believe!"

"In what, Father, in what? Do you believe in the life hereafter? Do you believe that when we die, we do not die altogether? Do you believe that we will see each other again, that we will love each other in the next world? Do you believe in the next life?"

The poor saint was sobbing.

"My child, leave off, leave off!"

Now, as I write this memoir, I ask myself: Why did he not deceive me? Why did he not deceive me as he deceived the others? Why did he torture himself? Why could he not deceive himself, or why could he not deceive me? And I prefer to think that he was tormented because he could not deceive himself into deceiving me.

"And now," he said, "pray for me, for your brother, and for yourself—for all of us. We must go on living. And giving life."

And, after a pause:

"Angelita, why don't you marry?"

"You know why."

"No, no; you must marry. Lázaro and I will find you a suitor. For it would be good for you to marry, and rid yourself of these obsessions."

"Obsessions, Don Manuel?"

"I know what I am saying. You should not torment yourself for the sake of others, for each of us has more than enough to do answering for himself."

"That it should be you, Don Manuel, saying this! That you should advise me to marry and answer for myself alone and not suffer over others! That it should be you!"

"Yes, you are right, Angelita. I am no longer sure of what I am saying since I began to confess to you. Only, one must go on living. Yes! One must live!"

And when I rose to leave the church, he asked me:

"Now, Angelita, in the name of the people, do you absolve me?"

I felt pierced by a mysterious and priestly prompting and said:

"In the name of the Father, the Son, and the Holy Ghost, I absolve you, Father."

We left the church, and as I went out I felt the quickening of maternal feelings within me.

My brother, now totally devoted to the work of Don Manuel, had become his closest and most zealous collaborator and companion. They were bound together, moreover, by their common secret. Lázaro accompanied the priest on his visits to the sick, and to schools, and he placed his fortune at the disposition of the saintly man. And he nearly learned to help celebrate Mass. All the while he was sounding deeper the unfathomable soul of the priest.

"What an incredible man!" he exclaimed to me once. "Yesterday, as we were walking along beside the lake he said: 'There lies my greatest temptation.' When I interrogated him with my eyes, he went on: 'My poor father, who was close to ninety when he died, was tormented all his life, as he himself confessed to me, by a temptation to commit suicide, by an instinct toward self-destruction, which had come to him from a time before memory—from birth, from his *nation*, as he said—and he was forced to fight against it always. And this struggle grew to be his life. So as not to succumb to this temptation he was forced to take precautions, to guard his life. He told me of terrible episodes. His urge was a form of mad-

ness—and I have inherited it. How that water beck-
ons me with its deep quiet! . . . an apparent serenity
reflecting the sky like a mirror—and beneath it the
hidden current! My life, Lázaro, is a kind of con-
tinual suicide, or a struggle against suicide, which is
the same thing. . . . Just so long as our people go
on living!' And then he added: 'Here the river eddies
to form a lake, so that later, flowing down the plateau,
it may form cascades, waterfalls, and torrents, hurl-
ing itself through gorges and chasms. Thus life eddies
in the village; and the temptation to commit suicide
is greater beside the still waters which at night reflect
the stars, than it is beside the crashing falls which
drive one back in fear. Listen, Lázaro, I have helped
poor villagers to die well, ignorant, illiterate villagers
who had scarcely ever been out of their village, and
I have learned from their own lips, or sensed it when
they were silent, the real cause of their sickness unto
death, and there at their deathbed I have been able
to see into the black abyss of their life-weariness. A
weariness a thousand times worse than hunger! For
our part, Lázaro, let us go on with our kind of suicide working for the people, and let them dream their
lives as the lake dreams the heavens.'

"Another time," said my brother, "as we were
coming back, we caught sight of a country girl, a
goatherd, standing tall, on the crest of the mountain
slope overlooking the lake and she was singing in a
voice fresher than the waters. Don Manuel stopped
me, and pointing to her said: 'Look, it's as though
time had stopped, as though this country girl had
always been there just as she is, singing the way she
is, and it's as though she would always be there, as
she was before my consciousness began, as she will be

when it is past. That girl is a part of nature—not of history—along with the rocks, the clouds, the trees, and the water.' He has such a subtle feeling for nature, he infuses it with feeling! I shall never forget the day when snow was falling and he asked me: 'Have you ever seen a greater mystery, Lázaro, than the snow falling, and dying, in the lake, while a headdress is laid upon the mountain?' "

Don Manuel had to moderate and temper my brother's zeal and his neophyte's rawness. As soon as he heard that Lázaro was going about inveighing against some of the popular superstitions he told him firmly:

"Leave them alone! It's difficult enough making them understand where orthodox belief leaves off and where superstition begins. And it's even harder for us. Leave them alone, then, as long as they get some comfort. . . . It's better for them to believe everything, even things that contradict one another, than to believe nothing. The idea that someone who believes too much ends up not believing anything is a Protestant notion. Let us not protest! Protestation destroys contentment and peace."

My brother told me, too, about one moonlit night when they were returning to the village along the lake, whose surface was being stirred by a mountain breeze, so that the moonbeams topped the white-crested waves, and Don Manuel turned to him and said:

"Look, the water is reciting the litany and saying: *ianua caeli, ora pro nobis*; gate of heaven, pray for us."

And two tears fell from his lashes to the grass, where the light of the full moon shone upon them like dew.

And time sped by, and my brother and I began to notice that Don Manuel's spirits were failing, that he could no longer control completely the deep-rooted sadness which consumed him; perhaps some treacherous illness was undermining his body and soul. In an effort to arouse his interest, Lázaro spoke to him of the good effect the organization of something like a Catholic agrarian syndicate in the Church would have.

"A syndicate?" Don Manuel replied sadly. "A syndicate? And what is that? The Church is the only syndicate I know of. And you have certainly heard 'My kingdom is not of this world.' Our kingdom, Lázaro, is not of this world. . . ."

"And of the other?"

Don Manuel bowed his head:

"The other is here. Two kingdoms exist in this world. Or rather, the other world. . . . Ah, I don't really know what I am saying. But as for the syndicate, that's a carry-over from your radical days. No, Lázaro, no; religion does not exist to resolve the economic or political conflicts of this world, which God handed over to men for their disputes. Let men think and act as they will, let them console themselves for having been born, let them live as happily as possible in the illusion that all this has a purpose. I don't propose to advise the poor to submit to the rich, nor to suggest to the rich that they submit to the poor; but rather to preach resignation in everyone, and charity toward everyone. For even the rich man must resign himself—to his riches, and to life; and the poor man must show charity—even to the rich. The Social Question? Ignore it, for it is none of our business. So, a new society is on the way, in which there will be neither rich nor poor, in which wealth will be justly divided, in which everything will belong to everyone—and so, what then? Won't this general well-being and comfort lead to even greater tedium and weariness of life? I know well enough that one of those leaders of what they call the Social Revolution said that religion is the opium of the people. Opium . . . Opium . . . Yes, opium it is. We should give them opium, and help them sleep, and dream. I, myself, with my mad activity am giving myself opium. And still I don't manage to sleep well, let alone dream well. . . . What a fearful nightmare! . . . I, too, can say, with the Divine Master: 'My soul is exceedingly sorrowful, even unto death.' No, Lázaro, no; no syndicates for us. If *they* organize them, well and good— they would be distracting themselves in that way. Let them play at syndicates, if that makes them happy."

The entire village began to realize that Don Manuel's spirit was weakening, that his strength was waning. His very voice—that miracle of a voice—acquired a kind of tremor. Tears came into his eyes at the slightest provocation—or without provocation. Whenever he spoke to people about the next world, about the next life, he was forced to pause at frequent intervals, and he would close his eyes. "It is a vision," people would say, "he has a vision of what lies ahead." At such moments the fool Blasillo was the first to burst into tears. He wept copiously these days, crying now more than he laughed, and even his laughter had the sound of tears.

The last Easter Week which Don Manuel was to celebrate among us, in this world, in this village of ours, arrived, and all the village sensed that the tragedy was coming to an end. And how those words struck home when for the last time Don Manuel cried out before us: "My God, my God, why hast Thou forsaken me?" And when he repeated the words of the Lord to the Good Thief—"all thieves are good," Don Manuel used to tell us—: "Today shalt thou be with me in paradise." And then, the last general Communion which our saint was to give! When he came to my brother to give him the Host—his hand steady this time—just after the liturgical ". . . *in vitam aeternam*," he bent down and whispered to him: "There is no other life but this, no life more eternal . . . let them dream it eternal . . . let it be eternal for a few years. . . ." And when he came to me, he said: "Pray, my child, pray for us all." And then, something so extraordinary happened that I carry it now in my heart as the greatest of mysteries: he leant over and said, in a voice which seemed to belong to the other world: ". . . and pray, too, for our Lord Jesus Christ."

I stood up weakly like a sleepwalker. Everything around me seemed dreamlike. And I thought: "Am I to pray, too, for the lake and the mountain?" And next: "Am I bedeviled, then?" Home at last, I took up the crucifix my mother had held in her hands when she had given up her soul to God, and, gazing at it through my tears and recalling the "My God, my God, why hast Thou forsaken me?" of our two Christs, the one of this earth and the other of this village, I prayed: "Thy will be done on earth as it is in heaven," and then, "And lead us not into temptation. Amen." After this I turned to the statue of the Mater Dolorosa—her heart transfixed by seven swords—which had been my poor mother's most sorrowful comfort, and I prayed again: "Holy Mary, Mother of God, pray for us sinners, now and at the hour of our death. Amen." I had scarcely finished the prayer, when I asked myself: "Sinners? Us, sinners? And what is our sin, what is it?'" And all day I brooded over the question.

The next day I went to see Don Manuel—now in the full sunset of his magnificent religiosity—and I said to him:

"Do you remember, my Father, years ago when I asked you a certain question you answered: 'That is a question you must not ask me; for I am ignorant; there are learned doctors of the Holy Mother Church who will know how to answer you'?"

"Do I remember? . . . Of course, I do. And I remember I told you those were questions put to you by the Devil."

"Well, then, Father, I have come again, bedeviled, to ask you another question put to me by my Guardian Devil."

"Ask it."

"Yesterday, when you gave me Communion, you asked me to pray for all of us, and even for . . ."

"That's enough! . . . Go on."

"I arrived home and began to pray; when I came to the part 'Pray for us sinners, now and at the hour of our death,' a voice inside me asked: 'Sinners? Us, sinners? And what is our sin?' What is our sin, Father?"

"Our sin?" he replied. "A great doctor of the Spanish Catholic Apostolic Church has already explained it; the great doctor of *Life Is a Dream* has written 'The greatest sin of man is to have been born.' That, my child, is our sin: to have been born."

"Can it be atoned, Father?"

"Go away and pray again. Pray once more for us sinners, now and at the hour of our death. . . . Yes, at length the dream is atoned . . . at length life is atoned . . . at length the cross of birth is expiated and atoned, and the dogma comes to an end. . . . And as Calderón said, to have done good, to have feigned good, even in dreams, is something which is not lost."

The hour of his death arrived at last. The entire village saw it come. And he made it his finest lesson. For he did not want to die alone or at rest. He died preaching to his people in the church. But first, before being carried to the church—his paralysis made it impossible for him to move—he summoned Lázaro and me to his bedside. Alone there, the three of us together, he said:

"Listen to me: watch over my poor flock; find some comfort for them in living, and let them believe what I could not. And Lázaro, when your hour comes, die as I die, as Angela will die, in the arms of the Holy Mother Church, Catholic, Apostolic, and Roman; that is to say, the Holy Mother Church of Valverde de Lucerna. And now farewell; until we never meet again, for this dream of life is coming to an end. . . ."

"Father, Father," I cried out.

"Do not grieve, Angela, only go on praying for all sinners, for all who have been born. Let them dream, let them dream. . . . Oh, how I long to sleep, to sleep, to sleep without end, to sleep for all eternity, and never dream! Forgetting this dream! . . . When they bury me, let it be in a box made from the six planks I cut from the old walnut tree—poor old tree!—in whose shade I played as a child, when I began the dream. . . . In those days, I really did believe in life everlasting. That is to say, it seems to me now that I believed. For a child, to believe is the same as to dream. And for a people too . . . You'll find those six planks I cut at the foot of the bed."

He was seized by a sudden fit of choking, and then, feeling better, he went on:

"You will recall that when we prayed together, animated by a common sentiment, a community of spirit, and we came to the final verse of the Creed, you will remember that I would fall silent. . . . When the Israelites were coming to the end of their wandering in the desert, the Lord told Aaron and Moses that because they had not believed in Him they would not set foot in the Promised Land with their people; and he bade them climb the heights of Mount Hor, where Moses ordered Aaron to be stripped of his garments, so that Aaron died there, and then Moses went up from the plains of Moab to Mount Nebo, to the top of Pisgah, looking into Jericho, and the Lord showed him all of the land promised to His people, but He said to him: 'Thou shalt not go over thither.' And there Moses died, and no one knew his grave. And he left Joshua to be chief in his place. You, Lázaro, must be my Joshua, and if you can make the sun stand still, make it stop, and never mind progress. Like Moses, I have seen the face of God—our supreme dream—face to face, and as you already know, and as the Scriptures say, he who sees God's face, he who sees the eyes of the dream, the eyes with which He looks at us, will die inexorably and forever. And therefore, do not let our people, so long as they live, look into the face of God. Once dead, it will no longer matter, for then they will see nothing. . . ."

"Father, Father, Father," I cried again.

And he said:

"Angela, you must pray always, so that all sinners may go on dreaming, until they die, of the resurrection of the flesh and life everlasting. . . ."

I was expecting "and who knows it might be . . ." but instead, Don Manuel had another choking fit.

"And now," he finally went on, "and now, at the hour of my death, it is high time to have me taken, in this very chair, to the church, so that I may take leave there of my people, who are waiting for me."

He was carried to the church and taken, in his armchair, into the chancel, to the foot of the altar. In his hand he held a crucifix. My brother and I stood close to him, but the fool Blasillo wanted to stand even closer. He wanted to grasp Don Manuel by the hand, so that he could kiss it. When some of the people nearby tried to stop him, Don Manuel rebuked them and said:

"Let him come closer. . . . Come, Blasillo, give me your hand."

The fool cried for joy. And then Don Manuel spoke:

"I shall say very few words, my children; I scarcely have strength except to die. And I have nothing new to tell you either. I have already said everything I have to say. Live together in peace and happiness, in the hope that we will all see each other again some day, in that other Valverde de Lucerna up there among the stars of the night, the stars which the lake reflects over the image of the reflected mountain. And pray, pray to the Most Blessed Virgin, and to our Lord. Be good . . . that is enough. Forgive me whatever wrong I may have done you inadvertently or unknowingly. After I give you my blessing, let us pray together, let us say the Paternoster, the Ave Maria, the Salve, and the Creed."

Then he gave his blessing to the whole village, with the crucifix held in his hand, while the women and children cried and even some of the men wept softly. Almost at once the prayers were begun. Don Manuel listened to them in silence, his hand in the hand of Blasillo the fool, who was falling asleep to the sound of the praying. First the Paternoster, with its "Thy will be done on earth as it is in heaven," then the Ave Maria, with its "Pray for us sinners, now and at the hour of our death"; followed by the Salve, with its "mourning and weeping in this vale of tears"; and finally, the Creed. On reaching "The resurrection of the flesh and life everlasting" the people sensed that their saint had yielded up his soul to God. It was not necessary to close his eyes even, for he died with them closed. When we tried to wake up Blasillo, we found that he, too, had fallen asleep in the Lord forever. So that later there were two bodies to be buried.

The whole village immediately went to the saint's house to carry away holy relics, to divide up pieces of his garments among themselves, to carry off whatever they could find as a memento of the blessed martyr. My brother kept his breviary, between the pages of which he discovered a carnation, dried as in a herbarium and mounted on a piece of paper, and upon the paper a cross and a certain date.

No one in the village seemed willing to believe that Don Manuel was dead; everyone expected to see him—perhaps some of them did—taking his daily walk along the shore of the lake, his figure mirrored in the water, or silhouetted against the background of the mountain. They continued to hear his voice, and they all visited his grave, around which a veritable cult grew up; old women "possessed by devils" came to touch the walnut cross, made with his own hands from the tree which had given the six planks of his coffin. And the ones least willing to believe in his death were my brother and I.

Lázaro carried on the tradition of the saint, and he began to compile a record of the priest's work. Some of the conversations in this account of mine were made possible by his notes.

"It was he," said my brother, "who made me into a new man. I was a true Lazarus whom he raised from the dead. He gave me faith."

"Faith? . . ." I interrupted.

"Yes, faith, faith in life itself, faith in life's consolations. It was he who cured me of my delusion of 'progress,' of my belief in its political implications. For there are, Angela, two types of dangerous and harmful men: those who, convinced of life beyond the grave, of the resurrection of the flesh, torment other people—like the inquisitors they are—so that they will despise this life as a transitory thing and work for the other life; and then, there are those who, believing only in this life . . ."

"Like you, perhaps . . ."

"Yes, and like Don Manuel. Believing only in this world, this second group looks forward to some vague future society and exerts every effort to prevent the populace from finding consolation in the belief in another world. . . ."

"And so . . ."

"The people should be allowed to live with their illusion."

The poor priest who came to replace Don Manuel found himself overwhelmed in Valverde de Lucerna by the memory of the saint, and he put himself in the hands of my brother and myself for guidance. He wanted only to follow in the footsteps of the saint. And my brother told him: "Very little theology, Father, very little theology. Religion, religion, religion." Listening to him, I smiled to myself, wondering if this were not a kind of theology, too.

And at this time I began to fear for my poor brother. From the time of Don Manuel's death it could scarcely be said that he lived. He went to the priest's tomb daily; he stood gazing into the lake for hours on end. He was filled with nostalgia for deep, abiding peace.

"Don't stare into the lake so much," I begged him.

"Don't worry. It's not this lake which draws me, nor the mountain. Only, I cannot live without his help."

"And the joy of living, Lázaro, what about the joy of living?"

"That's for others. Not for those of us who have seen God's face, those of us on whom the Dream of Life has gazed with His eyes."

"What; are you preparing to go and see Don Manuel?"

"No, Sister, no. Here at home now, between the two of us, the whole truth—bitter as it may be, bitter as the sea into which the sweet waters of our lake flow—the whole truth for you, who are so set against it. . . ."

"No, no, Lázaro. You are wrong. Your truth is not the truth."

"It's my truth."

"Yours, perhaps, but surely not . . ."

"His, too."

"No, Lázaro. Not now, it isn't. Now, he must believe otherwise; now he must believe . . ."

"Listen, Angela, once Don Manuel told me that

there are truths which, though one reveals them to oneself, must be kept from others; and I told him that telling me was the same as telling himself. And then he said, he confessed to me, that he thought that more than one of the great saints, perhaps the very greatest himself, had died without believing in the other life."

"It's not possible!"

"All too possible! And now, Sister, you must be careful that here, among the people, no one even suspects our secret. . . ."

"Suspect it!" I cried out in amazement. "Why, even if I were to try, in a fit of madness, to explain it to them, they wouldn't understand it. The people do not understand your words, they have only understood your actions. To try and explain all this to them would be like reading some pages from Saint Thomas Aquinas to eight-year-old children, in Latin!"

"All the better. In any case when I am gone, pray for me and for him and for all of us."

At length, his own hour came. A sickness which had been eating away at his robust constitution seemed to flare up with the death of Don Manuel.

"I don't so much mind dying," he said to me in his last days, "as the fact that with me another piece of Don Manuel dies, too. The remainder of him must live on with you. Until, one day, even we dead will die forever."

When he lay in the throes of death, the people, as is customary in our villages, came to bid him farewell and they commended his soul to the care of Don Manuel—Saint Manuel the Good, Martyr. My brother said nothing to them; he had nothing more to say. He had already said everything there was to say. He had become a link between the two Valverdes de Lucerna—the one at the bottom of the lake and the

one reflected on its surface. He was already one more
of us who had died of life, and, in his way, one more
of our saints.

I was disconsolate, more than disconsolate; but I was,
at least, among my own people, in my own village.
Now, having lost my Saint Manuel, the father of my
soul, and my own Lázaro, my more than flesh and
blood brother, my spiritual brother, it is now that I
realize that I have aged. But have I really lost them
then? Have I grown old? Is my death approaching?

Life must go on! And he taught me to live, he
taught us to live, to feel life, to feel the meaning of
life, to merge with the soul of the mountain, with the
soul of the lake, with the soul of the village, to lose
ourselves in them so as to remain in them forever.
He taught me by his life to lose myself in the life of
the people of my village, and I no longer felt the
passing of the hours, and the days, and the years,
any more than I felt the passage of the water in the
lake. It began to seem that my life would always be
like this. I no longer felt myself growing old. I no
longer lived in myself, but in my people, and my people lived in me. I tried to speak as they spoke, as they
spoke without trying. I went into the street—it was
the one highway—and, since I knew everyone, I lived
in them and forgot myself (while, on the other hand,
in Madrid, where I went once with my brother, I had
felt a terrible loneliness, since I knew no one, and
had been tortured by the sight of so many unknown
people).

Now, as I write this memoir, this confession of my
experience with saintliness, with a saint, I am of the
opinion that Don Manuel the Good, my Don Manuel,

and my brother, too, died, believing they did not believe, but that, without believing in their belief, they actually believed, in active, resigned desolation.

But why, I have asked myself repeatedly, did not Don Manuel attempt to convert my brother through deception, pretending to be a believer himself without being one? And I have finally come to the conclusion that Don Manuel realized he would not be able to delude him, that with him a fraud would not do, that only through the truth, with his truth, would he be able to convert him; that he knew he would accomplish nothing if he attempted to enact the comedy—the tragedy, rather—which he played out for the benefit of the people. And so, he won him over to his pious fraud; he won him over to the cause of life with the truth of death. And thus did he win me, and I never permitted anyone to see through his divine, his most saintly, game. For I believed then, and I believe now, that God—as part of I know not what sacred and inscrutable purpose—caused them to believe they were unbelievers. And that at the moment of their passing, perhaps, the blindfold was removed.

And I, do I believe?

As I write this—here in my mother's old house, and I past my fiftieth year and with my memories growing as dim and faded as my hair—outside it is snowing, snowing upon the lake, snowing upon the mountain, upon the memory of my father, the stranger, upon the memory of my mother, my brother Lázaro, my people, upon the memory of my Saint Manuel, and even on the memory of the poor fool Blasillo, my Saint Blasillo—and may he help me in heaven! The snow effaces corners and blots out shadows, for even in the night it shines and illuminates. Truly, I do not know what is true and what is false, nor what I saw and what I merely dreamt—or rather, what I dreamt and what I merely saw—nor what I really knew or what I merely believed to be true. Neither do I know whether or not I am transferring to this paper, white as the snow outside, my awareness, for it to remain in writing, leaving me without it. But why cling to it any longer?

Do I really understand any of it? Do I really believe in any of it? What I am writing about here, did it actually take place, and did it take place in just the way I am telling it? Can such things really happen? Can all this be more than a dream dreamed within another dream? Can it be that I, Angela Carballino, a woman in her fifties, am the only one in this village to be assailed by these far-fetched thoughts, thoughts unknown to everyone else? And the others, those around me, do they believe? At least they go on living. And now they believe in Saint Manuel the Good, Martyr, who, with no hope of immortality for himself, preserved that hope in them.

It appears that our most illustrious bishop, who set in motion the process of beatifying our saint from Valverde de Lucerna, is intent on writing an account of Don Manuel's life, something which would serve as a guide for the perfect parish priest, and with this end in mind he is gathering information of every sort. He has repeatedly solicited information from me; he has come to see me more than once; and I have supplied him with all sorts of facts and details. But I have never revealed the tragic secret of Don Manuel and my brother. And it is curious that he has never suspected anything. I trust that what I have set down here will never come to his knowledge. For, all temporal authorities are to be feared; I distrust all authorities on this earth—even when they are Church authorities.

And here I end this memoir. Let its fate be what it will. . . .

How, you may ask, did this document, this memoir of Angela Carballino, fall into my hands? That, dear reader, is something I must keep secret. I have transcribed it for you just as it was written, with only a few, a very few editorial emendations. Does it remind you of other things I have written? This fact does not gainsay its objectivity nor its reality. Moreover, for all I know, perhaps I created real, actual beings, independent of me, beyond my control, characters with immortal souls. For all I know, Augusto Pérez in my novel *Mist* was right when he claimed to be more real, more objective than I am, I who thought I had invented him. As for the reality of this Saint Manuel the Good, Martyr—as he is revealed to me by his disciple and spiritual daughter, Angela Carballino—it has not occurred to me to doubt his reality. I believe in it more than the saint himself did. I believe in it more than I do in my own reality.

And now, before I bring this epilogue to a close, I wish to remind you, patient reader, of the ninth verse of the Epistle of the forgotten Apostle, Saint Jude— what power in a name!—where we are told how my heavenly patron, Saint Michael Archangel (Michael means "Who such as God?" and archangel means arch-messenger) disputed with the Devil (Devil means accuser, prosecutor) over the body of Moses, and would not allow him to carry it off as a prize, to damnation. Instead, he told the Devil: "May the Lord rebuke thee." And may he who wishes to understand, understand!

I should like also, since Angela Carballino introduced her own feelings into the story—I don't know how it could have been otherwise—to comment on her statement to the effect that if Don Manuel and his disciple Lázaro had confessed their convictions to the people, they, the people, would not have understood. Nor, I should like to add, would they have believed the two of them. They would have believed in their works and not in their words. And works stand by themselves, and need no words to back them up. In a village like Valverde de Lucerna one makes one's confession by one's conduct.

And as for faith, the people scarcely know what it is, and care less.

I am well aware of the fact that no action takes place in this narrative, this *novelistic* narrative, if you will—the novel is, after all, the most intimate, the truest history, so that I scarcely understand why some people are outraged to have the Gospels called a novel, when such a designation actually sets it above some mere chronicle or other. In short, nothing happens. But I hope that this is because everything in it remains, remains forever like the lakes and the mountains and the blessed simple souls, who, beyond faith and despair, the blessed souls who, in the lakes and the mountains, outside history, took refuge in a divine novel.

Salamanca
November 1930

The Novel of
Don Sandalio, Chessplayer

Alors une faculté pitoyable se développa dans leur esprit, celle de voir la bêtise et de ne plus la tolérer.

Flaubert: *Bouvard et Pécuchet*

Prologue

NOT LONG AGO I received a letter from an unknown reader of mine and, with it, copies of some
letters this reader had received from a friend of his,
in which the friend spoke of a certain Don Sandalio, chessplayer, whose peculiarities he described at
length.

"I know," wrote my reader, "that you are always
in search of themes or plots for your novels and *nivolas*, and here you have one embodied in the enclosed
selection of correspondence. As you will see, I have
omitted the name of the place where the events occurred; as for the year, it was during the fall and
winter of 1910. I know you are not one of those writers who cares about situating events in a time and
place anyway—and perhaps you are right."

There was little more information in his covering
letter. And now I will say no more by way of Prologue, or *apéritif*.

I

31 August 1910

Here I am, Felipe, in this peaceful nook on the coast,
at the foot of mountains gazing at themselves in the
sea, here where no one knows me and where, thanks
be to God, I know no one. As you know, I'm in flight

from the society of what are called one's neighbors or fellow humans, and want the company of the waves of the sea, and of the leaves of the trees, which will soon be tumbling along, the leaves like the waves.

I've been driven here, as you know, by a new attack of misanthropy, or better, of anthrophobia, for I fear men more than I hate them. The truth is that I am prey to the same lamentable tendency as that which, according to Gustave Flaubert, marked the susceptible souls of his Bouvard and his Pécuchet, and that is the tendency to see stupidity everywhere and not be able to tolerate it. Although for me it is not so much seeing it, as hearing it. It is not a question of seeing folly, *bêtise*, as hearing follies, the follies which day after day pour out without cease or hindrance from young and old, from the foolish and the clever. For it is precisely those who pass for clever who say and commit the greatest number of follies. Though I know you will doubtless turn my own words against me, reminding me of what I have said so often to the effect that the greatest of fools is the one who dies without ever having said or committed a single folly.

And here I am acting the Robinson Crusoe, the hermit, even though it be among the human shadows which sometimes cross my path. Do you remember when we read that terrible passage from Defoe's book, of how one day as he was going toward his boat Crusoe was startled to see the print of a man's "naked foot" in the sand of the shore? He was "thunderstruck," to use the exact word used in the book, as if he had seen an apparition. He stopped to listen, he looked around him, but saw and heard nothing. He walked up and down the shore and—nothing! There was only the one and single footprint: toes, heel, all of it. And Crusoe returned to his lair, to his fortress, terrified to the last degree, looking behind himself at every two or three steps, mistaking every bush and tree, fancying every stump in the distance to be a man, and he himself filled with wild thoughts and forebodings.

I play the part of Crusoe with a will! And so I flee, not from the sight of prints of men's naked feet, but from their words, words out of souls clothed in folly, and I isolate myself against contact with their follies. And I repair to the shore to hear the waves breaking, or to the woods to hear the sound of the wind in the trees. I've no need of man, none! Nor of woman either, of course! At most, I'll abide some child who has not yet learned how to talk, who cannot yet recite the cute nonsense his parents have taught him to repeat like a parrot.

II

5 September

Yesterday I spent walking in the woods, in silent converse with the trees. But it's useless for me to flee from men: I find them on all sides: my trees are human trees. And not only because they've all been planted and cultivated by men, but for another reason—all these trees are domesticated and domestic!

I've found a friend in an old oak. You should see it, Felipe, you should see it! What a hero! It must be very old. And it's already dead in part. Mind, now, dead in part, not all dead. It bears a great wound which leaves its innards exposed. But the innards are hollow, a void. It shows its heart. But we know, no matter how poor our notions of botany, that its real heart is not there, and that the sap circulates between the alburnum and the bark. And still that wide wound with its flared borders is deeply impressive. The wind enters the opening and aerates the inside, which is large enough to give a wanderer refuge from a sudden storm, or to house a hermit or anchorite, some Diogenes of the forest! But the sap continues to run between the wood and the bark and carries the juice of life to the leaves, which turn green in the sun. They turn green, that is, until they turn yellow and sere and whirl along the ground at the foot of the woodland hero where, withering into rot they stick to the roots of the old oak and begin to form the leaf mold to feed the new leaves of the following spring. You should see the strong arms of the oak's roots whose fingers are sunk deep into the earth! The arms of its roots grasp the earth like the arms of its branches grasp at the sky.

You might think that when autumn comes the old oak will be left silent and bare. Not at all! For it is itself held in the grip of an equally heroic ivy. Treading among the knots of the exposed roots you can see the oaken, oak-like, veins of the ivy, which climbs the old oak and covers it in the bright shiny green of its perennial leaves. Even after the oak leaves fall, they doubtless make winter music when caught up in the ivy by the blast of the wind. And even when the oak itself dies, it will still shine green in the sun, and perhaps then a swarm of bees will settle in the wide wound and set up a hive.

I don't know why or how, but this old oak is beginning to reconcile me to humanity. And besides— why shouldn't I confess it? It's been so long since I've heard a piece of foolishness! In the long run, obviously, one can't live like this. I'm afraid I'm about to succumb.

III

10 September

Didn't I say so, Felipe? I've succumbed. I've become a member of the local Casino, I've joined the club! Though it's only to look rather than to listen. It happened when the first rains came. Neither the coast nor the woods offered any refuge then. And, as far as the hotel goes, what could I do there? Spend the days reading, or rather rereading? It wouldn't do. And so, in the end, I took refuge in the local clubhouse.

In the reading room I spend more time observing those who read than in reading myself. I certainly can't stand the newspapers for very long. They're somehow even stupider than the men who write for them. The latter sometimes have a certain talent for saying stupidities. But . . . to write them down? None show talent for that. Although, why write them down? And as for the readers, one must see it to believe it: the caricatures their faces become when they giggle at the cartoons!

After a spell in the reading room, I wander into the main salon where these men gather. But I studiously avoid all the regular groups and gatherings, all the *peñas* and *tertulias* so characteristic of our country. The splinters of conversation which reach me strike the rawest part of the wound I brought with me when I came here, retreating to this mountainous coastal region as to a sanitorium. No, I cannot endure, I cannot tolerate human stupidity. And I've decided to devote myself, with the utmost discretion, to the office of transient spectator, of mere bystander, at all these card games. In truth, these people have found a form of society almost without words, a word-less society. And I recall that supreme piece of fool-ishness uttered by that pseudo-pessimist Schopen-hauer to the effect that fools, since they have no ideas to exchange, invented little slips of painted cardboard to exchange instead, and called them playing cards. Well if fools invented playing cards, they were not such fools as Schopenhauer, who didn't even invent that, but only a system of mental card-shuffling called pessimism in which the worst of it, the *pessimus* of the pessimism, is the grief, as if there were not al-ready the boredom, the tedium, which is what the cardplayers kill when they kill time.

IV

14 September

I'm beginning to know the members of the club, my fellow members—for I have joined up, become a member, though transient. Of course, it's only a mat-ter of knowing them by sight. And I amuse myself in speculating on what they might be thinking—as long as they say nothing, that is, for as soon as they open their mouths I can no longer imagine what might really be taking place in their minds. And thus it is that I have certain preferences among the games when it comes time to play my role of spectator. In the game of *mus*, for example, all the verbal fireworks amuse me for a time, but I quickly tire of the yells of *envido*! and *quiero*! or *cinco más*! or *diez más*! or *órdago*! The last cry amuses me the most; the word *órdago* itself is apparently a Basque word meaning "There you are!" and when it is hurled at one player by another it sounds as if one fighting cock were challenging the other.

I am more attracted, in the end, by the chess games. Even in my youth, as you know, I fell into this solitary vice of two men together in company. If one can call that company. Although here in this Casino not all the chess games are silent, nor even are they the solitude of two men together in company. Instead, what usually happens is that a circle of spectators forms and they argue out the moves with the players and they even go so far as to move the pieces. There is the continuing game, for instance, played between a forestry engineer and a retired judge, and it is absolutely hilarious. Yesterday, the judge, who must have a weak bladder, was squirming about and, when someone suggested he go relieve himself, he vowed he would not go alone, but insisted the engineer go with him, for he was afraid that otherwise his opponent would shift the pieces. So they went together, the judge to urinate and the engineer as escort, and while they were gone the spectators slyly altered the composition of the game.

But there is one poor devil who has so far drawn my attention more than anyone else. The few who venture to address him at all—for he does not speak to anyone himself—call him Don Sandalio, and his sole activity seems to be that of chessplayer. I have not been able to ascertain a single detail of his life— though in all truth I am not much interested in finding out any of the details. I'd rather imagine them for myself. He goes to the Casino only to play chess, and he plays with scarcely a word and with the avid concentration of a sick man. Outside the world of chess there seems no world at all for him. The other members respect his silence, or perhaps merely ignore him, although I think I detect a certain measure of pity in their attitude. Or perhaps they think him a maniac, a monomaniac. Still, he always seems to find someone for a game, even if it be only from motives of compassion.

One thing he doesn't have is a circle of spectators. Everyone is aware that such a group only serves to annoy him and they keep their distance. Even I haven't ventured to go near his table, though he certainly does interest me. He seems so alone, so isolated in the midst of all the others! He's so withdrawn into himself! Or rather, withdrawn into the game, which seems like a sacred rite for him, a religious function. And I wonder to myself: what does he do when he's not playing chess? How does he make a living? What's his profession? Does he have a family? Does he love anyone? Has he known sorrow and disillusion? Is he the victim of some tragedy?

I've even ventured to follow him when he left the Casino for home. And I've watched to see whether, as he walked across the center of the town's Plaza, he would jump from square to square like a chesspiece. But shame forced me to cut short my pursuit.

V

I've been trying to shake the spell the Casino exerts over me. But it's impossible. The image of Don Sandalio follows me everywhere. He fascinates me like my favorite tree in the forest. And he's another tree, one more, a human tree, silent, vegetative. And he plays chess the way trees produce leaves.

It's two days now since I've gone to the Casino. I've made a great effort to stay away. I went as far as the door—only to tear myself away.

Yesterday I walked up into the woods. But I found I could not go along the highway, the man-made highroad that most men use, the one built for them by serfs, by hired workmen. The forest ways were made by free men with their feet. ("Free?") In any case I was forced to abandon the highway and climb through the woods. I was repelled by all those signs which ruin the freshness of everything. Why, they've even put signs on the trees by the side of the road! I imagine the very birds must avoid those trees, flee them more than they do the scarecrows which the farmers set up in the fields. Though it's interesting to think that the best way to make birds stay away from a place is to dress up some stick in the guise of a human, which suffices to drive away the graceful creatures which reap where they have not sown, the free creatures kept by our Father and theirs.

I plunged into the woods and came eventually upon the ruins of an old country house. All that was left were the walls, covered with ivy, like my old oak. Inside what had been the house proper was the half-ruined wall of the hearth, the family fireplace, in which there were still remains of a fire surrounded by the soot of the years. The green of the ivy shone over the black of the soot. Some birds fluttered among the leaves: doubtless they had built their nest close by the corpse of what had been the house.

I don't know why, but it all made me think of Don Sandalio, who is such an urban product, such a Casino-like figure. And I thought that no matter how much I tried to avoid men and their folly and their ridiculous civilization I am and remain a man myself, much more so than I thought, and that I cannot live far from my species. Why it's their very folly which attracts me most! It's the spur I need to goad me on!

It's obvious that I need Don Sandalio, that I can no longer live without him.

VI

20 September

Yesterday I finally couldn't stand it any longer! Don Sandalio arrived at the Casino at his usual hour, which is exactly the same time, chronometrically, every day, very early in the morning. He drank his coffee down and hurried over to his chess table, ordered the pieces to be brought to him, set them up, and awaited his opponent. And the opponent did not put in his appearance. Don Sandalio stared into the void with an anguished face. I felt sorry for him. So much so that I could not contain myself and went up to ask:

"Apparently your opponent is not coming today," I ventured.

"Apparently not," he answered.

"Well, if you like, until he comes, I could substitute for him. I am not a great player but, although I have not seen you play, I don't think you would find my game boring. . . ."

"Thank you," he said.

I thought that he meant to turn down my offer, in expectation that the other player would actually show up. But instead he accepted. He did not, of course, even ask who I might be. It was as if I did not exist in reality, exist as someone apart from himself, exist except for him. He, nevertheless, certainly existed for me. . . . That is, I think he did. He scarcely deigned to look at me, but stared instead at the board. In his eyes, obviously, the pawns and bishops and knights and castles and kings and queens have more soul than the people who manipulate them. And perhaps he's right.

He plays quite well, with assurance, not too slow, never arguing or changing his moves, and the only word he utters is "Check!" As I wrote the other day, he plays as if he were taking part in a religious service. Or better, like one composing some unheard religious music. Yes, his play is musical. He picks at the pieces as if he were picking a harp. One can almost hear his knight's horse musically breathing— not neighing, no!—as he moves in to checkmate. A winged horse, a Pegasus. Or more like a Clavileño, since both of them are wood. This horse doesn't jump on the table, it lands flying! And when Don Sandalio picks at the queen, it's pure music!

He won the game. And not because he plays better than I do, but because he didn't do anything else but play, while I lost myself in observing him. I don't know why, but I don't think he is by nature a highly intelligent man—although he puts all the intelligence he has, or rather, all his soul, into his play.

When, after several games, I finally called for a halt—for he never gets tired of playing and would have gone on—I asked him:

"What could have become of your playing-partner?"

"I don't know," he answered.

And he didn't seem much interested in knowing.

I left the Casino to take a stroll toward the beach, but then, once outside, I waited to see if Don Sandalio would follow me out. "Does he go for walks, that man?" I wondered. Presently, he did come out, proceeding absentmindedly. It would be hard to say where he looked when he walked. I followed him until he turned a corner and suddenly disappeared into a house, doubtless his own. I went on toward the beach again, no longer as alone as before, for now Don Sandalio, my Don Sandalio, kept me company. Before reaching the shore, I turned up toward the woods, and set out to pay a visit to my old oak, the oak dressed in ivy. I did not, of course, make any connection in my mind between the tree and Don Sandalio, not even between *my* oak and *my* chessplayer. The latter has now become, in any case, part of my life. Like Crusoe, I've found the print of a man's naked foot, the naked footprint of a soul, in the sand of the beach of my solitude. Still, I was not "thunderstruck." On the contrary, the footprint draws me on. Can it be the footprint of human stupidity? Of human tragedy? But

then, is not stupidity the greatest of all human trage-
dies?

VII

25 September

I continue fascinated, my dear Felipe, with the tragedy
of stupidity, or rather of simplicity. A couple of days
ago I overheard, without meaning to, a conversation
in the hotel, and I was indeed thunderstruck this time.
Two people were talking about a woman who was on
her deathbed and of how the confessor had told her:
"Well, now, when you get to Heaven, don't forget to
tell my mother, as soon as you see her, that we're living a Christian life here below in order to be able to
see her soon." Apparently the confessor, a most pious
priest, actually spoke in all earnest. One must assume
that this priest believed what he was saying, and it all
made me meditate on the tragedy of simplicity, or
rather, on the felicity of simplicity. For there really are
joys which are tragic. And that made me wonder if
my Don Sandalio is not perhaps a happy man!

Now, to return to Don Sandalio himself, I must
tell you that I continue to serve as his chess partner.
His former partner, it appears, has left town, something I found out, not precisely from Don Sandalio
himself, who never mentions his chess partners or any
other fellow mortal and who showed no interest in
whether his former partner had moved away or not,
or even in who he might have been, just as he has
never shown any interest in knowing who I might

be; in fact, I would consider it something of a miracle if he knew so much as my name.

Since I am a newcomer to the chess section, a few spectators have appeared to see what kind of a player I am; they are also probably curious to see if I am another Don Sandalio, someone whom they will have to classify and even perhaps define. I let them do what they wanted, for a time, but they soon began to realize that their presence only annoyed me, no less than it annoyed Don Sandalio and perhaps even more so.

Yesterday there were two men watching us play, and what a pair they were! They didn't confine themselves to looking or commenting on our moves, but launched into a political discussion! I couldn't contain myself and heard my own voice cry out: "Will you please keep quiet!" And they went away. What a look I got from Don Sandalio! A look of profound gratitude. It occurred to me that our man is as deeply wounded by human stupidity as I am myself.

We finished the game, and I went off to watch the waves die on the sands of the shore, without attempting to follow after Don Sandalio this time; doubtless he went straight home. I wondered if my chessplayer could believe that once this life was finished, we would go on to play chess in heaven for ever and ever, against men or against angels. . . .

VIII

30 September

I've noticed that Don Sandalio is worried about something. It must be his health, for it's plain that he has some trouble breathing. Sometimes he seems to be suppressing a moan or a complaint. But who'd dare ask him anything about it? Still, one day he seemed to have a dizzy spell and to be on the point of passing out, and I did say:

"If you like, we can postpone the game. . . ."

"No, no," he replied, "not on my account."

I thought that he was being heroic: "A heroic player!" I said to myself. But then I added aloud:

"Why don't you stay home for a few days?"

"Stay home? That would be worse!"

And I suppose it *would* be worse for him to stay home. Home? And what is home to him? Who lives there? What is it?

I hastened, in any case, to take my leave, giving a hurried excuse, and went off with a muttered "I hope you'll soon feel better, Don Sandalio!" He said simply, "Thank you!" And he did not add my name because surely he does not know it.

This Don Sandalio, not the one who plays chess with me in the Casino, but the other, the one *he* has imposed on my innermost soul, my Don Sandalio, follows me everywhere now, and I even dream of him, and almost suffer with him.

IX

8 October

Don Sandalio hasn't been back to the Casino since the day he felt ill and went home. I find this fact so extraordinary that I am greatly disturbed. When three days had passed since our man had gone, I caught myself beginning to set up the pieces on the board and waiting for him, or someone, to appear. . . . I was on the verge of trembling, for it occurred to me that I had thought so long on my Don Sandalio that we had changed places and that . . . in short, that I was suffering from a double personality. Really, one personality is enough!

But the day before yesterday one of the members of the Casino, seeing me so alone and, in his eyes probably bored, came over to tell me:

"You know what happened to Don Sandalio. . . ."

"No, I don't. What happened to him?"

"Well . . . he lost his son."

"Ah! He had a son . . . ?"

"Didn't you know? The one mixed up in the affair of the . . ."

I was overcome . . . with what? I don't know, but when I heard this I turned away, leaving the man with the words in his mouth, not caring what he thought of me. No, I didn't want to hear any stories about Don Sandalio's son. What for? I must keep the image I have formed of Don Sandalio, my Don Sandalio, pure and uncontaminated. And it's already spoiled by having a son suddenly appear, a son who, by dying, prevents me from playing chess with Don Sandalio for a certain number of days. No, I don't want to hear any stories. Stories? When I need any, I'll invent them.

As you know, Felipe, the only stories, the only histories, as far as I am concerned, are to be found in novels. And as regards the novel of Don Sandalio, my chessplayer, I don't need club members to make one up for me.

I left the Casino badly missing our man, and set off for the woods. I went to see my oak. The sun was striking the wide wound at its hollowed innards. Whenever an oak leaf fell from its height, it was caught up, for a while, between the leaves of the ivy.

X

10 October

Don Sandalio has come back, back to the Casino, back to our chess game. And he's come back intact, the same, the one I knew, mine, just as if nothing had happened.

"My sincerest condolences, Don Sandalio," I lied.

"Thank you, thank you very much," he replied.

And he made his first move on the chessboard. Just as if nothing had occurred at home, in his other life. Although, does he have any other?

It has occurred to me that, strictly speaking, he does not really exist for me nor I for him. And yet. . . .

When our round of games was finished I walked to the seashore. I was taken up with an idea which I'm sure you would find—for I know you well enough—absurd. I could not stop wondering what I might represent, what I might be like in the mind of Don

199

Sandalio. What must he think of me? How does he view me, how does he see me? What am I like to him? Who am I to him?

XI

12 October

I don't know what idiot devil tempted me today to suggest the solving of a chess problem to Don Sandalio.

"A problem?" he inquired. "I'm not interested in problems. The ones the game itself presents are enough for me. I don't mean to go looking for others."

Now that was the longest string of words I've ever heard from Don Sandalio. And what words! No other member of the Casino could have understood them as well as I did. And yet I later repaired to the seashore once again to look for whatever problems the waves of the sea might suggest to me.

XII

14 October

I'm incorrigible, Felipe, incorrigible. As if the lesson Don Sandalio gave me the day before yesterday were not quite enough, today I tried out on him a dissertation on the nature of the bishop, a chesspiece I do not handle well at all.

I told him that our Spanish *alfil*—which the French call *fou*, crazy—the bishop, in English, struck me as being a sort of crazy bishop, with something elephantine in its advance, for it proceeds obliquely, sideways, and never straight ahead, and from white to white or from black to black, never changing the color of its ground whatever its own color. And I went on and on about such things as a white bishop on a white ground and a white on black ground and a black bishop on black ground and a black on white ground! And in short I created a mountain of shavings from so much wood-turning! Don Sandalio looked at me as he might a mad bishop, rather taken aback, and then he looked as if he might bolt, as from a wild elephant. I told him as much, that later part, too, as we exchanged sets, black for white and white for black, the whites beginning the play as always. Don Sandalio's look made me shut up.

When finally I quit the Casino, I hurried along wondering if Don Sandalio's look did not prove that I had, indeed, taken leave of my senses. Had I gone mad? Was I crazy? I thought it probable. In my headlong flight from human stupidity I had doubtless fallen into madness. In my terror of stumbling upon the naked footprint of a fellow human's soul, was I not moving sidewise like a mad bishop? Black or white?

Don Sandalio is driving me mad, Felipe.

XIII

23 October

I haven't written to you for a week, my dear Felipe, because I've been sick. Perhaps I've been ill more from worry than from sickness. Besides, I've been enjoying the pleasures of bed, the kindly feel of the sheets! And from my bedroom window, from my bed itself, I can see the nearby mountain with its little waterfall. I keep a pair of binoculars on my night-table, and I study the falls through them for endless periods. And then there's the light and color changes on the mountainside!

I've called in the doctor with the best reputation in town, Dr. Casanueva. He appeared on the scene thoroughly equipped to dispute with me any notion I might have as to the cause of my indisposition. And he's only succeeded in increasing my concern for myself. He's made up his mind that I go about in-viting any number of ills, and all because I spend so much time in the woods. He began by recommending that I give up smoking, and, when I told him I never smoke, he no longer knew what to say. He simply didn't have the determination of that other medic who, in a similar situation, told the patient: "In that case, begin smoking!" And perhaps that doctor was right, because the main thing is to change one's regimen.

I've stayed in bed these many days, then, not be-cause I really needed to, but because it has afforded me the opportunity to study my relative solitude. In all truth I've spent most of the time, most of the week, between sleep and waking, uncertain as to whether I was dreaming the mountain in front of me or seeing the missing Don Sandalio before me.

You can well imagine that Don Sandalio, my Don Sandalio, has been the principal vision during my sickness. I've been taken with the notion, or illusion, that in these past days he's somehow taken on further qualities, has thus changed, and that when I see him again in the Casino and we play chess again, I'll find him to be another.

In the meantime, does he ever think of me? Does he

miss me at the Casino? Has he found another co-member (what a word!) to join him in a game of chess? Has he asked after me? Do I exist for him?

I've even lived through a terrible nightmare in which Don Sandalio appeared in the form of a terrifying black knight—a chessboard knight on his chessboard horse, of course!—who charged at me with the intention of devouring me, and I was a wretched white bishop, mad and elephantine, defending the white king against being checkmated. When I awoke from this nightmare it was dawn and a great weight pressed upon my chest, and I found myself breathing in and out like a gymnast, trying to put to rights that heart of mine which Dr. Casanueva thinks is somewhat damaged. Finally I was able to contemplate, through my binoculars, how the rays of the rising sun struck the water as it fell in a cascade down the mountainside in front of me.

XIV

25 October

Just a few lines on this postcard. I went to the beach, which was deserted. Even more deserted by virtue of the presence of a young girl walking beside the waves, which washed up and wet her feet from time to time. I could see her without being seen. I watched her take out a letter and read it. Then she lowered her arms, still holding the letter with both hands. After a while she raised them again, reread the letter, and then she tore it into the tiniest of pieces, folding and refolding the paper to do so. Finally she tossed the pieces, one by one, into the air, which carried them away toward the breakwater. They went like the butterflies of oblivion. Once they were all gone, she cried into her handkerchief and at last dried her eyes. The sea wind finished the job. And that's all.

XV

26 October

What I have to tell you today, my dear Felipe, is so startling as to be beyond the imagining of the most ingenious novelist. Which only goes to prove the good judgment of that friend of ours we called Pepe *El Gallego*, who, when he was translating a book of so-called sociology, said something to the effect that "I can't stand these sociological books. I'm translating one now on primitive marriage, and the author is all worked up as to whether the Algonquins get married in such and such a way, and the Kafirs in some other way, and another tribe or race in another way altogether. . . . Formerly books were filled with words; now they're filled with what they call facts or with documentation; ideas are nowhere to be found. . . . Now for my part, if I were to conceive a sociological theory, I'd base it on facts of my own invention, positive as I am that anything any man can invent has happened, is happening, or will happen." How right our good Pepe was!

But let's get to the facts, or, if you will, the events.

Just as soon as I felt a bit stronger, I shook off the comforts of the bed and—naturally!—made my way to the Casino. I was led thither, as you can imagine, by my urgent need to find Don Sandalio and resume our chess games. I arrived, but our man was nowhere about. And it was his regular hour to be there. I did not wish to ask after him.

I found myself unable to be patient and soon was asking for a board. I opened a newspaper in which a chess problem was set, and began to work it out. Presently one of the habitual spectators came over and asked me if I wanted to have a game. For a moment I was tempted to turn him down, for it seemed like a piece of treachery against Don Sandalio, but in the end I accepted.

This fellow member, formerly a spectator and now a partner, turned out to be one of those players who have no idea of how to be quiet. He announced all the moves, repeated the obvious, and even hummed snatches of popular songs. It was all too much. What a difference between this kind of game and the solemn, absorbed, silent play of Don Sandalio!

(*It occurs to me at this point that if the author of these letters were to write them now, in 1930, he would compare his play against Don Sandalio with pure graphic representational cinema, and his play against the newcomer with sound films. Thus, the latter game could be called play with sound track, or with accompanying hum.*)

For me it was like walking on live coals. I didn't dare order the fellow member to be quiet. Probably he sensed my state, for after two games he announced that he must leave. But, before going off, he came out with the following:

"I suppose you know about Don Sandalio. . . ."

"No. What is it?"

"He's in jail."

"In jail!" I exclaimed, thunderstruck.

"Of course, in jail! Naturally you understand . . . ,"
he began.

I cut him short:

"No, I understand nothing!"

I stood up and, scarcely taking leave, I hurried
from the Casino.

"In jail," I muttered over and over, "in jail! Why?"
Still, and after all was said and done, what business
was it of mine? Just as I had no wish to find out about
his son's death, I do not want to find out why he was
put in jail. I'm not interested in such matters. And
if he's anything like I think he is, anything like I've
figured him, like I've imagined him in my own mind,
he's not much more interested in such matters than
I am. Nevertheless, in spite of everything, this unex-
pected development totally changed the meaning of
my daily life. With whom am I to play chess, while
I hide from incurable human stupidity?

Now I'm beginning to think, intermittently, that I
should find out if he is or is not being held *incomu-
nicado*, and if he isn't, and if I'm allowed to see him,
I might go visit him and request permission to play a
daily game—without ever asking, naturally, anything
about the matter, nor even inquiring as to why he's
being held. Although, how do I know that he's not
already engaged in playing a daily game with one of
the guards?

As you can well imagine, all this has thoroughly
upset my plans for solitude.

XVI

28 October

Avoiding the Casino, avoiding the town, avoiding a human society which invents jails, I've taken to the woods, as far as possible from the highway. I shun the highway because of those trees used for signs, which are like prisoners, too, or like foundlings, which is almost the same, and then all those billboards. They all have something to proclaim, all kinds of products, some of them agricultural machinery, most of them liquor, others tires for automobiles that rush about everywhere. It all adds up to a dismal vision of humanity, which cannot live without fetters, manacles, shackles, chains, iron fences, and prisons.

I've been wandering in the woods, avoiding not only the highways, but even the paths beaten down by the feet of men, avoiding even the footprints of men, walking instead over the fallen leaves—they've begun to fall in plenty—and I've gone again to the ruins of the old homestead which I told you about, where the sooty remains of the hearth and chimney are covered with branches of ivy in which the birds of the fields build their nests. It may be that when the house was alive and the firewood burned on the hearth and the family kettle was at a boil, there was then a cage hanging nearby in which a linnet sang from time to time— from out of his prison!

I've sat among the ruins of the house, on a hewn stone, and meditated on whether Don Sandalio ever had a hearth, whether the house where he lived with the son who died was a home, whether he lived there with others, perhaps even a wife. Did he have one? Is he a widower? Is he married? But, after all is said and done, what does it all matter to me? Why do I set myself these problems, which are as abstract as chess problems and which are not those offered me by the play of my own life?

Ah, not offered me, I say, when the truth is . . . As you know, Felipe, I'm the one who's had no home these many years; my home and hearth were undone, and even the soot of the chimney has disappeared into the air. You know it is because I lost my home that human stupidity strikes me with such bitterness. Robinson Crusoe was a recluse; and Gustave Flaubert, who could not tolerate human stupidity, was another; and Don Sandalio, it seems to me, is also a recluse. And I am a recluse. And every recluse, every solitary man, my dear Felipe, is a jailed man, a prisoner, whether or not he walks abroad freely.

What can Don Sandalio be doing in his prison cell, now that he is more of a solitary than ever? Has he resigned himself and called for a chessboard and a book of problems to solve? Or has he himself perhaps begun to set problems? One thing I'm almost sure about, unless I'm greatly mistaken about our man's character—and I simply cannot conceive of being mistaken as regards my Don Sandalio—I'm sure that he doesn't give a fig about the problem or problems raised by the judge in the course of his investigations.

And what shall I do while Don Sandalio remains in jail here in this town, to which I've come in flight from my incurable anthropophobia? What shall I do in this corner of mountainous coast if they take my Don Sandalio away from me, for he had come to be my only tie with a humanity which attracts me at the same time as it repels me? And if Don Sandalio comes out of jail and returns to the Casino and in the Casino to chess—what else would he do?—how am I to play with him or even look him in the face knowing that he has been jailed for reasons altogether unknown to me? No, no! They've killed Don Sandalio, my Don Sandalio, by putting him in jail. And I have a feeling that he will never come out. Is he to emerge from prison so as to be a problem for the rest of his life? A problem on the loose? Impossible!

You can't imagine, Felipe, my state of mind when I last left the ruins of the old country house. I went off wondering whether it wouldn't be best to have a cell built for me within the ruins, a dungeon of my own making where I could lock myself in. Perhaps it would be better to be transported in a wooden cage, like Don Quixote, going abroad on a ox-drawn cart, seeing the open fields go by and watching sane men working them in the illusion that they are free—or free men who think they are sane, which comes to the same thing. Oh, Don Quixote! Another solitary like Robinson Crusoe and like Bouvard and like Pécuchet, a solitary whom a grave ecclesiastic, swollen with all the stupidity of sane men, called Don Tonto, Don Fool, calling him deputy-simpleton, and flinging in his face all manner of idiocies and vapidities!

And as regards Don Quixote, I should tell you, to bring this epistolary unburdening to a close, that it's my opinion that he did not die so soon after retiring back to his house when he was bested at Barcelona by Sansón Carrasco, but that he lived on a while longer in order to purge his generous, his holy, madness, among the hordes of people who came seeking his help to succor their sorrows and right their wrongs, but who, when they were not attended, insulted him and called him a treacherous impostor. And when he emerged from his house they murmured, "He's backed down, gone back on his boasts!" An even worse torment to fall upon him would be a swarm of reporters enveloping him and subjecting him to questionnaires and interrogations—what they nowadays call surveys. I can hear one of them asking: "And to what, Sir, do you owe your celebrity?"

Enough, enough, enough! Human stupidity is fathomless!

XVII

30 October

As regards disasters, it never rains but it pours, but all unforeseen wonders come upon one, as country people say, in litters and broods. I'll wager you couldn't guess what the latest is? Well, the judge has summoned me—to testify. "Testify to what?" you will ask. I asked the same thing: what?

He summoned me, had me swear on my honor to tell the truth and the whole truth, and then at once inquired if I knew Don Sandalio Cuadrado y Redondo, and if so, how long. I explained the extent of my "knowing" him: I knew only the chessplayer and had no knowledge or information at all on his life. Nevertheless, the judge thereupon attempted to wheedle out of me the unwheedlable and insisted on knowing whether I hadn't heard him make some mention of how he got along with his son-in-law. I was forced to confess that I had never heard that he had ever had a married daughter, just as I was ignorant until then of the fact that he had such mutually contradictory surnames as Cuadrado and Redondo.

"Well now, according to his son-in-law, who is

the person who suggested you be called to testify, Don Sandalio himself sometimes spoke of you at home," the judge informed.

"He spoke of me!" I was utterly surprised, thunderstruck. "Why, I don't even think he knows my name! I don't think I exist in his eyes!"

"You are wrong, Sir. According to his son-in-law . . ."

"I assure you, Your Honor, that I know no more of Don Sandalio than what I've told you and that I do not want to know more."

The judge seemed satisfied and he let me go without further probing.

But I'm confused by what's happening to my Don Sandalio. Shall I go back to the Casino? Shall I again expose myself to the snatches of talk coming from these faithful representatives of average humanity, of humanity at its average? I'm really in a quandary, Felipe, and don't know what to do.

XVIII

4 November

And now comes the most extraordinary, the most incredible part of all. Don Sandalio is dead! Dead in jail! I'm no longer sure how I first heard the news. Perhaps I heard it at the Casino, for surely they spoke of his death. I fled from their talk, fled to the hills, to the woods. I know I walked like a somnambulist. I wasn't sure what was happening to me. I arrived at the oak tree, my old oak tree, and, since it was beginning to drizzle, I took refuge inside its open innards, in its wound, like Diogenes might have crouched in his barrel, and I nodded off while the wind whirled the dry leaves around me in my tree trunk.

And then . . . I found myself crying. I was overcome by a black anguish and cried, Felipe, for the death of my Don Sandalio. Why? I felt a great void within me. For the man who was not interested in problems systematically formulated, in problems of the kind expostulated in newspapers, not interested in charades and puzzles and riddles, that man who had lost a son, who had a married daughter and a son-in-law, that man who had been sent to jail and who had died there, that man . . . had died on me. I would no longer hear him keep quiet while he played, I would no longer hear his silence, a silence heightened by the unique word "Check!" uttered liturgically. Sometimes, however, he did not even utter that single word, for if the checkmate was obvious, why say so in words?

And that man had sometimes spoken of me in his own house, according to his son-in-law. But that's impossible! The son-in-law must be an impostor. How could he speak of me, when he didn't even know me? He had scarcely heard me utter a dozen words! Unless . . . unless he invented me, just as I was inventing him! Could he have been doing with me what I was doing with him?

It was the son-in-law, no doubt, who had him put in jail. But what for? And I don't ask *why*, but *what for*? For as regards prison, what counts is not the reason but the purpose. And why did he ask the judge to summon me? What was I supposed to testify? Was I part of the defense? But what was the charge? Is it conceivable that Don Sandalio, my Don Sandalio could do anything deserving imprisonment? A silent chessplayer! Chess understood as it was by my Don Sandalio, as a religion, places one beyond good and evil.

And now I remember those solemn laconic words of Don Sandalio: "Problems? I'm not interested in problems. I have enough with those the game itself presents without looking for others." Could he have been brought to jail by one of those problems presented by the game of life? But . . . did my Don Sandalio really exist? Still, he died, and therefore he must have lived. And yet I've come to doubt he's dead. Such a man, such a Don Sandalio, could not die just like that, could not make such a bad choice. Even the report about his dying in jail smacks of some trick. He meant to imprison death. Will he be resurrected?

XIX

6 November

Gradually I'm coming to believe—what else can I do? —in the death of Don Sandalio. But I'm still not ready to return to the Casino; I'm not willing to find myself awash in that sea of mediocre foolishness, the more mediocre the worse, in that societary folly of the human race which makes men come together (Imagine!) to associate with each other. And I certainly don't care to hear their comments on Don Sandalio's "mysterious" death in jail. Although: do they ever really find mystery in anything? Most of them die without any awareness at all; some reserve their greatest follies for the end and transmit them in testamentary form to their children and heirs. And their children are just that: their heirs, without inner life, without even a hearth.

All those cardplayers, and the chessplayers who hum to themselves and sing snatches of tunes, who play without any religiosity whatever! They're all simply bored spectators.

Who ever invented clubs and Casinos? After all, public cafés are tolerable, especially when there are no games being played, when the noise of dominoes is stilled, when conversation is possible and easy and no one is taking notes. Cafés are even refreshing for the spirit, for in such a context human folly is refined and purified, for it laughs at itself, and, when folly laughs at itself, it ceases being folly. Folly is redeemed by foolery.

But the Casinos are regulated, and the regulations usually include the infamous clause prohibiting discussion of religion and politics—so what, then, is there left to discuss? And their libraries are more demoralizing than courthouses. They are libraries to show to visitors, and they're never without the standard dictionary, "for the settling of arguments," settling of bets regarding the value of a word and whether it is best used in this way or that! . . . In the café, on the other hand. . . .

Of course you mustn't think, Felipe, that I'm going to take refuge now, to console myself for the death of Don Sandalio, in one of the cafés in town. No, I've scarcely entered any. I went and had a drink in one, at a time of day when there was no one else around; it boasted great mirrors, rather opaque, each facing others, and I saw myself in them, reproduced endlessly, each time more dimly, the farther the dimmer, until I was lost in the distance, as in a sad dream. What a monastery of hermits we all made, the numberless images of the one original! I was already disquieted, when another individual entered the place. Seeing his myriad reproductions invade that vast camp of dreamland, I fled.

Once, when I found myself in a Madrid café, musing as usual, four city sports came in and began a loud discussion about bullfighting. I was amused that they argued about what they had read in the bullfight-papers rather than what they had actually seen in the bullring. Presently, another entered and sat down nearby; he ordered coffee, took out a notebook and began to write. As soon as the fellows noticed him, they stopped talking; one of them, in a loud voice and with a certain challenge announced: "Do you know what? That fellow there with his notebook, who pretends he's making up some kind of report on the place, is actually one of those types who goes around the cafés to listen to what we're saying and write us up in the papers. . . . He should write up his grandmother!" The four of them, with their commentaries and tone of voice, made it so hot for the poor fellow—who may well have been no more than a humble bullfight critic after all—that he had to quit the place. Of course, if instead of being a poor critic, he was actually one of those novelizers of realist novels, a writer of historical novels, and he was there to provide himself with material, then he deserved all he got.

No, I won't be going to any café for material. At best, I'll go in to see myself reproduced in a series of mirrors, and to join the silent far-off company of some other human shadows losing themselves in the distance. In any case, I'm certainly not going back to the Casino.

You might very well point out that the Casino is

a species of gallery of tarnished mirrors wherein we're reproduced. . . . But, remember that Pindar, who said, "Be what you are!", also said and in relation to that very thought, "Man is the dream of a shadow." Well, then: the members of the Casino are not dreams of shadows, but shadows of dreams, which is not the same thing. And if Don Sandalio fascinated me, it was because I could feel him dream, I sensed him dreaming chess, while all the others. . . . The others are merely shadows of my own dreams.

No, I won't be going back to the Casino. Anyone who didn't go mad among so many fools would be a greater fool than they.

XX

10 November

For days I've felt more withdrawn from people than ever, more than ever fearful of overhearing their foolishness. I go from the beach to the high woods and from the height of the woods down to the beach, to watch the waves tumble along and to watch the leaves do the same. Sometimes I've been able to watch the leaves tumble into the waves.

That was until yesterday when—who do you suppose called on me? None other than Don Sandalio's son-in-law! He came to the hotel intending "to have a talk" with me.

"I've come to see you," he began, "so as to bring you up to date on my poor father-in-law. . . ."

"Now just a minute," I interrupted him. "No use your going on. . . . I don't want to know a word of what you're thinking of telling me. I'm not interested in anything you may have to say about Don Sandalio. I'm not interested in stories about other people. I'm not interested in getting mixed up in other people's lives. . . ."

"But I've heard my father-in-law speak of you so often that I thought . . ."

"Speak of me? Why, your father-in-law scarcely knew me. . . . He probably didn't even know my name. . . ."

"You're wrong."

"Well if I'm wrong, I prefer it that way. Moreover, I'd be very surprised if Don Sandalio spoke *of* me, for he never spoke *to* me of anyone else. He barely spoke at all."

"That's the way he was outside the house."

"In that case, what he said at home is no concern of mine."

"I had thought, Sir," the youth said then, "that you had formed some attachment, perhaps had even felt some affection for Don Sandalio. . . ."

"Yes, but for *my* Don Sandalio," I interrupted him. "Do you understand me? *My* Don Sandalio, the one who silently played chess with me, and not *yours*, not your father-in-law. I could be interested in silent chessplayers, but never in fathers-in-law! And for that reason I will ask you not to insist on telling me the story of *your* Don Sandalio. My own Don Sandalio's story I know better than you."

"But at least you will not deny a young man some advice. . . ."

"Advice, advice? From me? I'm not in a position to offer any kind of advice to anybody."

"You mean you refuse. . . ."

"I refuse utterly to know any of the things you

might want to tell me. I have enough with what I invent on my own."

The son-in-law looked at me in a way not very different from the way his father-in-law had looked at me when I spoke of the mad bishop advancing sideways; he shrugged his shoulders, took his leave, and left my quarters. My thoughts wandered and I wondered if Don Sandalio had ever spoken at home of my discourse on the mad elephantine bishop of the chessboard. Who knows? . . .

And now I am preparing to quit this town, to abandon this mountainous corner of the coast. Still: will I be able to leave it behind? Am I not bound to it by the memory of Don Sandalio? No, I really can't leave.

XXI

15 November

And now I begin to remember all over again, to recall and to reconstruct certain obscure dreams I dreamt along the way: they are shadows which do not appear in front of one or come alongside, but are like those which evanesce into the distance of dim tarnished mirrors. On returning home some nights I would meet a human shadow falling across my inner awareness; it would project itself into my dormant consciousness and rouse it strangely; and the shadow would then lower its head, as if to avoid recognition. And I have now begun to wonder if it was not Don Sandalio, another Don Sandalio, the one I never knew, not the chessplayer but the one whose son died, the one who had a son-in-law, the one who spoke of me at home, the one who died in jail. Doubtless he avoided me, wished to escape.

But, when I met that shadow, or thought I did, that human shadow out of some tarnished mirror, a figure now grown mysterious in the distance of the past, was I awake or dreaming? Or am I now simply imagining these images of things past? Of course, as you know, I think, however paradoxical it may seem, that there are memories of things-to-come just as there are hopes of things past, and these are called nostalgia. And I must confess to you, friend Felipe, that I am forging new memories every day, inventing what happened, what passed, and what passed before me and in front of me. I am convinced that no one can be sure of what happened as distinguished from what he is continually inventing as regards what happened. Now, I am afraid I may well be inventing, out of the death of Don Sandalio, another Don Sandalio. But why do I say "I am afraid"? Fear? Why?

That shadow I see before me now, off the beaten track, in retro-time, walking by with head bowed—his? or mine?—could it be Don Sandalio returning from an encounter with some problem treacherously presented by the game of life, perhaps from an encounter with the problem which landed him in jail, and in jail caused him to encounter death?

XXII

Don't waste your time, Felipe, asking me for the impossible. It's no use your insisting. I am not prepared to search out the facts of Don Sandalio's private life. And I certainly will not seek out his son-in-law so that he can tell me why and how Don Sandalio went to jail, nor why and how he came to die there. I'm not interested in his story, his history; I'm satisfied with his novel of himself. And as regards this novel, the point is to dream it.

And as for your asking me to at least inquire what his daughter was like, what she was, in the past, since the son-in-law is a widower, and how she came to get married, suffice it to say that you need expect nothing from me. I know what you're after, Felipe. Quite simply: you've missed, in the course of this long correspondence, the presence of a single woman. And now, you expect the novel you're looking for from me to take shape, to jell, with the appearance of a woman. The missing She! The old story of "her." As in: *Cherchez la femme*. But I don't intend to seek out Don Sandalio's daughter nor any other "she" or "her" who might have been involved with him. Moreover I imagine that for Don Sandalio there was no woman other than the chess queen, the queen who advances in a straight line, like a chess tower or castle, from white to black or from black to white, and sideways, too, like a mad elephantine bishop, from white to white and from black to black, the queen who dominates the chessboard—but to whose high estate of dignity and imperiousness the least of pawns may aspire, whose high estate he may achieve, though it involve a change of sex. I think that queen was the only queen in his mind.

I don't recall what writer obsessed with the sex "problem" said that woman is a sphinx without a riddle. Perhaps. But the most profound problem of the novel or play of our life does not lie in the sexual "question," any more than it lies in our stomach; the most profound question of our novel, yours and mine, Felipe—Don Sandalio's novel, too—is the problem of personality, of being or not being, and is not a question of eating or not eating, of loving or being loved. Our novel, the novel of each one of us, revolves around the question of whether we are anything more than chessplayers, or cardplayers, or Casino members, or . . . serve in whatever profession or function you like, of whatever religion, in whatever sport, as whatever we may be. . . . For my part I leave this novel to each one to dream as best suits him, distracts him, or consoles him. There may well be sphinxes without riddles—and those are the novels which most please members of Casinos—but there are also riddles without sphinxes. The queen of chess does not have the female face or breasts of the sphinx squatting on the desert sands under the sun, but she has her riddle. Perhaps Don Sandalio's daughter was sphinxlike and the cause of his private tragedy, but I don't expect she was enigmatic or that she possessed a riddle. On the other hand, the queen of his thoughts was enigmatic even if not sphinxlike. The queen of his thoughts did not recline on the desert sands under the sun but traveled the length of the chessboard, sometimes straight on and sometimes sideways. Would you want any better novel than that?

XXIII

You insist to the end! Now you want me to "at least" write the novel of Don Sandalio, chessplayer. Write it yourself, if you want. You've got all the data, the "facts," for there are no others but the ones I've furnished you in these letters. If you need more, invent them in the manner of Pepe "el Gallego." Though why would you really want any more novel than I've provided you? Everything is there. If it isn't enough for some people, let them add whatever is missing, out of their own imagination. My correspondence with you contains the whole of my novel of the chessplayer, the entire novel of *my* chessplayer. For me there is no other.

You want more? Well now, go find yourself a quiet café in your own town, preferably on the outskirts, a café with mirrors, dim tarnished mirrors facing each other, and sit there and dream. And talk to yourself in the various mirrors. And you will almost certainly find your own Don Sandalio in the course of the dialogue. But, you say, he won't be mine? What of it? And he may not even be a chessplayer. He can be a billiardplayer or a footballplayer, or whatever. Or he might be a novelist. And you yourself, while you dream him and construct a dialogue, will become a novelist. Become a novelist, my dear Felipe, and you won't need to ask others for novels. A novelist ought not to read the novels of others, even though Blasco Ibáñez says the opposite and asserts that he scarcely reads anything but novels.

Now if it's a terrible thing to fall into the profession of novel-manufacturer, it's even more terrible to fall into the profession of novel-reader. And believe me, there would be no factories of mass-produced goods, American style, if there were not a clientele to consume the mass produce, the factory-brand goods.

And now, I'll bring this correspondence to an end. I'll leave this city at once so as not to have to write any more about the enigmatic shadow of the chessplayer Don Sandalio, who pursues me in all parts of this hideaway. I'll quit it once and for all and go to join you, so we can continue this dialogue on his novel in personal conversation.

Until we meet, shortly, a final salute in writing from your friend.

Epilogue

I MYSELF have just gone over all this correspondence again. The more I read it—and I've read it all several times now—and the more I examine the letters sent to me by an unknown reader, the more I've come to suspect that the whole thing is a ruse, an attempt to "place" a piece of fiction, to find an outlet for a contrived autobiography, even if contrived only in part. In other words, I suspect that Don Sandalio himself is the author of the letters, and that he has simply situated himself outside himself the better to represent as well as disguise himself and conceal his own truth. Naturally, he was able to narrate the manner of his own death or the conversation maintained between the son-in-law and Felipe's supposed correspondent, that is, himself. Mere novelistic trickery!

On the other hand, is it not possible that Don Sandalio, the "my" Don Sandalio of the letter writer, is none other than "Dear Felipe" himself? May not the entire correspondence be a novelized autobiography of Felipe, the recipient of the supposed letters and so-called unknown reader of Miguel de Unamuno? The author of the letters! Felipe! Don Sandalio, chessplayer! All of them figures in a gallery of tarnished mirrors!

It is well known, in any event, that all biography, whether historical or novelized—and both are the same for the present purpose—is autobiography, always, and that every author who presumes to be speaking for someone else is speaking in reality for himself and of himself, no matter how different this "himself" is from the one he thinks he is. Novelists are the greatest historians, especially the ones who put themselves most into their stories, their histories, the histories they invent.

It is also true that every autobiography is nothing less than a novel. All *Confessions* are novels, from those written by Saint Augustine to those by Jean Jacques Rousseau; and the *Dichtung und Wahrheit* of Goethe is also a novel, though Goethe, in giving this title of Poetry and Truth to his own autobiography, saw with all his Olympian insight that there is no truer truth than poetic truth, that there is no truer history than the novel.

Every poet, every creator, every novelist (and to novelize is to create) creates himself as he creates his characters, and if they are stillborn, if they are born dead, then it is because he himself is one of the living dead. When I say every poet, that is, every creator, I include the Supreme Poet, the Eternal Poet, I include God, who in creating the Creation, the Universe, while creating it continuously, versifying it, is doing no more than creating Himself in His Poem, in His Divine Novel.

For all these reasons, and for others which I keep to myself, I cannot help but believe that the author of these letters, which narrate the biography of Don Sandalio, the chessplayer, is none other than Don Sandalio himself, though he writes of his own death and of events following it, in order to throw us off the track.

In spite of all the evidence, there will be people of a materialist nature—the kind of people who do not dispose of "material time" to plumb the depths of the

problems offered by the game of life—who will think
that I should have used the data in these letters to
write the novel of Don Sandalio; that is, invent a solution to the mysterious problem of his life and thus
create a novel, a real novel. But I live in a spiritual
time of my own, and have merely set myself the task
of writing the novel of a novel—which is something
like the shadow of a shadow—and not the novel of a
novelist; the novel of a novel set down for my readers,
whom I have made in the measure that they have
made me. Neither I nor my readers—mine—are
either of us interested in any other kind of creation.
My readers—mine—do not look for the coherent
world of so-called realist novels. Isn't that so, readers,
my readers? My readers—mine—know that a plot is
no more than the pretext for a novel, and that a novel,
the novel, is left more integral, purer, more interesting, more novelistic, if there is no plot, if the plot is
removed. In any case, I no longer need my readers—
readers like the unknown reader who offered me those
"Letters to Felipe"—I no longer need my own readers
to suggest plots so that I may give them back novels.
I prefer—and I am sure they prefer my doing so—
to give them novels and let them supply or add the
plots. My readers are not the type to go out and buy
the story-synopsis before they go to the opera, or to
the films (with sound track or otherwise), so they
will know what to expect.

Salamanca
December 1930

The Madness of Doctor Montarco

I FIRST MET Dr. Montarco just after his arrival in the city. A secret attraction drew me to him. His appearance was obviously in his favor, and his face had an open and guileless look about it. He was tall, blond, robust, yet quick in movement. He immediately made friends with everyone he knew, because if he was not to make a person his friend, he refrained from making him his acquaintance. It was difficult to know which of his gestures were natural and which were studied, so subtly had he combined naturalness and art. From this proceeded the fact that while there were some who criticized him for affectation and found his simplicity studied, others of us thought that whatever he did was natural and spontaneous. He himself told me later: "There are gestures which, natural enough to begin with, later become artificial after they have been repeatedly praised. And then there are other gestures which, though we have acquired them through hard work and even against our very nature, end by becoming completely natural and seemingly native to us."

This observation should be enough to show that Dr. Montarco was not, while he was still of sound mind, the extravagant personality which many claimed. Far from it. He was, on the contrary, a man who in conversation expressed discreet and judicious opinions. Only on rare occasions, and even then only with persons completely in his confidence (as I came to be), did he unbridle his feelings and let himself go; it was then he would indulge in vehement invective against the people who surrounded him and from whom he had to earn his livelihood. And this was a foreboding of the abyss into which his spirit was finally to fall.

He was one of the most orderly and unpretentious men I have ever known. He was not a "connoisseur" or collector of anything, not even of books, nor did I ever detect in him any monomania whatever. His practice, his home, and his literary work: these were his only preoccupations. He had a wife and two daughters, aged eight and ten, when he arrived in the city. He was preceded by a very good reputation as a doctor; nevertheless, it was no secret that he had been forced by his peculiar conduct to leave his native town. His greatest peculiarity, in the eyes of his medical colleagues, lay in the fact that although he was an excellent practitioner and very well versed in medical science and biology, and that although he was a voluminous writer, it never seemed to occur to him to write about medical matters. As he told me once, in his characteristically violent manner: "Why must these idiots insist on me writing about professional topics? I studied Medicine simply to cure sick people and earn my living doing so. Do I cure them? I do; and therefore let them leave me in peace and spare me their nonsense, and let them keep out of my business. I earn my living as conscientiously as I can, and, once my living is made, I do with my life what I want, and not what these louts want me to do. You can't imagine what profound misery of a moral sort there is in the attempt, which so many people make, to confine everybody to a speciality. For my part, I find a tremendous advantage in living *from* one activity and *for* another. . . . You probably don't need to be reminded of Schopenhauer's justified denunciation of professional philosophers and busybodies."

A short while after arriving in the city, and after he had built up a better-than-average practice and had acquired the reputation of a serious, careful, painstaking, and gifted doctor, a local journal published his first story, a story halfway between fantasy and humor, without descriptive writing and without a moral. Two days later I found him very upset; when I asked the reason, he burst out: "Do you think I'm going to be able to resist the overwhelming pressure of the idiocy prevailing here? Tell me, do you think so? It's the same thing all over again, exactly the same as in my town, the very same! And just as happened there, I'll end by becoming known as a madman. I, who am a model of sanity. And my patients will gradually fall away and I'll lose my practice. Then the dismal days will come again, days filled with despair, disgust, and bad temper, and I will have to leave here just as I had to leave my own town."

"But what has happened?" I was finally able to ask.

"What has happened? Simply that five people have already come up to me to ask what I meant by writing the piece of fiction I have just published, what I intended to say, and what bearing did it have. Idiots, idiots, what idiots! They're worse than children who break dolls to find out what's inside. This town has no hope of salvation, my friend; it's simply condemned to seriousness and silliness, two blood sisters. People here have the souls of schoolteachers. They believe no one could write except to prove something, or defend or attack some proposition, or from an ulterior motive. One of these blockheads asked me the meaning of my story and by way of reply I asked *him*: 'Did it amuse you?' And he answered: 'As far as that goes, it certainly did; as a matter of fact, I found it quite amusing; but . . .' I left the last word in his mouth, because as soon as he reached this point in the conversation, I turned my back on him and walked away. That a piece of writing should be amusing wasn't enough for this monster. They have the souls of schoolteachers, the souls of schoolteachers!"

"But, now . . ." I ventured to take up the argument.

"Listen," he interrupted, "don't you start coming at me with any more 'buts.' Stop that. The infectious disease, the itch of our Spanish literature, is the urge to preach. Sermons everywhere, and bad sermons at that. Every little Christ sets himself up to dispense advice, and does it with a poker face. I remember picking up the *Epístola moral a Fabio* and being unable to get beyond the first three verses; I simply couldn't stomach it. This breed of men is totally devoid of imagination, and so all their madness is merely silly. An oysterlike breed—there's no use of your denying it—; oysters, that's what they are, nothing but oysters. Everything here savors of oyster beds, or ground-muck. I feel like I'm living among human tubers. And they don't even break through the ground, or lift their heads up, like regular tubers."

In any case, Dr. Montarco did not take heed and he went and published another story, more fantastic and satirical than the first. I recall Servando Fernández Gómez, one of Dr. Montarco's patients, discussing it with me.

"Well, sir," said the good Fernández Gómez, "I really don't know what to do now that my doctor has published his stories."

"Why not?" I asked him somewhat surprised.

"Frankly, it seems rather risky, putting oneself in the hands of a man who writes things like that."

"Come, now, he gives you good medical attention, doesn't he?"

"There's no question of that. I've no complaint on that score. Ever since I put myself in his hands, consulting with him and following his advice, I've been much better and every day I notice a further improvement. Still, those pieces of his . . . he must be a bit strange in the head. He's got bats in his belfry, I should think, a head full of crickets."

"Don't be alarmed, Don Servando. I have many dealings with him, as you know, and I've observed nothing at all wrong with him. He is a very sensible man."

"When one talks to him he answers normally enough and what he says is very sensible, but . . ."

"Listen, I'd rather have a man operate on me who had a steady hand and eye even if he did speak wildly (though Montarco doesn't do that either), than a man who was exquisitely proper, full of sententious wisdom and every kind of platitude and then went ahead and threw my whole body out of joint."

"That may be. Still . . ."

The next day I asked Dr. Montarco about Fernández Gómez, and he responded drily: "A constitutional fool!"

"What's that?"

"A fool by physiological constitution, *a nativitate*, a congenital, irremediable fool."

"Sounds like the absolute and eternal fool."

"No doubt . . . for in this area an Absolute fool and a Constitutional one are the same thing; it's not as in politics, where the Absolutists and the Constitutionalists are at opposite poles."

"He says you've got bats in your belfry, a head full of crickets. . . ."

"And his head, and those of his kind, are full of cockroaches. And cockroaches are merely mute crickets. At least mine can sing, or chirrup, or creak out something."

A short time later the doctor published his third tale; and this time the narrative was more pointed, full of ironies, mockery, and ill-concealed invective.

"I don't know whether you're doing the wisest thing by publishing these stories," I told him.

"But I have to. I simply have to express myself and work off my feelings. If I didn't write out these atrocities I'd end up committing them. I know well enough what I'm doing."

"There are some people who say that all this doesn't suit a man of your age, position, and profession . . . ," I said by way of drawing him out.

At this, he jumped to his feet and exclaimed:

"Just as I told you, exactly what I've said a thousand times: I'll have to go away from here, or I shall die of hunger, or they'll drive me crazy, or all of these things together. Yes, that's it, all of them at once: I shall have to leave, a madman, to die of hunger. And they talk about my position, do they? What do those blockheads mean by position? Listen, believe me, we shall never emerge from barbarism in Spain, we shall never be more than fancy Moroccans, fancy and false, for we'd be better off being our simple African selves, until we stop insisting that our chief of state be illiterate, that he write not a word, not even a volume of epigrams, or some children's tales, or a farce, while he is in office. He risks his prestige by literacy, they say. Meanwhile, we risk our history and our evolution with the opposite. How stupid and heavy-handed we are!"

Thus compelled by fatal intuition did Dr. Montarco set himself to combat the public feeling in the city where he lived and worked. At the same time he strove to be more and more conscientious and meticulous in his professional duties and in his civic and domestic obligations. He took extreme care to attend to his patients in every way, and to study their ills. He greeted everyone with great affability; he was rude to no one. In speaking to a person he would choose the topic he thought most likely to interest him, seeking thus to please each one. In his private life he continued to be the ideal, the exemplary, husband and father. Still, his tales continued to grow more fanciful and extravagant: such was the opinion of the masses, who also thought he was straying further and further from the "normal," the "usual." And his patients were beginning to leave him, creating a void around him. Whereupon his ill-concealed animosity became evident once more.

And this was not the worst of it, for a malicious rumor began to take form and to spread: he was said to be arrogant. Without foundation of any sort, it began to be whispered that the doctor was a haughty spirit, a man concerned only with himself, who gave himself airs and considered himself a genius, while he thought other people poor devils, incapable of understanding him. I told him about this consensus and this time, instead of breaking out into one of his customary diatribes, as I had expected, he answered me calmly:

"So, I'm haughty and proud, am I? No! Only ignorant people, fools, are ever really haughty; and frankly, I don't consider myself a fool; my type of foolishness doesn't qualify me. As if we actually could peer into the depths of each other's conscience like that! I know they think I am disdainful of others, but they are wrong. The fact is merely that I don't have the same opinion of them that they have of themselves. And besides—I might as well tell you what I'm really thinking—what is all this talk about pride and striving for superiority? For the truth is, my friend, that when a man tries to get ahead of others he is simply trying to save himself. When a man tries to sink the names of other men into forgetfulness he is merely trying to insure that his own be preserved in the memory of living men, because he knows that posterity is a close-meshed sieve which allows few names to get through to other ages. For instance, have you ever noticed the way a flytrap works?"

"What do you mean? What kind of a . . . ?"

"One of those bottles filled with water, which in the country are set around to catch flies. The poor flies try to save themselves and, since there is no way out but to climb on the backs of others, and thus navigate on cadavers in those enclosed waters of death, a ferocious struggle takes place to see which one can win out. They do not mean to drown each other at all; they are only trying to stay afloat. And that's the way it goes in the struggle for fame, which is a thousand times more terrible than the struggle for bread."

"And the struggle for life," I added, "is the same, too. Darwin . . ."

"Darwin?" he cut me off. "Do you know the book *Biological Problems* by William Henry Rolph?"

"No."

"Well, read it. Read it and you will see that it is not
the growth and multiplication of a species which
necessitates more food and which leads to such struggle, but rather that it is a tendency toward needing
more and more food, an impulse to go beyond the
purely necessary, to exceed it, which causes a species
to grow and multiply. It is not an instinct toward self-
preservation which impels us to action, but rather an
instinct toward expansion, toward invasion and en-
croachment. We don't strive to maintain ourselves
only, but to be more than we are already, to be everything. In the forceful words of Father Alonso Rodríguez, that great man, we are driven by an 'appetite
for the divine.' Yes, an appetite for the divine. 'Ye
shall be as gods!': thus it was the Devil tempted our
first parents, they say. Whoever doesn't aspire to be
more than he is, will not be anything at all. All or
nothing! There is a profound meaning in that. Whatever Reason may tell us—that great liar who has invented, for the consolation of failures, the doctrine of
the golden mean, the *aurea mediocritas*, the 'neither
envied nor envying' and other such nonsense—whatever Reason may tell us—and she is not only a liar
but a great whore—in our innermost soul, which we
now call the Unconscious, with a capital *U*, in the
depths of our spirit, we know that in order to avoid
becoming nothing sooner or later, the best course to
follow is to attempt to become all.

"The struggle for life, for super-life, rather, is an
offensive and not a defensive struggle. . . . In this
Rolph is quite right. And I, my friend, do not defend
myself; I am never on the defensive, instead I believe
in the attack. I don't want a shield, which would only
weigh me down and hinder me. I don't want anything

but a sword. I would rather deliver fifty blows, and receive ten back, than deliver ten and not receive any. Attack, attack, and no defense. Let them say what they like about me; I won't hear them, I'll take no notice, I'll stop my ears, and if in spite of my precautions, word of what they say reaches me, I will not answer them. If we had centuries of time to spare, I would sooner be able to convince them that they are fools—and you may imagine the difficulty in doing that—than they would convince me I am mad or arrogant."

"But this purely offensive system of yours, Montarco my friend . . . ," I began.

"Yes, yes," he interrupted me again, "it has its flaws. And even one great danger, and that is that on the day my arm weakens or my sword is blunted they will trample me underfoot, drag me around, and make dust of me. But before that happens they will have already accomplished their purpose: they will have driven me mad."

And so it was to be. I began to suspect it when I heard him talk repeatedly about the character of madness, and to inveigh against reason. In the end, they succeeded in driving him mad.

He persisted in issuing his stories, fictions totally different from anything current at this time in Spain; and he persisted, simultaneously, in not departing one whit from the reasonable sort of life he outwardly led. His patients continued to leave him. Eventually, dire want made itself felt in his household. Finally, as a culmination to his troubles, he could no longer find a journal or paper to print his contributions, nor did his name make any headway or gain any ground in the republic of letters. It all came to an end when a few of us who were his friends took over responsibility for his wife and his daughters, and arranged for him to go into an asylum. His verbal aggression had been growing steadily more pronounced.

I remember, as if it were yesterday, the first day I went to visit him in the asylum where he was confined. The director, Dr. Atienza, had been a fellow student of Dr. Montarco and manifested affection and sympathy for him.

"Well, he is quieter these days, calmer than at the beginning," the director told me. "He reads a little, very little; I think it would be unwise to deprive him of reading matter altogether. Mostly, he reads the *Quixote*, and, if you were to pick up his copy of the book and open it at random, it would almost certainly open to Chapter 32, of the Second Part, where is to be found the reply made by Don Quixote to his critic, the ponderous ecclesiastic who at the table of the duke and duchess severely reprimanded the knight-errant for his mad fancies. If you like, we can go and see him now."

And we did so.

"I am very glad that you've come to see me," he exclaimed as soon as he caught sight of me, raising his eyes from the *Quixote*, "I'm glad. I was just thinking and wondering if, despite what Christ tells us in the twenty-second verse of the fifth chapter of Saint Matthew, we are ever permitted to make use of the forbidden weapon."

"And what is the forbidden weapon?" I asked him.

" 'Whosoever shall say to his brother . . . Thou fool, shall be in danger of hell fire.' You see what a terrible sentence that is. It doesn't say whosoever calls him assassin, or thief, or bandit, or swindler, or coward, or whoreson, or cuckold, or liberal; no, it says, whosoever shall say 'fool.' That, then, is the forbidden weapon. Everything can be questioned except the intelligence, wit, and judgment of other people. When a man takes it into his head to have aspirations, to presume to some special knowledge or talent, it's even more complicated. There have been popes who, because they considered themselves great Latinists, would rather have been condemned as heretics than as poor Latinists guilty of solecisms. And there are weighty cardinals who take greater pride in the purity of their literary style than in being good Christians, and for them orthodoxy is no more than a consequence of literary purity. The forbidden weapon! Just consider the comedy of politics: the participants accuse one another of the ugliest crimes, they charge each other covertly with grave offenses, but they are always careful to call each other eloquent, clever, well-intentioned, talented. . . . For 'Whosoever shall say to his brother . . . Thou fool, shall be in danger of hell fire.' Nevertheless, do you know why we make no real progress?"

"Maybe because progress has to carry tradition on its back," I ventured to say.

"No, no. It's simply because it is impossible to convince the fools that they *are* fools. On the day on which fools, that is to say, mankind, become truly convinced that they are just that, fools, on that day progress will have reached its goal. Man is born foolish. . . . And yet whosoever shall say to his brother . . . 'Thou fool,' shall be in danger of hell fire. And in danger of hell fire he was, that grave ecclesiastic, 'one of those who presume to govern great men's houses, and who, not being nobly born themselves, don't know how to instruct those that are, but would have the liberality of the great measured by the narrowness of their own souls, making those whom they govern stingy, when they pretend to teach them frugality. . . .' "

"Do you see," Dr. Atienza whispered to me, "he knows chapters 31 and 32 of the second part of our book by heart."

"He was in danger of Hell Fire, I say," the poor madman went on, "this grave ecclesiastic who came out with the duke and duchess to receive Don Quixote, and who sat down at table with him, face to face while they ate. For, a little while later, furious, stupidly envious, and animated by low passions decked out as high wisdom, this boor charged the duke with responsibility before Our Lord for the actions of this 'good man.' . . . *This good man* is what the ridiculous and pompous cleric called Don Quixote, and he then went on to call him Mister Fool. Mister Fool! and he the greatest madman of all time! But he condemned himself to hell fire for calling him that. And in hell he lies."

"Perhaps he is only in purgatory, for the mercy of God is infinite," I ventured to say.

"But the guilt of the grave ecclesiastic—who clearly stands for our Spain in the book, and nothing else —is an enormous one, really enormous," he continued, ignoring my qualifying suggestion. "That ponderous idiot, a genuine incarnation and representative, if there ever was one, of that section of our population which considers itself cultured, that insufferable pedant, after rising peevishly from the table and questioning the good sense of his lord, who was feeding him—though it is doubtful if he did anything to earn his keep—said: 'Well may fools be mad, when wise men celebrate their madness. Your Grace may remain with this pair, if you please, but for my part, as long as they are in this house, I shall keep to my quarters, and thus save myself the labor of reprehending what I cannot mend.' And with that, 'leaving the rest of his dinner behind him, away he went.' He went away; but not entirely, for he and his like still prowl about, classifying people as sane or mad, and deciding which persons are which. . . . It's scandalous and hypocritical, but these great judges call Don Quixote 'the sublime madman' in public—and another pack of phrases they have heard somewhere—and in private, alone with themselves, they call him Mister Fool. Don Quixote, who, in order to go off in pursuit of an empire, the empire of fame, left Sancho Panza the government of an Island! And what office did Mister Fool keep for himself? Not even a ministry! And after all, why did God create the world? For His greater glory, they say, to make it manifest. And should we do less? . . . Pride! Pride! Diabolic pride! That's the cry of the weak and impotent. Bring them here, all those grave and ponderous gentlemen infected with common sense. . . ."

"Let's leave," Dr. Atienza whispered, "he is getting excited."

We cut short the visit with some excuse or other, and I took leave of my poor friend.

"He has been driven mad," Dr. Atienza said as soon as we were alone. "One of the wisest and sanest men I ever knew, and he has been driven mad."

"Why do you say that?" I asked. "Why do you say 'driven'?"

"The greatest difference between the sane and the insane," he answered me, "is that the sane, even though they may occasionally have mad thoughts, neither express them nor carry them out, while the insane—unless they are hopeless, in which case they do not think mad thoughts at all—have no power of inhibition, no ability to contain themselves. Who has not thought of carrying out some piece of madness— unless he is a person whose lack of imagination borders on imbecility? But he has known how to control himself. And if he doesn't know, he evolves into a madman or a genius, to a greater or lesser extent of one or the other depending on his form of madness. It is very convenient to speak of 'delusions' in this con- nection, but any delusion which proves itself to be practical, or which impels us to maintain, advance, or intensify life, is just as real an emotion and makes as valid an impression as any which can be registered, in a more precise manner, by the scientific instru- ments so far invented for the purpose. That necessary store of madness—to give it its plainest name— which is indispensable for any progress, the lack of balance which propels the world of the spirit and without which there would be absolute repose—that is, death—this madness, this imbalance, must be made use of in some way or other. Dr. Montarco used it to create his fantastic narratives, and in doing so he freed himself from it and was able to carry on the very orderly and sensible life which he led. And really, those stories . . ."

"Ah!" I interrupted, "they are deeply expressive, they are rich in surprising points of view. I can read and reread them because of their freshness, for I find nothing more tedious than to be told something in writing which I have already ruminated. I can al- ways read stories like these, without a moral and without description. I have been thinking of writing a critical study of his work, and I entertain the hope that once the public is put on the right track they will finally see in them what they don't today. The public isn't as slow-witted or disdainful as we sometimes think; their limitation is that they want everything given them already masticated, predigested, and made up into capsules ready to be swallowed. Everyone has enough to do simply making a living and can't take the time to chew on a cud which tastes bitter when it is first put in the mouth. But a worthwhile commentary can bring out the virtues of a writer like Dr. Montarco, in whose work only the letter and not the spirit has so far been perceived."

"Well, his stories certainly fell on rocky ground," Dr. Atienza resumed. "His very strangeness, which in another country would have attracted readers, scared people away here. At every step of the way and confronted with the simplest things, people surfeited with the most didactic and pedantic junk asked insistently: 'Now what does he mean here, what is this man trying to say in this passage?' And then, you know how his patients all deserted him, despite the fact that he gave them perfect care. People began to call him mad, despite his exemplary life. He was accused of passions which, in spite of appearances, did not really dominate him. His writings were all rejected. And then, when he and his family found themselves in actual need, he gave way to mad talk and acts; and it was this madness which he had previously vented in his writings."

"Madness?" I interrupted.

"No, you're right. It wasn't madness. But now they have succeeded in making it turn into madness. I have been reading his work since he has been here and I realize now that one of their mistakes was to take him for a man of ideas, a writer of ideas, when fundamentally he is no such thing. His ideas were a point of departure, mere raw material, and had as much importance in his writing as earth used by Velázquez in making the pigments for his painting, or the type of stone Michelangelo used for his *Moses*. And what would we say of a man who, equipped with a microscope and reagent, made an analysis of the marble by way of arriving at a judgment of the *Venus of Milo*? At best, ideas are no more than raw material, as I've already said, for works of art, or philosophy, or for polemics."

"I have always thought so," I said, "but I have found this to be one of the doctrines which meets with the most resistance on the part of the public. I remember that once, in the course of watching a game of chess, I witnessed the most intense drama I ever saw. It was a truly terrible spectacle. The players did no more than move the chessmen, and they were limited by the canons of the game and by the chessboard; nevertheless, you cannot imagine what intensity of passion there was, what tension of a truly spiritual nature, what flow of vital energy! Those who only followed the progress of the game thought they were attending an everyday match, for the two players certainly played without great skill. For my part I was watching the way they picked out the chessmen and played them; I was attentive to the solemn silence, the frowns on the players' brows. There was one move, one of the most ordinary and undistinguished no doubt, a check which did not eventuate in checkmate, which was nevertheless most extraordinary. You should have seen how one player grasped his knight with his whole hand and placed it on the board with a rap, and how he exclaimed 'Check!' And those two passed for two commonplace players! Commonplace? I'm certain that Morphy or Philidor were more so. . . . Poor Montarco."

"Yes, poor Montarco! And today you have heard him speak more or less reasonably. . . . Rarely, only rarely, does he rant. When he does, he imagines he is a grotesque character whom he calls the Privy Counsellor Herr Schmarotzender; he puts on a wig, gets up on a chair, and makes a wild speech—full of spirit, however, and in words which somehow echo all the longing and eternal seeking of humanity. At the end, he gets down and asks me: 'Don't you think, Atienza, my friend, that there is a good deal of truth, basically, in the ravings of the poor Privy Counsellor Herr Schmarotzender?' And, in fact, it often strikes me that the feeling of veneration accorded madmen in certain countries is quite justified."

"You know, it seems to me that you should give up the management of this place."

"Don't concern yourself, my friend. It's not that I believe that the veil of a superior world, a world hidden from us, is lifted for these unfortunates; it's simply that I think they say things we all think but don't dare express through timidity or shame. Reason, which we have acquired in the struggle for life and which is a conservative force, tolerates only what serves to conserve or affirm this life. We don't understand anything but what we must understand in order to live. But who can say that the inextinguishable longing to survive, the thirst for immortality, is not the proof, the revelation of another world, a world which envelops, and also makes possible, our world? And who can say that when reason and its chains have been broken, such dreams and delirium, such frenzied outbursts as Dr. Montarco's, are not desperate leaps by the spirit to reach that other world?"

"It seems to me, and you will forgive my bluntness in saying so, that instead of your treating Dr.

Montarco, Dr. Montarco is treating you. The speeches of the Privy Counsellor are beginning to affect you adversely."

"It may be so, I don't know. The only thing I am sure of is that every day I dedicate myself more to this asylum; for I would rather watch over madmen, than have to put up with fools. The only trouble, really, is that there are many madmen who are also fools. But now I have Dr. Montarco to devote myself to. Poor Montarco!"

"Poor Spain!" I said. We shook hands and parted.

Dr. Montarco did not last long in the asylum. He was gradually overcome by a profound melancholy, a crushing depression and finally he sank into an obstinate state of muteness. He emerged from his silence only to murmur: "All or nothing. . . . All or nothing. . . . All or nothing. . . ." His illness became worse and ended in death.

After his death, his desk drawer was searched and a bulky manuscript was found with these words on the title page:

ALL OR NOTHING
I request that on my death this manuscript be burned without being read.

I don't know whether Dr. Atienza resisted the temptation to read it or not; nor whether, in compliance with the madman's last wish, he burned it or not.

Poor Dr. Montarco! May he rest in peace, for he deserved both peace and final rest.

February 1904

The Other

A Mystery in Three Acts and an Epilogue

Cast of Characters

THE OTHER
ERNESTO, brother to LAURA
LAURA, wife to COSME
DAMIANA, wife to DAMIÁN
DON JUAN, family doctor
The AMA

ACT ONE

Scene i

ERNESTO and DON JUAN

ERNESTO: Very well, Don Juan, I entreat you, as family doctor and something of a psychiatrist as well, to shed some light on this mystery here and on the condition of my poor sister Laura. There's something mysterious going on all right, something which makes it hard to breathe. This place is part jail, part cemetery, part . . .

DON JUAN: Madhouse!

ERNESTO: Exactly! And this mystery . . .

DON JUAN: A horror mystery!

ERNESTO: Of course I didn't know him. . . . The two of them met and married while I was in America, and, when I returned I found myself with this . . . madman!

DON JUAN: Yes, your brother-in-law, poor Laura's husband, has gone completely mad.

ERNESTO: I thought so. But what about her?

DON JUAN: She's caught it, too. It's contagious. They're united and at the same time separated by mutual terror. . . .

ERNESTO: Separated . . . ?

DON JUAN: Yes. Ever since the day this horror began and he lost his mind, they no longer sleep together. He sleeps by himself, locked in his room so that no one can hear what he says when he talks in his sleep. And he speaks of himself as The

251

Other One, or The Other. When his wife calls him by his own name, Cosme, he answers: "No, I'm The Other One, The Other." The worst of it is that Laura doesn't seem to find it strange at all that he should indulge in such fantasy. In fact his calling himself The Other seems to make some sense to her, to possess some meaning hidden from anyone else. I didn't know them until they came to live here just after their marriage. At first they got along in great good harmony, a perfect couple. But one fatal day, when Laura returned from a trip, madness entered this house. And this madness, which is enough to drive even me mad, is called . . . The Other!

ERNESTO: And what of her?

DON JUAN: Either she pretends not to know what's happening, or she really doesn't know.

ERNESTO: Has it been very long since . . . ?

DON JUAN: A little over a month. It must have been building up, but then it exploded all of a sudden. But she'll be here soon, and you, as a brother, will sound her out better than I can. [*As he starts out*, LAURA *arrives*.] I'll leave you both together, to explain matters.

Scene ii

ERNESTO: Look, little Laura, I've spoken to your doctor because there's an air of mystery here which makes it hard to breathe. He calls it a horror mystery. What is it?

LAURA: [*Looking around in agitation*] I don't know . . .

ERNESTO: [*Taking her by the arm*] What is it? Why

does your husband lock himself in at night? Why is he afraid to be caught asleep and dreaming? Why? And what's all this about The Other? Who or what is The Other?

LAURA: Oh, Ernesto! My poor husband seems to have gone mad and is pursued by the one he calls The Other. He seems possessed, bedeviled, as if The Other were his Guardian Devil. . . . I've found him more than once apparently trying to rid himself of his devil, trying to tear him out. He doesn't want to be seen. And he's had all the mirrors in the house covered over. And once, when he surprised me looking into my little hand-mirror, which I must use . . .

ERNESTO: Of course, a woman must have a mirror. . . .

LAURA: Naturally. But he yelled at me and said: "Don't look at yourself in the mirror! Don't look for the Other Woman!"

ERNESTO: Well! . . . why doesn't he go out? Go out and forget it? It's no good being locked up. . . .

LAURA: He says that everyone else resembles a mirror and that he doesn't want even to be with himself. . . .

ERNESTO: And what does he read?

LAURA: Oh, it's not a matter of what he reads. . . .

ERNESTO: Are you sure?

LAURA: His madness is nothing like Don Quixote's. He's not mad from reading, it's not something out of a book. . . . I'm sure of *that*.

ERNESTO: What else are you sure of? What else do you know?

LAURA: I don't want to know anything else about it.

ERNESTO: Well, now, you can't live like that. You

must find out the truth. I'm not prepared to leave
you in the hands of a madman. Why, he's capable
of . . .

LAURA: No, Ernesto, he wouldn't. . . .

ERNESTO: How can you be sure? But in any case I
want you to tell me the truth, because you must
know what it is. . . . And I ask for the truth because I'm sure there's more than mere madness in
all this. Your husband Cosme is obviously mad,
totally mad, even though he reasons, or precisely
because he reasons too much. But his madness has
some basis, some cause, some beginning, and
you, his wife, must know what it is. . . .

LAURA: This kind of thing. . . .

ERNESTO: No, no, no. You must know very well
why it suddenly happened, and what happened
on that "fatal day," as Don Juan calls it. . . .

LAURA: What day?

ERNESTO: The day you were away on a trip, and he
was here alone, and he suddenly went mad. . . .

LAURA: But I was away. . . .

ERNESTO: And when you came back and found him,
you must have known what was happening. A
madness like this does not suddenly happen without any rhyme or reason, whatever the cause.
What could have happened on that fatal day?

LAURA: Don't torture me anymore. Ask him. He's
coming now.

Scene iii

THE OTHER: [*Entering*] What is it you should ask
me?

ERNESTO: You, Cosme . . .

THE OTHER: No! I'm the other one!

LAURA: My brother, who never met you, merely
wants to ask . . .

ERNESTO: It's true I can't say I know you. . . .

THE OTHER: I don't know myself. . . .

LAURA: He wants to ask you about the mystery, the
mystery of this house. . . .

THE OTHER: My mystery?

ERNESTO: Yes, yours, and the mystery of the fatal
day when your wife was away and you, all alone
here with . . .

THE OTHER: With The Other!

ERNESTO: That day you fell into this mania. And
now I beg you, Cosme, to stop all this talk about
The Other and stop confusing us with . . .

THE OTHER: *Forget* him? That's easily said. . . .

ERNESTO: Well then, out with it! Tell us once and
for all what you're talking about. Unburden yourself.

THE OTHER: [*He stalks about in silence while the
brother and sister follow him with their eyes, as if
watching a man talking to himself.*] All right,
then. If I keep it all to myself I'll soon begin
screaming what I doubtless do already when I'm
asleep. I'll rid myself of it. And it's you I'll tell,
Ernesto, you'll be the one to know it. Laura,
leave the room!

LAURA: But . . .

THE OTHER: I've asked you to leave! Leave the
room! You're the one who shouldn't know about
it. Although . . . do you already know?

LAURA: Me? Your Laura . . .

THE OTHER: My Laura lives as if she were living
with a dead man. Go away! I want to see if by

confessing to your brother I can live again. Leave us! I've already told you! Go away, go away!

[LAURA *leaves the room.*]

Scene iv

ERNESTO and THE OTHER

[*The latter goes to the door and locks it. Of a sudden he bites the key, and then puts it in his pocket. He approaches* ERNESTO *and offers him an upright chair, on the other side of a small table. He sits down and, putting his elbows on the table, rests his head in the palms of his hands.*]

THE OTHER: Well, you're about to hear a confession. . . . But don't worry, you're safe. . . .

ERNESTO: I'm easy in my mind. . . .

THE OTHER: People are as frightened of remaining alone with a madman, who's always dangerous, as they are of going to a cemetery alone at midnight. A madman is like a dead man to them. And they're right, for a madman carries a dead man within him. . . .

ERNESTO: Make an end of it!

THE OTHER: I haven't even begun . . . !

ERNESTO: Begin then!

THE OTHER: I'm beginning! It must be some time ago now. . . . I don't remember. My wife, your sister, went off to settle up some family matters, and I let her go by herself because I wanted to be alone, go over some papers, set fire to some memories, make some ash fertilizer in my memory. . . . I needed to come to accounts, make peace with myself. One late afternoon, sitting here where I'm sitting now . . . but am I really here?

ERNESTO: Calm down, Cosme.

THE OTHER: Not Cosme! The other one, The Other!

ERNESTO: Be calm. You're with me. . . .

THE OTHER: With you? With me? I was with my-self, I tell you, here with myself, when the other one, The Other, was announced, and I saw myself enter through that door there. . . . No, don't be alarmed. Here, take the key if you want it. [*He hands* ERNESTO *the key.*] Incidentally, now, you don't happen to keep a small mirror on you, do you, a little mirror to see if your hair and beard are in order?

ERNESTO: Yes, I've got this one. [ERNESTO *takes out a mirror and hands it over.*]

THE OTHER: A mirror and a key don't go together. [*He breaks the mirror and throws it away.*]

ERNESTO: Well! . . . In any case, go on with your story. You're beginning to . . .

THE OTHER: Don't worry. . . . As I was saying, I saw myself coming in that door as if I was walk-ing out of a mirror. And I saw myself sit down there, just where you're sitting. . . . Don't think you're dreaming. You don't need to pinch your-self. You're not dreaming. . . . It's you all right. . . . I saw myself come in, and then The Other . . . that is to say, I myself . . . sat like I'm sitting now, like you. . . . [ERNESTO *shifts in his chair.*] And he went on looking at me, looking into my eyes, looking at himself in my eyes. . . . [*Growing uneasy,* ERNESTO *lowers his gaze.*] I felt myself becoming unconscious, my soul turned to water. I began to live—or rather to un-live—backwards, in retro-active time, as in a film run backwards. . . . I began to live backwards, toward the past, like a horse reined in and backing up. . . . And my whole life passed before me and once again I was

twenty years old, and then ten, and five, and I
became a child. A child! And then, when I could
taste the milk from my mother's breast, the sacred
milk of the breast on my innocent infant's lips . . .
I was un-born. . . . I died. . . . I died when I
reached the age of birth, the age of our birth. . . .

ERNESTO: [*Starting to get up*] Better rest!

THE OTHER: Rest? You want *me* to rest? Didn't you
tell me to unburden myself? How can I rest without unburdening myself? Now don't get up. . . .
Sit down again. . . . And you can put away the
key. . . . I'm harmless and unarmed. Or, are you
still upset about my breaking your mirror?

ERNESTO: The fact is . . .

THE OTHER: Yes, of course it's dangerous to be
locked up with a madman, with a dead man. Isn't
that it? But, listen . . .

ERNESTO: Finish with it then.

THE OTHER: After a while I returned to consciousness, I was resurrected. But there, sitting where
you're sitting, and here, where I'm sitting, sat my
corpse. . . . Right here, in this same chair, here
sat my corpse . . . here . . . here it is! I am my
corpse, I am the dead man! Here it sat . . . livid!
[*He covers his eyes.*] I can still see myself! Everything is a mirror to me! I can still see myself!
Here it sat, livid, looking at me with its dead eyes,
with its eyes out of eternity, its eyes which reflected, as in a tragic photographic plate, the scene
of my death. . . . Forever . . . forever . . .

ERNESTO: Do calm down now! Calm down!

THE OTHER: Ah, I shall never be able to be calm
again, never to rest . . . never, never. . . . My dead
man . . . I took hold of him and—how heavy he
was! how heavy he is! And I carried him down

to the cellar, and locked him in, and there he stays, locked away. . . .

ERNESTO: Well, now . . .

THE OTHER: Nothing well about it! Because you're going with me right now, to the cellar, to see the corpse of The Other, of the one who died here! . . . He's down there, in the dark, dying in the dark. . . .

ERNESTO: But Cosme! . . .

THE OTHER: Come with me! Come on! And don't be afraid of the dead man! Come! . . . I'll go in front and you follow behind me. If you're carrying a gun, you can point it at me. . . .

ERNESTO: Don't say such things. . . .

THE OTHER: Say? To the devil with saying things! . . . The worst is to do things, to act . . . act. . . . Come and see the other dead man. . . . I'll go in front. . . . [*They go out and the scene is left deserted. After a while, there is a rapping at the door.* LAURA's *voice is heard outside.*]

LAURA: Cosme! Cosme! Open the door! [*Silence*] Cosme! Cosme! Open the door!

AMA: Why have they locked the door? Cosme, child!

LAURA: There's no sound of anyone in there. . . . Where can they be?

AMA: Don't worry. Ernesto is with him. . . .

LAURA: Ernesto! Ernesto! Someone will have to break in the door.

AMA: Wait. Cosme, my child!

LAURA: Cosme! Ernesto!

AMA: What are you afraid of?

LAURA: I don't know. But I'm more afraid of him now than ever before. . . . Cosme! Cosme!

AMA: Cosme, my child, open the door.

LAURA: Cosme, open the door. Don't lock us out!

THE OTHER: [*Coming into the room, followed by* ERNESTO, *who seems horrified*] I'm coming, I'm coming! Open the door with your key, Ernesto!

ERNESTO: We're coming. [*He opens the door, his eyes fixed on* THE OTHER.]

LAURA: [*Entering*] Thank God! It's you!

THE OTHER: What do you want, Laura? What do you two want from me?

LAURA: You?

THE OTHER: Yes, it's me . . . me, the very same.

ERNESTO: [*To* LAURA, *pointing with his key in the direction of* THE OTHER] I'll leave you there with him, your husband, I've got to talk to the Ama. [*He takes the* AMA *aside*.] What's going on in this house? What is the mystery here?

AMA: In every house, in all . . .

ERNESTO: But when a corpse is being mummified in the cellar of the house and the corpse being mummified is, as far as one can fathom with one's senses, Cosme himself, what then?

AMA: My poor child!

ERNESTO: Whose is it?

AMA: Come now, he's infected you with his madness as he did his wife. . . .

ERNESTO: But I saw it, I tell you, with these eyes that the earth will one day swallow. . . . He showed it to me by the light of a candle, and turned his face away. . . . Oh, there's something terrible going on here. A mystery . . .

AMA: Let the mysteries be mummified too. . . .

ERNESTO: Perhaps a crime . . .

AMA: Let all crimes rot. My poor children! And I'm not going to tell poor Laura about some corpse in the dark. She must hear nothing of any such thing. . . .

ERNESTO: But the mystery must be cleared up. . . .

AMA: Then, do it without her finding out. . . . And you must try to calm her down now. For some reason she's become more frightened than ever. . . . I don't know what she wants from her husband. Nor why he frightens her. . . . Try to calm her down. [*Speaking to* THE OTHER] Come, my child. . . .

[THE OTHER *leaves* LAURA *to her brother and joins the* AMA.]

AMA: My son, what have you done?

THE OTHER: Ama!

AMA: What have you done to yourself?

THE OTHER: What did he do to me, you mean. . . .

ERNESTO: [*To* LAURA] Don't carry on. For you haven't told me the truth, the whole truth. Everything that's happened in this house.

LAURA: What happened?

ERNESTO: You haven't told me anything about the other one, Laura.

LAURA: You, too? Are you with him? Talking the same . . .

ERNESTO: I don't know which one is your husband.

LAURA: Neither do I.

ERNESTO: Where did you meet him? How did you come to marry?

LAURA: I'll tell you the story. But, just now, you must leave me alone. Cosme frightens me more than ever. When he told me to get out before he locked himself in here with you, I saw to the bottom of his soul. Look at him, he seems to be looking through the floor while he listens to the Ama.

ERNESTO: Yes, he's looking through the floor.

AMA: I suspected it all. . . . I guessed it. . . . I

divined the Day of Destiny, I read it in your eyes. . . .

THE OTHER: The eyes of a dead man . . .

AMA: I guessed, I divined what you did with . . .

THE OTHER: Don't say his name! I am him, the the other one, The Other! And you, Ama, you no longer know who I am. . . . You've forgotten. Isn't that true?

AMA: Yes, I've forgotten! And I've forgiven you!

THE OTHER: And the other one?

AMA: I've forgiven the other one as well. I've forgiven you both.

THE OTHER: But, do these two know?

ERNESTO: [*To* THE OTHER] A new life is about to begin, from now on. . . .

THE OTHER: Another death, you must mean. . . .

ERNESTO: Light must be shed here, this house must be cleansed. . . . Light! Light!

THE OTHER: Light? Why light?

ERNESTO: So that you may see each other, so that we may all see each other.

AMA: It would be better not to see each other. . . .

THE OTHER: To see oneself is to die, Ama, or to kill oneself. And one must live, even if it be in the dark. Better in the dark.

AMA: Now is the time to be yourself. You must save yourself.

CURTAIN

ACT TWO

Scene i

ERNESTO, LAURA, and the AMA

ERNESTO: And now for the truth, the whole truth!

AMA: The whole truth? No one could stand that. I don't want to know anything. I've forgotten everything. I no longer know any one. Both of them were like my own children. . . . I raised one, his mother the other. But I loved both of them like a mother, I suckled them both, I was their wet nurse, their ama. The two of them . . .

ERNESTO: What two?

AMA: The twins. Cosme and Damián . . .

ERNESTO: What's this, Laura?

AMA: Yes, let your sister tell you. I don't want to think of it again, I don't want to know. I'm leaving. [*To* ERNESTO, *apart*] And of the other matter . . . not a word. [*She leaves.*]

Scene ii

ERNESTO and LAURA

ERNESTO: What's it all about?

LAURA: I'll tell you. . . . When I first came to Renada with Father—may God keep him!—I met Cosme and Damián Redondo, twins. They resembled each other so closely that there was no way of telling them apart. They were both impetuous and passionate. They fell in love with me, both of them! And they did so with such fury that they ended up by hating each other. They grew to hate each other deeply, with a hate based on intense jealousy, a fraternal jealousy and a fraternal hatred. I couldn't tell them apart—there wasn't a visible sign of difference between them—and so I had no reason to prefer one to the other. And then, there was the danger that if I married either one, the other would not be far away. . . .

ERNESTO: You should have rejected them both!

LAURA: Impossible! They courted me like two tornados! They won me over! Or won over me! And then their rivalry was ferocious, and their mutual hatred unspeakable. I began to fear, and they began to fear, that one would kill the other. It became a kind of mutual suicide pact. As for me, I was afraid they would tear me to pieces, morally and emotionally. There was no way of resisting, resisting them both. And so they won me over, or won over me, with their violence. . . .

ERNESTO: Which one of the two?

LAURA: The two of them . . . One of them . . . the other. And they decided that whoever did not marry me would go away. I wasn't present when they decided that. I was terrified whenever I saw them both together. It must have been a frightful spectacle. . . .

ERNESTO: No. I imagine it must rather have been a hellishly quiet scene, infernally icy. . . .

LAURA: I don't know, I never knew, how they decided the matter. I didn't know and I didn't want to know. They were supposed to separate forever. . . . I married the one who remained behind, this one, this Cosme. . . .

ERNESTO: But is this one Cosme?

LAURA: Well if it isn't, who is it?

ERNESTO: The Other, as he says. . . .

LAURA: Who? Damián? What madness!

ERNESTO: Don't get excited!

LAURA: It's enough to drive one mad. . . . Anyone

would say that you've gone mad yourself. . . . Just
to imagine that this one, my one, is the other
one. . . .

ERNESTO: Go on! . . .

LAURA: I married Cosme, and Damián went away.
It was then that father died. I don't doubt that my
two ferocious lovers played a part in his death by
driving him to distraction. . . . Shortly afterwards,
Damián wrote saying he was getting married. I
was delighted, for it meant one less worry, the
fear that one day he would return. . . . Cosme
went off to attend his brother's wedding. . . .

ERNESTO: And you?

LAURA: No, I didn't want to go. I wasn't meant to
go. And I never saw him again. . . .

ERNESTO: Which one?

LAURA: For heaven's sake, Damián of course. . . .
But then, when I was away myself, all this happened and my husband changed. When I returned I found him . . . an other!

ERNESTO: Which is what he calls himself. . . . He
had changed into . . .

LAURA: The Other. . . . Yes . . .

ERNESTO: Damián?

LAURA: No, not Damián. . . . The Other!

AMA: [*Entering*] There's a woman here, Laura, who
says she must see you. She's quite excited. . . .
Shall I have her come in?

LAURA: Show her in. Please stay, Ernesto.

[*The* AMA *goes out.*]

Scene iii

ERNESTO, LAURA, and DAMIANA

DAMIANA: [*Enters*] Laura, the wife of Cosme Redondo?

LAURA: I am Laura. And this is my brother Ernesto.

DAMIANA: Well, I am Damiana, the wife of Damián, your brother-in-law, and I've come to find out what you've done with my husband. . . .

LAURA: What *I've* done with your husband?

DAMIANA: It has been over a month since he told me he was going to visit his brother, your Cosme, that he was coming to visit you both. When he did not write me, I wrote Cosme asking after Damián. I had no answer, so I wrote again, and yet again. And . . . still no answer. And so now I've come to ask him what he's done with his brother. . . .

LAURA: What *who* has done with his brother . . . who?

DAMIANA: Your husband. . . . Or what *you've* done with my husband. . . .

LAURA: I?

DAMIANA: Yes, you. In any case, what both of you, you and your husband, have done with *mine*.

LAURA: Yours?

DAMIANA: Yes, mine! What have you done with mine? . . .

LAURA: But I . . .

DAMIANA: Where have you got him?

LAURA: Where have we got him? I? . . .

DAMIANA: I . . . I . . . I . . . ! Enough! Where do you have him?

LAURA: But . . .

DAMIANA: Call your husband, or whoever . . . call him and let him tell me what you've done with *mine*. . . . Call him!

LAURA: Don't scream like that. . . .

DAMIANA: I'll scream all right. . . . Call him, I said, bring him here. And give me back what belongs to me!

The Other

Scene iv

[THE SAME *as above and* THE OTHER, *who comes into the room slowly.* DAMIANA *goes to embrace him, but he draws back, stares at his hands, and then covers his eyes with them, while he shakes his head negatively.*]

DAMIANA: Damián!

LAURA: No! It's Cosme!

THE OTHER: Me, I'm the other one. I've already said so: The Other!

LAURA: [*Who comes to his defense*] But you're Cosme, my Cosme. . . .

THE OTHER: The Other I said! The Other of the other one! And now you two furies are here. Did you come to pursue me? To torment me? To avenge yourselves? To avenge the other one? You two furies . . . you, Laura . . . and you, Damiana . . .

DAMIANA: But, where is my Damián?

ERNESTO: Your Damián, Madame, or the other one, your Cosme, Laura, is dead and locked up in the dark of the cellar. [*Turning on* THE OTHER] Assassin! Murderer! Fratricide!

THE OTHER: [*Crossing his arms*] I? An assassin? But who am I? Who is the assassin? Who the assassinated? Who the hangman? Who the hanged? Which one is Cain? And which one Abel? Which one am I, Cosme or Damián? Yes, the mystery has been exploded, madness has become reasonable, the shadow has given birth to light. The two twins, who like Esau and Jacob struggled with each other in their mother's womb, bore each other a fraternal hatred, a hatred which was demoniacal love, the two brothers finally

found each other. . . . It was at dusk, the sun
having just died, when the shadows merge and
the green of the fields turns black. . . . Hate your
brother as you hate yourself! And filled with
hatred for themselves, intent on committing mutual suicide . . . for a woman . . . another woman
. . . they fought. And one of them felt, in hands
frozen with terror, the neck of the other going
cold. . . . And he looked into the dead eyes of his
brother to see if he saw himself dead there. . . .
The shadows of the night which was falling
shrouded the other one's pain. . . . And God
remained silent. . . . And He remains silent still!
Who is the dead one? Who is the more dead? And
who the assassin?

ERNESTO: You're the assassin, the executioner! You!
Your brother came to see you that day at dusk,
and you fought, out of jealousy surely, and you
killed your brother. . . .

THE OTHER: Exactly! In self-defense. And who
am I?

ERNESTO: Cain!

THE OTHER: Cain! Cain! I call myself that name
every night, in my dreams, and that's why I sleep
alone, behind locked doors and away from everyone. So that no one will hear me . . . so that I don't
hear myself. . . . Poor Cain! Poor Cain! And I
tell myself that if Cain had not killed Abel, Abel
would have killed Cain. . . . It was fated! Even
in our schooldays, it was one of the chief jokes to
ask someone all of a sudden: "Who killed Cain?"
And the boy who was asked usually fell for it and
would answer: "His brother Abel." And so it was.
In any case, does one become Cain for having

killed one's brother, or does one kill one's brother
because one is Cain?

ERNESTO: In other words, if . . .

THE OTHER: In other words, if . . . whichever one
you choose of the two, if one of them . . .

ERNESTO: Yes?

THE OTHER: If one had not killed the other, the
other would have killed the one.

ERNESTO: And you?

THE OTHER: I? One and the other, Cain and Abel,
hangman and hanged!

Scene v

THE SAME as above, the AMA and DON JUAN

AMA: [*Entering with* DON JUAN] We've begun to
realize what's happening and . . .

DAMIANA: Ama!

AMA: Wait, Damiana! I've begun to realize what's
happening, and I see the mystery being unfolded
—though not cleared up—and so I've brought
Don Juan, for all this must be covered up, buried
here. . . .

ERNESTO: The one buried is the other one.

THE OTHER: No, I'm the one that's buried!

AMA: Listen to me, Don Juan, one of my two children—for the one I brought up is as much but
no more mine than the other one, even if I did not
give birth to either—one of my children has killed
the other, and he seems to be down there below,
buried or not. And now we must fix up all this,
Don Juan. Between us all, between the six of us,
we must bury the mystery within this house, so
that it never gets out, so that nothing is ever

heard of it on the outside, so that nobody in the world ever finds out. And you, Don Juan, must find no reason to report anything, you must not make any report at all. Just as if nothing were known of the one who . . . has disappeared. My poor child!

DAMIANA: There's still the matter of the child . . . my child!

DON JUAN: What child, señora?

AMA: Whoever's!

DON JUAN: But you could tell them apart, you can still tell them apart. . . .

AMA: Not now, now that they've become one. . . .

DON JUAN: But the dead man . . .

AMA: They're both dead men now. . . .

THE OTHER: Yes, now and later!

DON JUAN: Better, yes, to keep it quiet. That is, if the widow . . .

ERNESTO: And who is that?

THE OTHER: What, no one can answer? Which one of you claims to be a widow? Or would you both like to be widows? Or both be wives to me? Whom do either of you love? The dead man or The Other, the deader of the two? Ah, I know! You both love the killer, Cain, even if only out of pity. Poor Cain! But I tell you that Abel also deserves pity. Poor Abel!

ERNESTO: Let us leave him with his conscience. And now [*to* DAMIANA] please make yourself at home in this house of ours . . . or your house . . . and wait for everything to become clear. But first, please accompany me to the cellar so that I may show you . . . The Other.

[*Exit* ERNESTO, LAURA, DAMIANA, *and* DON JUAN]

Scene vi

THE OTHER and the AMA

AMA: My child, what have you done with your
brother?

THE OTHER: [*sobbing*] I carry him within me, dead.
He's killing me. . . . He's killing me. . . . He'll
destroy me, Ama. He's implacable. Abel is implacable. Abel never forgives. Abel is evil! Yes,
yes, if Cain hadn't killed him, Abel would have
killed Cain. And now he's killing him. . . . Abel
is killing me. Abel! What hast thou done with
thy brother? Whoever gets himself executed is as
evil as whoever acts as executioner. To let oneself
become a victim is a diabolic vengeance. Oh, Ama!

AMA: Listen . . .

THE OTHER: [*Covering her mouth with his hand*]
I've told you not to name him. . . .

AMA: But tell me, tell my heart's ear. . . . I've forgotten him, I tell you, I've forgotten him. . . .
You are and will be both of you. For the two of
you are one. Victim or executioner, either way.
What difference is there? One is the other!

THE OTHER: That, Ama, that is the sacred truth.
We are all one. . . .

AMA: Come here to me. [*Drawing him to her breast*]
Can you remember when they were not dry?
When you sucked life from them? Sometimes I
would exchange you with your mother. Both of
you sucked at my breasts, both of you sucked
hers. . . . We would exchange you and I would
change breasts. Sometimes from this one, on the
heart's side, sometimes the other. . . .

THE OTHER: On the liver's side!

AMA: And now . . . they're dry.

THE OTHER: Drier still are those of the mother who gave us birth!

AMA: By now they're part of the earth. . . .

THE OTHER: And the other one is earth . . . and I'm earth. . . .

AMA: Why did you hate him, my child?

THE OTHER: Ever since we were small I've suffered at seeing myself outside myself. . . . I couldn't stand that mirror image. . . . I couldn't stand being outside myself. . . . The way to hate oneself is to see oneself outside oneself, to see oneself as someone else. Oh, the terrible rivalry as to who would learn the lesson best! And if I knew it, and he didn't, and they thought the one who knew it was he! . . . And they would have to make a distinction between us by name alone, or by a ribbon, or by some other token! . . . To become a name! It was he, he who taught me to hate myself. . . .

AMA: But he was good. . . .

THE OTHER: The two of us made ourselves bad. . . . When one is not always oneself one becomes bad. . . . In order to grow bad one need only to have a mirror continuously before one, especially a living, breathing mirror. . . .

AMA: And then . . . the woman!

THE OTHER: The women, Ama, the women . . . one and then another, seduced and seducing. . . .

AMA: We live on earth. . . .

THE OTHER: We live in mystery, Ama, in mystery. . . . And you and my mother showed us how to pray. . . . Everything double, doubled. . . . God doubled too! . . .

AMA: Doubled? God?

THE OTHER: His other name is Destiny!

AMA: Fatality!

THE OTHER: She is another . . . Destiny's wife. . . . God is also Other! . . .

AMA: How confused your poor mind is, my child . . . !

THE OTHER: No! It's He, God, Destiny, The Other in heaven who's brought on this confusion! And it's not my head that's confused, but my heart! It's ready to burst! And one's heart is earth!

AMA: Resign yourself!

THE OTHER: I remember, Ama, when he and I, the two of us together, saw the tragedy of Oedipus, that grand inquirer, that divine detective. . . . His drama seemed like something out of the Grand Guignol, absurd and, at the same time, of the essence of life and truth. Oedipus, too, had to resign himself. . . .

AMA: Resign yourself, then!

THE OTHER: But what of the furies? Those furies Destiny uses to pursue and torment me? The furies of my Destiny and of the other's. Destiny . . . Fatal furies, those two widows . . . unleashed furies . . . What of them?

AMA: They must be placated!

DAMIANA: [*From within*] Give me mine!

THE OTHER: Hers?

DAMIANA: [*Still within*] Let them give me mine!

THE OTHER: Which one is hers, Ama?

AMA: Do you know?

THE OTHER: I? I don't know who I am. . . .

DAMIANA: [*Still within*] Give me the father. . . .

THE OTHER: The father? I don't even know who I am. . . .

AMA: Even less do I. . . .

CURTAIN

273

ACT THREE

Scene i

THE OTHER

[*In the background, a full-length mirror behind a folding screen.* THE OTHER *paces about; head bent, he gesticulates as if talking to himself. Suddenly he makes up his mind and, pushing the screen aside, stands before the mirror. He crosses his arms and stares at himself for a moment. Presently he covers his face with his hands. Next he stares at his hands; he extends them toward his own image in the mirror as if to seize it by the throat, but then, on seeing other hands come toward him, he draws them back, and puts them to his own neck, as if to strangle himself. Overcome by black despair, he falls at the foot of the full-length mirror and, leaning his head against the glass and staring at the floor, he breaks down sobbing.*]

Scene ii

THE OTHER and LAURA

[LAURA *appears. She stands apart, observing him, and then silently comes up behind him, until she is close enough to put her hand on his shoulder.*]

THE OTHER: [*Turning about with a start*] Who is it?

LAURA: I. Your Laura.

THE OTHER: You . . . my . . . my what? My . . .

LAURA: Yes, your Laura!

THE OTHER: You, my wife?

LAURA: Yes, aren't you the one who's mine?

THE OTHER: Mine, mine? No! Yes . . . my assassin!

And I don't know if I was a homicide or a suicide.

LAURA: Don't think about it. Let the dead man be! And . . .

THE OTHER: Which one is the dead man? Your brother has set himself up as my jailer until all this is cleared up . . . But I . . .

LAURA: [*Raising him from the floor*] First of all, leave the mirror alone, and don't torment yourself. . . . Don't stare at yourself. . . .

THE OTHER: [*Rising*] At the dead man?

LAURA: [*Takes hold of the screen and covers the mirror as it was before. She helps* THE OTHER *to a couch, where she has him sit down.*] Don't look at yourself again. . . . Don't kill yourself like this. . . . Live! Live! . . . I know it's you well enough. . . .

THE OTHER: Your brother, Ernesto, my brother-in-law. . . .

LAURA: Your brother-in-law! So! I am your wife, then?

THE OTHER: Make your own deductions. Whoever I am . . .

LAURA: But you are . . .

THE OTHER: The Other. I've already told you. Your brother has set himself to be my jailer, my keeper, until the matter is cleared up. But I . . .

LAURA: You . . . I know very well who you are. . . . Why wouldn't I know! And I am yours. . . .

THE OTHER: Whoever I am . . .

LAURA: Yes, whoever you are, because . . . [*She curls herself up into his lap coquettishly, and he kisses her head.*] Ever since your first kiss after the . . . deed . . .

THE OTHER: The murder you mean. . . . Call it by
its right name!

LAURA: Ever since what you did in self-defense . . .

THE OTHER: Every murder is committed in self-
defense. Every murderer commits murder in the
course of defending himself. Defending himself
from himself . . .

LAURA: Forget all those arguments and come. . . .

THE OTHER: Yes, to you. You want me to forget. . . .

LAURA: Of course!

THE OTHER: Well, I can't forget. . . .

LAURA: Ever since your first kiss, Damián . . .

THE OTHER: [*Rejecting her*] What! I'm not Damián. . . . I'm not . . . Cosme. I've already told
you. . . .

LAURA: [*Leaning against him again*] No, you can't
deceive me. . . . I know you. . . . That kiss of
yours tasted of blood, and I know you killed
him. . . .

THE OTHER: For you, of course?

LAURA: Yes, for me!

THE OTHER: I don't recognize you. Who are you?

LAURA: Laura, your Laura . . .

THE OTHER: My Laura! But to whom do you belong?

LAURA: To any one of the two of you, to either . . .
To you!

THE OTHER: What you want is to know the taste of
the other one's kisses. . . . You love Cain rather
than Abel, the one who killed. . . .

LAURA: For me! For my sake!

THE OTHER: Supposing it was your man, but supposing he killed the one belonging to the other
woman so that he could have his pleasure with
her?

LAURA. Impossible! That's impossible! Although
. . . I don't know. . . .

THE OTHER: You know plenty! A woman in love
knows. . . . So you were in love with Damián,
and not with Cosme, not with your Cosme? . . .
Come now, answer me! You were in love with
another woman's husband? Answer me, Laura!

LAURA: I . . . was in love . . . with you!

THE OTHER: Tell me, when you came to Renada
and we both laid siege to you, when we both almost laid you waste with love, which of the two
did you prefer? Or was it the two of us?

LAURA: Since I could never tell the difference between you . . .

THE OTHER: Still, love should be able to tell. . . .

LAURA: But there simply was no telling which of
you was which. . . .

THE OTHER: No? . . . It's terrible to be born double!
Terrible never to be one and the same!

LAURA: Is that the reason you began to hate each
other?

THE OTHER: And each of us himself. The jealous
man hates himself. Whoever does not feel that he
is different, obviously different, distinguishably
different, hates himself. . . . And you . . . you. . . .
[*He presses his head between his hands*] you desired . . .

LAURA: You!

THE OTHER: No, the other one! You always desired
the one you didn't have, the one who wasn't there,
and whenever you saw us together you hated us
both. But . . . which one did you desire? Come
now, which one?

LAURA: You! I've already told you. You, you, you.
The Other!

THE OTHER: One always desires the one one doesn't have. . . . And now?

LAURA: Now . . .

THE OTHER: Yes, now . . .

LAURA: You, you, you. Always you!

THE OTHER: No, the dead man . . . the other one!

LAURA: But the other . . .

THE OTHER: I am The Other!

LAURA: Mine . . .

THE OTHER: Yours . . . Who?

LAURA: You.

THE OTHER: And I, who am I? How do you know me? Where is the sign? [LAURA *playfully tries to open his shirt.*] Hands off!

LAURA: Won't you let me look for it?

THE OTHER: Yes, yes, you're a woman after all, more curious than amorous, always wondering what the other one is like. What is he like? How is he different? Where is the mole, where the hidden mark to tell them apart? But . . . how do you know the other one doesn't have the same markings?

LAURA: The marking I made?

THE OTHER: Hands off! Just as well I didn't let myself fall asleep naked within your reach. Women are naturally dissemblers. . . .

LAURA: Ever since that day . . .

THE OTHER: You mean you don't know me, the murderer. . . .

LAURA: Of course, I know you!

THE OTHER: [*Rising*] Do you really know me? Come here. [*He takes her head in his hands and looks into her eyes.*] Look at me well. What do you see?

LAURA: Blood!

THE OTHER: Do you know Cain?

LAURA: Damián! . . . Cosme!

THE OTHER: Do you know Abel?

LAURA: Cosme! . . . Damián!

THE OTHER: Do you know the other one?

LAURA: You're killing me. . . . I hear her . . . the other woman! [*She flees.*]

THE OTHER: The other woman!

Scene iii

THE OTHER and DAMIANA

DAMIANA: This must come to an end. . . .

THE OTHER: No. It must begin!

DAMIANA: True. This must begin, Cosme. . . .

THE OTHER: Cosme? No, you know well enough who I am. . . .

DAMIANA: You're mine!

THE OTHER: Yours, yes, the one you've won, with blood and terror. . . . [*Once seated,* DAMIANA *draws him down to her and begins to soothe and caress him as if he were a child.*]

DAMIANA: Ah, I see how you suffer. . . . All for me! You killed him for my sake!

THE OTHER: Be quiet!

DAMIANA: Why don't you call me Damiana?

THE OTHER: That name . . .

DAMIANA: It reminds you of . . . I know who it reminds you of. . . .

THE OTHER: Of the other one! Of me!

DAMIANA: Ever since the day you showed up at the wedding I have never stopped wanting you. Even in the arms of another I would ask myself: "What must he be like, the other one? What are his kisses like? Could he be the same?"

THE OTHER: So that even as you were giving yourself to me you weren't really mine?

DAMIANA: You mean that you're . . .

THE OTHER: The Other!

DAMIANA: Whoever you are . . . You're mine!

THE OTHER: But who am I? Do you know?

DAMIANA: I should say!

THE OTHER: Well, I don't! They say that to be mad
is to be alienated, alien to oneself, to be in another . . .

DAMIANA: But we still haven't seen each other . . .
that is, we haven't seen each other again since . . .
we've never been alone, altogether alone. . . .

THE OTHER: Yes, seen . . . and touched each other.
Altogether alone and naked. . . .

DAMIANA: Yes, I must strip you naked, as if you
were a little child, put you to bed and croon to
you. . . .

THE OTHER: So you can find the birthmark, the
sign? . . .

DAMIANA: I have no need for that! I can see it
through your clothes . . . the mark I put on you,
my own marking!

THE OTHER: Really? What mark? What marking?

DAMIANA: The mark of my own!

THE OTHER: Between the two of you you're destroying me. . . . The two of you killed the one . . .
and the two of you will kill the other. . . . [*He
begins to sob.*]

DAMIANA: What weakness! Yes, I *will* kill you. I'll
make you die of remorse if you don't admit you're
mine, the man I won, and if you don't quit this
awful house which belongs to Laura and a dead
man, if you don't leave her, if you don't come with
me to be for me alone, mine alone. . . . Leave the

dead man, leave his wife, his widow, leave your
jailer, and come with me, the two of us alone. . . .
She's the widow. . . . Whoever she belongs to,
she's the widow! Because . . . now that we're
alone, let's tell the whole truth . . . because the
truth is that you were both in love with me, and
I made the two of you mine. And now you won't
admit who you are because you don't dare. You're
a coward, a coward!

THE OTHER: You got us to hate each other, you
made us hate each other!

DAMIANA: Me? Or the other one?

THE OTHER: Are you jealous?

DAMIANA: Yes, horribly so! Whether you're the one
or the other, you can't be hers! I'll tear you away
from her! You two took her to separate yourselves
one from the other, so you could hate each other,
and I made you both love me so that you could
join in my love. . . .

THE OTHER: It was you who finished the job of
separating us. . . . It was you who poisoned our
life. . . .

DAMIANA: Not I, but the other one!

THE OTHER: The two of you are the other! And
you're no different one from the other. You're both
the same. You're both women. And all women
are as one. Cain's woman was the same as Abel's.
There's no difference between you. . . . The same
fury . . .

DAMIANA: Now you've grown to hate us. . . .

THE OTHER: As much as I hate myself . . .

DAMIANA: [*Whispering to him.*] But you took me
. . . you've possessed me. Or rather, I took you,
I've possessed you. . . .

THE OTHER: Don't you know? Don't you know me?

DAMIANA: Yes, I've possessed you!

THE OTHER: If you had, you wouldn't be desiring to possess me again. . . .

DAMIANA: That's why!

THE OTHER: Damiana, don't give yourself away!

DAMIANA: The point is that the other woman. . . .

THE OTHER: Ah, now I understand! Whoever I may be, Cosme or Damián, the one you possessed or not, what you want is to take me away from the other woman. . . .

DAMIANA: In those days, just after the wedding— do you remember?—in those days, I . . . Well, now at this moment of total truth we must confess everything to each other, and I don't mind saying that during those first days of the honeymoon . . .

THE OTHER: Bitter memory!

DAMIANA: I had the two of you, I took my pleasure with both of you, you and the other one, and I deceived you both. . . .

THE OTHER: That's what you thought. But both of us agreed to deceive you even while we pretended to believe in your little game. And you only had one of us. For just as both of us desired the other woman, the one we didn't have—and that's what gave rise to our mutual hate—so we both wanted to protect ourselves against your fury. . . . Of the two of us, the one you had in those days was your own—poor man!—and the one who rejected you, pleading satiation, was the other one—poor man! And both of us feared your fury. . . .

DAMIANA: My love!

THE OTHER: Your self-love! It was a tragic struggle. But when you thought you had us both, you had only one.

DAMIANA: One and the other!

THE OTHER: As you like. . . .

DAMIANA: It was you!

THE OTHER: You say you know, don't you? . . .

DAMIANA: It's enough to drive one mad!

THE OTHER: And not from love . . . Or rather, yes, from self-love . . . woman's pride . . .

DAMIANA: Look here, I'm going to give you proof that you, whoever you are, belong to me, that you must be mine. . . .

THE OTHER: Proof?

DAMIANA: Yes, proof.

THE OTHER: Let's have it.

DAMIANA: I'm going to be a mother.

THE OTHER: [*Horrified*] What? What do you mean? . . .

DAMIANA: I mean I'm going to be a mother. I'm carrying the child of . . .

THE OTHER: Who? Whose is it?

DAMIANA: Yours.

THE OTHER: Mine or the other's?

DAMIANA: Of both. Of the one which the two of you are. . . . And perhaps I'm carrying two . . . for I can feel them fighting already.

THE OTHER: Two? Two more? No! More madness . . .

DAMIANA: Only the mad can breed and beget.

THE OTHER: And kill. And God cannot, should not, condemn me to have children, to become again . . . Other.

DAMIANA: Well, you will be again. For I'm going to give you . . . an other, another you.

THE OTHER: To be born again? To die again? No, no, no!

DAMIANA: Whose child is it now, tell me?

THE OTHER: I cannot have children. God cannot

condemn me to have children . . . to become once
more an Other.

DAMIANA: And Laura?

THE OTHER: Ah, the other woman! . . . The two of
you together are another woman! Be quiet, will
you . . . ?

DAMIANA: Is that what you tell the other woman?

THE OTHER: The other woman . . . The two of you
are another woman!

DAMIANA: Let her show herself. . . . You can choose
from the two of us! Between us we'll strip you
naked. I'm going to bring her here right now!

THE OTHER: [*Attempting to hold* DAMIANA *back*]
No, no, don't bring her here! No! I don't want to
see you both together!

DAMIANA: Let me get her, Cain, my Cain!

Scene iv

THE OTHER, alone

THE OTHER: Cain! Cain! And now I'm in the hands
of the furies, of the two furies, especially in the
hands of this last one. And between the two of
them, the seduced and the seductress, woman
conquering and woman conquered, I'll be torn
to shreds. . . .

Scene v

THE OTHER, DAMIANA, and LAURA

DAMIANA: We must put an end to all this, Laura.
We must put an end to it at once. [*Addressing*
THE OTHER] You . . .

THE OTHER: Who?

DAMIANA: Cain! Whoever you are! Cain, my Cain.
You're my Cain, and for my sake you killed . . .

LAURA: No! He killed for me. And he was defending himself. . . .

DAMIANA: Defending himself or attacking, what difference does it make? Anyway, it is all up to him. Cain, choose one of us, me, the mother, and turn the other one out . . . or kill her! Stay with the mother of your child!

THE OTHER: I . . . The Other, will stay with the other woman!

DAMIANA: Which of us is that?

THE OTHER: My woman!

DAMIANA and LAURA: [*At the same time*] Me . . . me . . . me . . .

THE OTHER: The one who hates herself as I hate myself, the one who bears the weight of the crime . . .

DAMIANA: I do! I. And as proof, I tell you to kill *her*! Because if you don't do it, I . . .

THE OTHER: More death?

DAMIANA: Yes, more death! Blood calls for blood and only blood will avenge blood. Kill her and bury her down there below, with the dead man, *her* man. . . . She belongs to the dead man, whoever he is, the man who was beaten, whoever he was. . . .

THE OTHER: The man who was beaten? Who was beaten? He or I?

DAMIANA: You are the survivor, you are the father!

LAURA: And the father, who is *he*?

DAMIANA: Not your man.

THE OTHER: No, I am the more dead of the two!

DAMIANA: Good enough. If you are, kill *her*!

LAURA: Oh no, no, no! No more killing! I'll go away so that he may live and the crime never be discovered, whoever the killer was—though I know

well enough who it was. I'll give him to you. . . .
We can't divide him up. . . . I'll leave him for
you. . . .

DAMIANA: Just as in the judgment of Solomon, is
that it? Oh, you're so smart, so sharp, so generous.
Just like all cowards, like all girls who've been
seduced and been made into mistresses. . . .

LAURA: You think I was his mistress?

DAMIANA: Yes, you're the mistress type.

LAURA: And you?

DAMIANA: I? The seductress, the she-conquistador,
the one who wants and wins. I'm woman! And I'm
woman and wife to the one and the other, to both
of them! And you're merely a mistress. Cain never
had a mistress. He had a woman and wife, a crea-
tive woman who won him. The mistress was
Abel's . . . Abel was a conquistador. Poor Cain
was one of the conquered, one of the seduced, one
of those . . . who are loved! Abel did not know
how to suffer! And as for you, you've only had the
one man, and it was he who had you, and I've had
them both, the two of them, the one who made
you his and the other one . . . both!

LAURA: You lie, you lie, you lie! . . .

DAMIANA: The two of them were mine . . . and they
killed for my sake. . . . And the one who survives
is more mine because he had more strength, or
more luck, because he could kill the other one.
And he could kill him because he was more mine.
I gave him the strength, or the luck. . . . I bear
here in my womb . . . And now to avenge that
death . . . And a death can be expiated only with
. . .

THE OTHER: With another death . . . I know!

DAMIANA: So?

LAURA: You're both killing me! Your Laura will die. . . .

DAMIANA: Not his Laura . . . He's mine, he belongs to me, my Cain. . . . The crime made him mine. . . .

THE OTHER: Don't scream so. The jailer will hear you, the madhouse attendant. . . . And so will Destiny, The Other above [*He points upward.*] and down below. [*Indicates downward*]

DAMIANA: Let him hear and come. Let's get this over with once and for all. . . . We're all mad now. . . .

Scene vi

THE SAME and ERNESTO

ERNESTO: [*Entering*] The madhouse attendant is here!

THE OTHER: The jailer and presiding judge!

ERNESTO: Will the truth ever be known?

DAMIANA: This woman, your sister Laura, the seduced maiden, the maiden made, the mistress, provoked Damián into killing her Cosme. She wanted to have a taste of the other one, to know what he tasted like. . . .

LAURA: No. It was she, the she-conquistador, the rabid tigress, who, desiring my Cosme, sent her own husband to his death at the hands of my husband, so that she could have my husband for her lover. It was she who wanted a taste of the other one, to see what he tasted like. . . .

DAMIANA: I already knew!

ERNESTO: [*To* THE OTHER] And you?

THE OTHER: I? I can no longer stand this. I'm leaving. One woman pulls at the one, the other pulls at the other, and between the two of them they tear me apart. It's horrible to be saddled with these furies of Fatality, of Destiny, furies unbound and unleashed. . . . Two women on the back of one dead man . . . It's the punishment of any man who has ever won a woman to be in some way won by still another woman. The seducer always becomes someone else's seduced. And it's awesome that one cannot become, ever, oneself forever, one and the same one forever. . . . We are born alone merely to die alone! To die alone, alone, alone! . . . To have to die with another, with the other, with the others . . . The other one is killing me. . . . And yet . . . Thy will be done under the earth as it is over the heavens! I'm going! [*He leaves.*]

Scene vii

ERNESTO, LAURA, and DAMIANA

ERNESTO: That's enough, Damiana, there's an end to it. This house can no longer continue to be a madhouse, or a cemetery . . . Or a hell. . . . We'll bury the crime along with the dead man, but . . .

DAMIANA: And am I supposed to leave, to go away without my . . . Cain? No. That cannot be, it should not be! I'll take what belongs to me, my . . . lover, far away from here, and *she* shall remain here as befits a widow, with her dead man, her husband. . . .

LAURA: Take him, take him away with you! . . .

ERNESTO: No, she won't. She's not taking him . . . she cannot take him away. . . .

LAURA: I'll lose my . . .

DAMIANA: Yours? The crime, whoever the killer was, made him mine, mine. . . . [*She seizes* LAURA *by the arms.*] Look here! Look into my eyes. Don't you see him there?

LAURA: Let go of me, you devil!

DAMIANA: Don't you see? Don't you see the whole thing? Don't you see that the man—one or the other: it makes no difference—who took you was taken by me and became entirely mine? Because . . . when I came here, it was because I was summoned here by . . . Cain.

LAURA: Lies, lies, lies! You lie!

DAMIANA: I lie, do I? The lie was to say that he did not answer my letters. He answered them all right. He asked me to come. . . .

LAURA: You're lying, lying, lying!

ERNESTO: Everyone here is lying. There's no way to find out the truth. The only certainty is that whoever did it . . . is a fratricide and that he's brought black hell to this house and that in God's justice he deserves . . .

THE OTHER: [*From within*] Death! Death to Cain! Cain, Cain, Cain: Where is Abel thy brother? What have you done with him? [ERNESTO *bars the way to the two women, who attempt to join* THE OTHER.]

THE OTHER: [*Within*] Laura!

LAURA: It's *his* voice!

THE OTHER: [*Within*] Damiana!

DAMIANA: *That's* his voice.

THE OTHER: [*Within*] Damiana! You can have our accursed seed, we leave it to you. More Others . . . The furies . . . the furies! Death to Cain! Death to Abel! Die by key, die by mirror! [*There is the* thud of a body falling to the ground. *The women are frozen with fear.* ERNESTO *goes to see what has happened.*]

Scene viii

LAURA and DAMIANA

LAURA: You've killed him . . . and he was mine!

DAMIANA: Both of them belonged to me! [*She stops* LAURA, *who attempts to leave.*] Where are you going? To see the other dead man? The two of them really are one now. The two dead men . . . Leave the dead in peace!

LAURA: You killed him. . . .

DAMIANA: Nonsense! They killed themselves. . . . Poor men! I'm the mother. . . .

LAURA: And who is the father? Are you sure that the child you're expecting . . .

DAMIANA: The child I already have . . .

LAURA: . . . is your husband's . . . Or is it?

DAMIANA: My husband or yours . . . What's the difference? It's all one to me.

LAURA: How horrible!

DAMIANA: Happiness is woven out of horror, and that's a triumph. That's life, poor little female Abel, little barren Abela! To give life is to give death. A maternal womb is a cradle. . . .

LAURA: Yours is a tomb.

DAMIANA: The tomb is a cradle, and a cradle a tomb. It's what gives a man life so that he may dream it, for only dreams are life. And what gives a man life gives death to an angel who was sleeping the terrible joy of eternity . . . eternal but empty. The cradle is a tomb. The maternal womb is a sepulcher.

Scene ix

THE SAME, AMA, and then ERNESTO

AMA: Is it over then? [*She gazes into the room where* THE OTHER *lies.*] My child! My son! I was afraid this might happen. . . .

ERNESTO: [*Returning*] Which one is it?

AMA: Now? The Other! Both! Let them be buried together.

LAURA: [*To* DAMIANA] Assassin! Murderer! Female Cain, Caina! You've killed them both!

DAMIANA: Poor little victim! Poor little . . . mistress! Poor little widow . . . widow to them both! Poor little barren Abela! Abela the innocent, the seduced shepherdess, the enamored shepherdess! Either of the two was the same to her. . . . She belonged to the first who took her, prey to the first predator. . . . Poor meek lamb! Poor little Abela! Poor little enamored shepherdess! Go and offer up your little lambs to your own God, Abela! I'm going off with mine, with my child . . . or children . . . and I'll take their father with me. . . .

AMA: Will you furies both be quiet! Let the dead rest in peace!

ERNESTO: The dead won't leave us in peace, they won't leave the living in peace. They're our dead . . . the others!

LAURA: I want to die. . . . Why live on now?

DAMIANA: I don't want to die. I must live in order to give life to another, to the son, or sons, I carry. . . .

LAURA: More horror!

DAMIANA: Horror? Two, like Jacob and Esau. And didn't those two fight in their mother's womb,

Ama, to see which one would come into the world
first?

LAURA: How would you know?

DAMIANA: I can feel the struggle going on in my
womb. Each one trying to come into the world
first so as to be the first to get the other one out
of the world. You go lull your dead, and I'll lull
my living. Since you had no man, you won't be
giving life to another. Life kills, but it gives life,
it gives life from death itself. [*She crosses her
hands in her lap, over her womb.*] What peace
we'll have now, my child, a sweet sad peace without any meaning or content! My . . . dead, and
you, my living, my life! [*To* LAURA] Go in peace
with your brother. I found maternity in battle, and
I don't expect peace. Here, in the mysterious peace
of my womb, a cradle and a tomb, the eternal war-
fare between brothers is reborn. Here they wait to
leave off sleeping and begin to dream . . . others.

CURTAIN

Epilogue

ERNESTO, DON JUAN, and the AMA,
seated around a table

ERNESTO: From the legal point of view, the case is
of no further interest. Whoever the murdered
man and whoever the suicide, the two widows are
now taken care of and there is no reason to probe
any further into a madman's crime.

DON JUAN: But still the mystery remains, and mysteries should be dissipated, cleared up. . . .

AMA: What for? Let the mystery rot along with the
two dead men, my poor sons!

ERNESTO: But tell us, Ama, since you must know,
who was the dead man? And why did they fight
with each other?

AMA: What dead man? The first or second? The one
who killed the other, or the one who killed himself? Or, better, the one who was killed by the
. . . one.

ERNESTO: It's all the same now. But who was the
only one I knew, the suicide?

AMA: Ask him!

DON JUAN: He was mad!

AMA: Of course! We are all mad, more or less. No
one can live with madmen unless he's already
mad. . . . Probably he himself didn't know who
he was.

DON JUAN: And what of the women?

AMA: Mad, too . . . the two of them! Mad with desire . . . for Cain. Each one desired the other man,
the one they didn't know in private, and their desire blinded them, so that they thought he was
the other man, the man who belonged to the other

293

woman. . . . Besides, the two of them fell madly
in love at the end with the killer, Cain, each one
convinced, each wanting to believe, that he had
killed for her sake. . . . Any woman who is a
woman, that is, a mother, falls in love with Cain,
and not with Abel, for it is Cain who suffers, who
hurts. . . . No one has inspired greater passions
than great criminals. . . .

ERNESTO: But when Damiana came here looking for
her husband, did she really believe he was missing, or did she come here in response to The
Other, Laura's husband, and did she come with
the intention of giving herself to him? Or was it
Damián who summoned her?

AMA: Who knows? . . .

ERNESTO: Damiana gave one version of the matter
when she first arrived, and then, shortly before
the suicide, gave another. . . . Which was the lie?

AMA: Who knows? Perhaps both were lies.

ERNESTO: Impossible!

AMA: One even lives a lie when one lives the truth
in which one does not believe. . . . Ah, and what's
the use of picking at the mystery anyway?

DON JUAN: But what about *him*? Tell us, Ama, did
he, in his madness, really believe he was someone
else?

AMA: My poor child! He, the murderer, was driven
by guilt into thinking he was the victim, the dead
man! The hangman may think he is the hanged
man. He carries the victim's corpse within him,
and therein lies his suffering. Cain's punishment is
to feel himself Abel, and Abel's is to feel himself
Cain. . . .

ERNESTO: Ever since death entered the world with

the fall of our first parents, Cain and Abel's parents, we live dying. . . .

AMA: The fact is that life is a crime. . . .

DON JUAN: But you surely could distinguish between them. . . . If the two women were blinded by desire and did not know which was which, you, Ama, guided by maternal love, did know, did distinguish. . . . Who was he?

AMA: I've forgotten! Compassion, charity, love . . . all make you forget. I loved Cain as much as I did Abel, one as much as the other. And I loved Abel as a potential Cain, . . . I loved the innocent one for what he suffered because he could sense the guilty one within himself. Honor is a great burden for honorable men! Just as much as vice is a burden for the vice-ridden!

ERNESTO: "Charity shall cover the multitude of sins," said Saint Peter.

AMA: Charity forgets and forgiveness is oblivion. Woe to whoever forgives without forgetting! That's the most diabolic vengeance. . . . The criminal must be forgiven his crime, the virtuous man his virtue, the proud man his pride, the humble man his humility. Everyone must be forgiven for having been born. . . .

DON JUAN: But the mystery remains. . . .

AMA: The mystery? Mystery is fatality . . . Destiny. And why clarify it? Could we live at all if we knew our destiny, our future, the exact day of our death? Can a man with a summons from death really live? Close your eyes to the mystery! It's the uncertainty of our supreme hour which allows us to live at all, and it is the secret of our destiny, of our true personality, which allows us to dream. . . .

Let us dream, then, and not seek a solution to the dream. . . . Life is a dream. Let us dream *la forza del destino, la fuerza del sino.* . . .

DON JUAN: But what of the secret! To live without knowing the secret of the past . . . not to know who he was, what it was that was . . . to resign oneself not to know . . . Not ever to find the solution . . .

AMA: After all is said and done, you *are* a scientist. . . .

DON JUAN: No, I am merely a man. . . . A man who wants to know the secret, the enigma. . . .

AMA: Very well, Don Juan. You are a wise man, and all you need do is to gather together all your recollections of the dead man, and join them to all the recollections of everyone else, then study them, restudy them, compare them, and . . . you will find your solution.

DON JUAN: My solution! It's not my solution I want, but everyone's.

ERNESTO: Exactly what I want!

DON JUAN: Let's assume the matter became public knowledge. . . . I seek the public solution!

ERNESTO: That's it! The public solution!

AMA: The public solution? That's the one which should least concern us. Let each one keep to his own solution . . . and there's an end to it!

DON JUAN and ERNESTO: [*Together*] But what of the mystery?

AMA: You want to know, gentlemen, what the mystery is?

DON JUAN: Truth cures!

ERNESTO: Truth solves!

AMA: [*Stands up, solemnly*] The mystery! I don't know who I am, you don't know who you are, the teller of this story does not know who he is [*This last phrase may be changed to read "Unamuno does not know who he is."*], and he doesn't know who any of those who listen to us may be. Every man dies, whenever Destiny arranges it, without ever having known himself, and every death is a suicide, a Cain's death. Let us forgive each other so that God may forgive us all!

ERNESTO: And you, Ama, will you go on living in this house of the dead, your house, Ama?

AMA: Mine?

ERNESTO: Yes, yours, and the house of the dead. [*He leaves.*]

AMA: [*To* DON JUAN] They've left us alone, with them. . . .

DON JUAN: With the mad and the dead.

AMA: And the two greatest mysteries, Don Juan, are madness and death.

DON JUAN: All the more so for a doctor.

CURTAIN

Notes

Notes

xiii. *I have compassion only* . . . Number 194 of the *Pensées*, according to the edition of Léon Brunschvigg, which we shall use throughout this Introduction.

xv. "*The last act* . . . *play*": *Pensées*, 210.

xvi. *Diario*: *Miguel de Unamuno*: *Diario íntimo* (Madrid: Alianza Editorial, 1970), p. 108.

xvii. *As regards religion* . . . *as they do.*: "My Religion," in *The Agony of Christianity and Essays on Faith*, Vol. 5 of this edition, 211–12.

. . . *what matters* . . . *God*: Karl Jaspers, *Way to Wisdom* (New Haven, 1960), p. 47.

The first word . . . *religion.* . . . : Paul Tillich, *The Protestant Era* (Chicago, 1957), p. 185.

xviii. "*The comic apprehension* . . . *of a way out*": Søren Kierkegaard, *Concluding Unscientific Postscript*, tr. by David F. Swenson and Walter Lowrie (Princeton, 1941, 5th printing), pp. 462–63.

xx. "*Simplicity, simplicity!* . . . *myself alone!*": *Miguel de Unamuno*: *Diario íntimo*, pp. 27–28.

"*Like those poor creatures* . . . *interesting beings*": *Diario íntimo*, p. 143.

"*excitator Hispaniae*": Ernst Robert Curtius, "Unamuno," in *Essays on European Literature* (*Kritische Essays zur europäischen Literatur*), tr. by Michael Kowal (Princeton, 1973), pp. 246–47.

xxii. "*from the obsession* . . . *personal continuity*": Quoted from the *Heraldo de Madrid*, December 14,

1932, by Andrés Franco, *El teatro de Unamuno* (Madrid, 1971), p. 210.

xxvi. *"If you gave yourself . . . Christian faith?"*: *Miguel de Unamuno: Diario íntimo*, p. 131.

xxvii. *Pascal had asserted*: *Pensées*, 88.

xxix. *"condemned to death"*: *Pensées*, 199.

". . . there are two kinds of people . . . do not know Him": *Pensées*, 194.

Tía Tula

Title: The alliterative and doubled-edged *Tía Tula* of the original title *La Tía Tula* has been retained in order to convey the equivocal meaning of *tía* ("formidable" as well as "aunt"). Throughout the book, where "Aunt Tula" is used, the first sense is, unfortunately, lost. Tula is the diminutive for Gertrudis: thus, the literal title would be "Aunt Gert," an impossible pair of monosyllables in English.

4. *. . . she has led me back to herself*: Taken from *The Life of the Holy Mother Teresa of Jesus*, Described by Herself at the Command of Her Confessor, in *The Complete Works of Saint Teresa of Jesus*, translated and edited by E. Allison Peers (London and New York, 1950), Vol. i, Ch. i, p. 11.

"God be praised forever, . . . than see her suffer here.": Cf. *Santa Teresa de Jesús. Obras completas*, ed. Luis Santullano (Madrid, 1963), p. 1254.

Unamuno indicates in the text: "From a letter written in Avila on December 15, 1581, by the Holy Mother and Aunt Teresa de Jesús to her nephew don Lorenzo de Cepeda, who was in the New World, in Peru, where he had married doña María de Hinojosa, who is the doña María referred to in the letter."

a lo divino: The conversion of a profane theme

into a religious one, frequent in 16th- and 17th-century Spanish literature.

Rosary of Sonnets: *Rosario de sonetos líricos* (1911), in Vol. xiii of Unamuno's *Obras completas*; the sonnet is cxviii, "Irrequietum cor," p. 629.

4. (*uncle to his immortal niece*): Don Quixote lived with his niece and a housekeeper.

5. *Mist*: *Niebla*, Unamuno's novel or *nivola*, published in 1914. Cf. Vol. 6 of this edition.

Life Is a Dream: The most famous drama (*La vida es sueño*) of the Spanish Golden Age dramatist Pedro Calderón de la Barca (1600–1681).

6. *Sophocles*: In his *Antigone*, Sophocles has her commit suicide in the cave where she was imprisoned by Creon. Euripides, however, in his version of these events, has Antigone escape and live with Creon's son, Haemon, after the death of her brothers. The dialogue is from Sophocles' drama, lines 511-21.

8. *Lucan, the Spaniard*: Marcus Annaeus Lucanus, Roman epic poet, A.D. 39–65, born in what is today Cordoba.

Aristotle . . . zoon politicon: *Politics*, Book i, Ch. 2.

9. *Abishag*: The "entire book" Unamuno planned to dedicate to Abishag the Shunammite became Ch. 5 in his *La agonía del cristianismo*. Cf. Vol. 5 in this edition.

nivola: The term Unamuno applied to all his novels starting with *Niebla*, 1914.

10. *Abel Sánchez*: Cf. Vol. 6 of this edition.

14. *to take care of holy images*: It was not uncommon for spinsters in Spain to devote themselves to the care of holy images, especially to dressing them for holidays.

65. *what Saint Teresa . . . "He is by condition very childlike in things . . ."*: "El es de condición en cosas

muy aniñado. . . ." From letter dated *24 de julio de 1576*, in *Santa Teresa. Obras completas*, ed. Luis Santullano (Madrid: Aguilar, 9th ed., 1963), p. 870.

70. *'It is better to marry than to burn. . . .'*: I Cor. 7:9.

" *'To marry is to give grace to the married couple and allow them to raise children for heaven.'* ": Although Unamuno's Spanish text does not contain quotation marks between 'To marry' and 'for heaven,' such punctuation has been added to show that the author is quoting directly from P. Gaspar Astete, S.J. (1539–1601), *Catecismo de la Doctrina Cristiana*: "El Sacramento del Matrimonio es para casar, y dar gracia a los casados, con la cual vivan entre sí pacíficamente y críen hijos para el cielo" (Oviedo: Secretariado Catequístico de Oviedo, 1956, p. 41).

93. *'Behold the handmaid . . . to thy word'* . . . : Luke 1:38.

'Woman . . . is not yet come': John 2:4.

Saint Manuel Bueno

135. *Saint Manuel Bueno*: *Bueno* is not an uncommon surname in Spanish; it was chosen specifically by the author because with a small "b" it means "good," and suggests Saint Manuel the Good, a denomination we use whenever appropriate.

Bertoldo: Comic figure of Italian legend and protagonist of the stories of Giulio Cesare Croce (1550–1609), which were very popular in Spain.

139. *his holy . . . Himself*: One's saint's day is the day dedicated to the saint whose name one bears. Jesus Christ was Don Manuel's patron saint, since in Hebrew Immanuel (Manuel) means "God with us."

the fool Blasillo: Blasillo, diminutive for Blas, in French Blaise, the given name of Pascal who wrote (*Pensées*, 233): "Suivez la manière par où ils ont commencé: c'est en faisant tout comme s'ils croyaient, en prenant de l'eau bénite, en faisant dire des messes, etc. Naturellement même cela vous fera croire et vous abêtira." Unamuno quotes these words often throughout his works, and they no doubt suggested to him the idea of Blasillo the "congenital" fool who accepts faith simply and purely, without analyzing ("cela vous abêtira").

140. "*My God . . . me?*": Matt. 27:46.

142. *the city . . . lake*: The setting of Unamuno's story was suggested by the lake of San Martín de Castañeda in Sanabria, at the foot of the ruins of a Bernardine monastery, and containing, according to legend, the submerged city of Villaverde de Lucerna.

144. *a tree . . . six planks from it*: This idea was suggested to Unamuno by the planks he had gazed upon, during his visit to Yuste, which had been cut from the trees of the Sierra and formed the coffin that had contained the remains of the Emperor Charles V a dozen years before they were transferred to the Escorial.

"*from cradle to heaven*" . . . "*little angels belong in heaven*": The Spanish expressions "teta y gloria" and "angelitos al cielo" are formulas of consolation offered to parents who have lost children of tender age.

149. *what the catechism says*: Unamuno here quotes part of the catechism, much used in Spain, of Fr. Gaspar Astete, S.J. (1537–1601). Unamuno often railed against this catechism as fostering passive acceptance of dogma and narrowness of thought.

157. *as someone said*: The reference is to Pascal's *Pensées*, 233. Cf. note to "the fool Blasillo."

166. *one of those leaders . . . Revolution*: Karl Marx.

'*My soul . . . death*': Matt. 26:38.

167. "*Today . . . paradise*": Luke 23:43. Instead of "today" Unamuno has "mañana" or "tomorrow."

168. *the great doctor of* Life Is a Dream: *Pedro Calderón de la Barca* (1600–1681), whose best-known drama is *La vida es sueño* (1635). The first quotation ("pues el delito mayor/del hombre es haber nacido") is from Act I, Scene ii; the second (". . . pues no se pierde/obrar bien, aun entre sueños"), which Unamuno changes a bit, is from Act III, Scene iv.

170. *When the Israelites . . . Aaron died there*: Num. 20:22–28.

and then Moses . . . grave: Deut. 34:1–6.

and if you can . . . stop: Josh. 10:12–14.

he who sees God's face . . . forever: Gen. 32:30 reads: "And Jacob called the name of the place Peniel: for I have seen God face to face, and my life is preserved." Also Judg. 13:22: "And Manoah said unto his wife, We shall surely die, because we have seen God."

DON SANDALIO

Epigraph: *Alors une faculté pitoyable . . . ne plus le tolérer*: "Then a pitiable faculty developed in their spirit, that of perceiving stupidity and no longer tolerating it." *Bouvard and Pécuchet*, translated by T. W. Earp and G. W. Stoner (Norfolk, Conn.: New Directions, 1954), p. 258.

183. *nivolas*: Unamuno's ingenious term applied to the unconventional novels he wrote after *Paz en la guerra* (*Peace in War*), 1897.

184. *the greatest of fools . . . a single folly*: Cf.

La Rochefoucauld, "The man who lives free from folly is not so wise as he thinks."

187. *peñas and tertulias*: We have added "characteristic of our country," for there is no satisfactory equivalent in English for these Spanish, strictly male, talkfests, where, as Unamuno might well have added, had he been thinking of foreign readers when he wrote, one or two or three "mono-dialoguists" hold sway day after day. The closest talk-circle in English to a *tertulia* might well have been the meetings presided over by Samuel Johnson: such a gathering in Spain, even today, would certainly be called *la tertulia de S. J.* A *peña* is associated with enthusiasm for a given activity: there are *peñas* of bullfight addicts (the classic *peña*), those devoted to a certain bullfighter, those nowadays devoted to one football (soccer) team, usually expressing a merely local patriotism in the present un-individualist society.

188. *Schopenhauer . . . playing cards.*: From *Parerga und Paralipomena*, Vol. 1, *Arthur Schopenhauer's Sämmtliche Werke*, ed. by Julius Frauenstädt, 2nd ed. (Leipzig, 1923), Vol. 5, p. 350.

"To counteract this miserable feeling [boredom], men run to trivialities which please for the moment they are taken up . . . card games and the like, which have been invented for this very purpose. . . . Hence, in all countries the chief occupation of society is card-playing, and it is the gauge of its value, and an outward sign that it is bankrupt in thought. Because people have no thoughts to deal in, they deal cards, and try and win one another's money. Idiots!" Translated by T. Bailey Saunders, "Personality, or What a Man Is," in *The Pessimist's Handbook*, *a Collection of Popular Essays*, *by Arthur Schopenhauer* (Lincoln: Univ. of Nebraska Press, 1964), pp. 25–26.

193. *Clavileño*: the wooden horse Don Quixote and Sancho are gulled into riding in Part II, Ch. XLI.

207. *fetters, manacles*: Omitted, at the end of this sentence, is a passage, in the original, based on a play on words in Spanish: "And you will observe that some of these instruments of torture, the fetters and manacles, are called *esposas* and *grillos*. Poor *grillos!* Poor *esposas!*" *Grillos* are, as well as fetters, crickets; *esposas* mean, as well as manacles, wives.

209. *Perhaps it would be better . . . like Don Quixote*: Cf. *Don Quixote*, Part I, Ch. XLVI ff.

whom a grave ecclesiastic . . . called Don Tonto: Cf. *Don Quixote*, Part II, Ch. XXXI.

Sansón Carrasco: Don Quixote's neighbor, "bachelor of arts" from the University of Salamanca, who eventually is responsible for Don Quixote's return home.

210. *Cuadrado y Redondo*: "Square and Round"; the writer of the letter is indicating the meaninglessness—to him—of any exterior properties or characteristics belonging to Don Sandalio, by conferring on him two such ridiculous and confining (defining) adjectives for names.

216. *"Be what you are!"*: *Pythian Odes*, II, line 72, from *The Odes of Pindar* (Loeb Classical Library, 1968). The entire quote is: "Be true to thyself, now that thou has learnt what manner of man thou art."

"Man is the dream of a shadow": *Pythian Odes*, VIII, line 95.

222. *Blasco Ibáñez*: Vicente (1867–1928), famous Spanish novelist, defender of Republican ideals. His best novels are those he wrote about life in the region of Valencia, at the end of the last century and beginning of this one. Later such popular novels as

Los cuatro jinetes del Apocalipsis (*The Four Horse-men of the Apocalypse*) made him rich.

THE MADNESS OF DOCTOR MONTARCO

232. *Epístola moral a Fabio*: poem on the transitoriness and disillusionments of life, written in solemn tercets, probably by Andrés Fernández de Andrada, c. 1600.

237. *Father Alonso Rodríguez*: (1538–1616), Jesuit author of the treatise *Ejercicio de perfección y virtudes cristianas* (1609). Unamuno is mistaken, however, in attributing the quotation that "we are driven by an 'appetite for the divine' " to Rodríguez; it comes from *The Ascent of Mount Carmel* (*Subida del Monte Carmelo*, 1583), by Saint John of the Cross, San Juan de la Cruz), 1542–91.

'Ye shall be as gods!': Gen. 3:5.

245. *Morphy or Philidor*:

Paul Charles Morphy (1837–84), celebrated American chessplayer.

Philidor: François André Danican (1726–95), French chessplayer and operatic composer.

THE OTHER

Cast of Characters: *Ama*: nurse. We have retained the Spanish word, however, because (1) *ama*, like the infantile oenomatopeic *mama*, is found in several of the world's languages, (2) English uses the spelling "amah" for the same meaning (though dictionaries give it as derived from the Portuguese, where the spelling, however, is the same as the Spanish: *ama*), (3) it would appear to be associated, in Unamuno's mind, with his obsessive memory of maternal milk, through its derivation from the basic verb *amamantar*, to nurse, suckle, and (4) the word also means—and suggests—"in the early Christian church, the vessel in which the wine for the Eucharist was consecrated" (Webster's *New International Dictionary*, 1921).

296. *la forza del destino, la fuerza del sino*: *Don Álvaro, o la fuerza del sino* was written in prose, in France in 1831 when its author Ángel de Saavedra, later the Duque de Rivas (1791–1865) was in exile, and rewritten in prose and verse in Spain in 1835; the play, a fate-drama, later inspired Verdi's opera *La forza del destino* (1862).